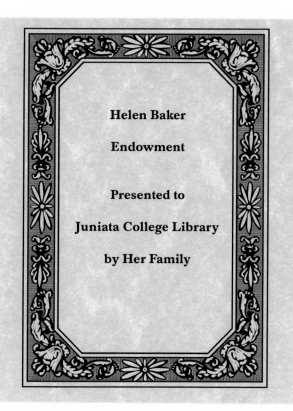

The Rules of Federalism

The Rules of Federalism

*Institutions and
Regulatory Politics in the
EU and Beyond*

R. Daniel Kelemen

HARVARD UNIVERSITY PRESS

Cambridge, Massachusetts, and London, England

Library of Congress Cataloging-in-Publication Data

Kelemen, R. Daniel.
    The rules of federalism : institutions and regulatory politics in the EU
and beyond / R. Daniel Kelemen.
        p.   cm.
    Includes bibliographical references and index.
    ISBN 0-674-01309-3 (alk. paper)
    1. Environmental policy. 2. Environmental policy—European Union
countries. 3. Federal government. 1. Title.

GE170.K45 2004
363.7′056′094—dc22   2003056904

For my parents, Peter and Sandra Kelemen

Contents

Acknowledgments

In writing this book, I benefited from the comments and insights of a number of mentors and colleagues. I am grateful to them all. I especially thank Philippe Schmitter, Geoffrey Garrett, David Vogel, and John Ferejohn, all of whom provided valuable advice and suggestions from the earliest stages of the project. Robert Kagan, Alberta Sbragia, and Susan Rose-Ackerman also read the entire manuscript and provided important suggestions. For helpful comments on various aspects of the manuscript, I also wish to thank Alison Alter, Gerrit Betlem, James Caporaso, Wolfgang Durner, Christian Egenhoffer, Charles Epp, Thomas Heller, Nicolas Jabko, Joseph Jupille, Robert Kaufman, Kathleen McNamara, Sophie Meunier, Terry Moe, Roger Noll, Jacques Pelkmans, Mark Pollack, Richard Revesz, Armin Rosencranz, and Frans van Waarden.

Thanks also to those who helped make my research in Brussels such a rewarding experience. The Fulbright Foundation provided the financial support that made my time there possible and the Centre for European Policy Studies (CEPS) and CEPS director Peter Ludlow both provided institutional support and opened many doors for me in Brussels. My CEPS colleagues shared both their insights and encouragement.

I am grateful to Rutgers University's Department of Political Science and to Princeton University's Center of International Studies for their financial and institutional support as I completed research and writing for this book. A big thank you to Michael Aronson and Benno Weisberg at Harvard University Press for supporting this book. Some material in Chapter 1 appeared in my article "Regulatory Federalism: EU Environmental Policy in Comparative Perspective," in *Journal of Public Policy* 20, no. 2, and is reprinted with the permission of Cambridge University Press. Some material in Chapter 6 is taken from my article "The Politics of 'Eurocratic' Structure and the New European Agencies" in *West European*

Politics 25, no. 4, and is reprinted with the permission of Frank Cass Publishers.

Finally, I am especially grateful to my wife, Tasha, and to my family—Mom, Dad, Paula, Mike, Amy, Laura, Paul, and all the rest of you—whose love and encouragement through the years made this book possible.

The Rules of Federalism

1 | Regulatory Federalism and the EU

The European Union (EU) specializes in regulation. While the role of EU institutions in a range of policy areas—including monetary policy, foreign policy, and policing—has increased in recent years, most EU activity still focuses on regulatory policy. Indeed, so much of the EU's activity concentrates on regulatory policy that some analysts have labeled the EU a "regulatory state" (Majone 1996, pp. 54–56; McGowan and Wallace 1996). The EU's regulatory agenda has come to dominate regulatory policymaking in the member states. The EU plays a powerful role in economic regulation, steering the operation of markets through its far-reaching regulation of mergers and state aid to industry and its sector-specific regulation in areas ranging from financial markets to telecommunications to agriculture. The EU also plays a prominent role in social regulation, acting to protect the health and safety of humans and the environment in areas such as environmental protection, occupational health and safety, public health, and consumer protection.[1] Explaining the development and operation of regulatory policy in the EU may not account for the European integration process in its entirety, but it provides a central piece of the EU puzzle.

In this book, I argue that the development of EU regulatory policy can best be understood by viewing the EU as a federal system. While the EU lacks important attributes of a full-fledged federal state, it operates as a federal system in the area of regulation. I examine the development of social regulation in the EU through the lens of comparative federalism. I develop a theory of regulatory federalism to explain how the basic institutional structures of federal systems mediate struggles over regulation and shape the development of regulatory policy. I then conduct structured, focused comparisons of regulatory policy in the EU and four federal polities.

The theory of regulatory federalism makes two basic claims. First, the *vertical* division of authority between central and state governments pro-

1

duces a similar *politics of competence*[2] in all federal systems. As the two levels of government interact strategically, the division of authority concerning regulation moves through a similar series of stages and reaches a broadly similar outcome: federal governments take on a large role in policymaking, and state governments control most implementation. Second, differences in the *horizontal* fragmentation of power within the structure of the federal government explain differences in the *politics of discretion*. The greater the fragmentation of power in the structure of the federal government, the lower the discretion granted to state governments in implementing federal laws. In other words, as the number of "veto players" (Tsebelis 1995, 2002) at the federal level increases, the discretion of state governments decreases. The fragmentation of power at the federal level encourages an adversarial, litigious approach to regulation that reduces the discretion of states in implementing federal statutes. By contrast, the concentration of power at the federal level encourages a less judicialized, more flexible approach to regulation that allows wide discretion for state governments.

Viewing the EU in light of regulatory federalism leads to surprising predictions. The EU's central institutions are widely held to exercise less control over the EU member states than federal governments of well-established federal polities do over their constituent units. The European Commission staff is a tiny fraction of the size of other federal bureaucracies, and the commission plays very little direct role in policy implementation. Working from the premise that the EU is something less than a federal system, one would expect its central institutions to allow member states more discretion in implementing EU policies than do federal governments. One would at least expect the degree of state discretion in the EU to be closer to that in Canada and Australia, where the federal governments play little role in policy enforcement, than to that in the United States, where the federal government plays a more powerful role. However, the theory of regulatory federalism yields an opposite prediction. The theory suggests that as a system with a high fragmentation of power, the EU is likely to follow the U.S. model of detailed, inflexible rulemaking and litigious enforcement that constrains state discretion.

The theory of regulatory federalism is significant not only for students of the EU, but for students of other federal systems as well. While there is a great deal of literature on various aspects of federalism, there is little systematic, comparative research assessing the impact of federalism on regulation. Most studies that examine the relationship between federalism and social regulation focus on assessing the optimal allocation of regulatory authority between state and federal governments (Stewart 1977, 1993b; Revesz 1992, 1997a, 1997b; Vogel 1995; Swire 1996; Engel 1997; Scharpf 1996b; Oates 1997; Esty and Geradin 2001). These studies ask such questions as: How much potential, if any, is there for competition between jurisdictions to lead to a "race to the bottom" in regulatory standards? Does the potential for a race to the bottom justify the enactment of regulations by the federal government, or does competition between jurisdictions enhance public welfare? While these studies may help us identify the optimal level for various types of regulation, they tell us little about the actual patterns of regulation that are likely to develop in federal systems, because these patterns are determined more by politics than by considerations of efficiency.

A few authors have conducted insightful positive analyses of regulatory federalism (Mashaw and Rose-Ackerman 1984; Elliott, Ackerman, and Millian 1985; Rose-Ackerman 1981; Noam 1982). This literature, however, has not yielded a well-developed positive theory of regulatory federalism to explain the actual political process that determines the allocation of regulatory authority and the relationships between levels of government in federal polities. This book offers a positive political theory of regulatory federalism that explains how federal institutional structures influence strategic interactions between the various branches of the federal government, state governments, and courts and how these structures shape the development of regulatory policy.

I assess the theory of regulatory federalism with structured, focused comparative case studies (George 1979). In addition to the EU, I examine four federal polities: the United States, Germany, Canada, and Australia. This case selection allows for variation in the structure of the federal government. In both the EU and U.S. systems, power at the federal level is highly fragmented. Federal institutions in Canada and Australia are variants of the Westminster-style parliamentary model, which provides for a high concentration of power within the federal government.[3] Germany falls in the middle, as a parliamentary system that provides for more fragmentation of power given the significant power of the *Bundesrat*. The theory of regulatory federalism suggests that the division of jurisdictional competences should develop along similar lines in all these cases, but that the degree of discretion granted to states should vary depending on the structure of the federal government. By comparing across cases, I assess how the structures of the federal governments influence the role of courts in the regulatory process and the degree of discretion granted to state governments.

In comparing the development of regulatory federalism in these five cases, my focus is on environmental regulation, which I take to be characteristic of the development of other areas of social regulation. In order to demonstrate the generalizability of my findings to other areas of social regulation, I analyze the development of food and drug safety regulation in the EU.

In the remainder of this chapter, I present and critique alternative theoretical perspectives on the EU and introduce the theory of regulatory federalism. In the next four chapters, I present comparative case studies of the development of environmental regulation in the EU (Chapter 2), the United States (Chapter 3), Germany (Chapter 4), and Canada and Australia (Chapter 5). In Chapter 6, I extend my analysis beyond the area of environmental policy and examine the development of food and drug safety regulation in the EU. Finally, in Chapter 7, I speculate on the prospects for future development of social regulation in the EU.

Alternative Perspectives

Few studies of regulation in the EU employ the perspective of comparative federalism. While several pioneering scholars have analyzed regulation in the EU from this perspective (Capelletti, Seccombe, and Weiler 1986; Scharpf 1988; Weiler 1991; Sbragia 1992a; Dehousse 1992; Nicolaidis and Howse 2001), most studies of EU regulation are informed by one of the two rival theoretical perspectives on European integration that have dominated academic debates for years: intergovernmentalism and supranationalism.[4] Although these approaches may offer convincing explanations of general trends or critical junctures in the process of European integration, neither provides an adequate explanation of the development of regulation in the EU.

Intergovernmentalists view the EU as an international regime controlled by sovereign states and used by them to facilitate international policy coordination (Moravcsik 1991, 1993, 1998; Garrett 1992; Keohane and Hoffman 1991; Hoffman 1966, 1982; Milward 1992).[5] While they recognize that the EU is more highly developed than other regimes, they emphasize that the difference is one of degree and not one of kind. EU member governments delegate tasks to Community institutions for essentially the same reasons that other groups of governments delegate tasks to international institutions such as the World Trade Organization, the International Atomic Energy Agency, or the office of the United Nations High Commissioner for Refugees: they recognize that they can benefit from coordinating their policies but face a number of collective action problems. In order to facilitate negotiation and to make their commitments more credible, EU member states delegate extensive agenda setting, monitoring, and enforcement powers to supranational institutions.

Some intergovernmentalists analyze the relationships between the member states and EU institutions using principal-agent theory (Garrett and Weingast 1993; Moravcsik 1993, 1995, 1998). They explain that the member states (the principals) may choose to delegate authority to EU institutions (their agents) in order to make their commitments to cooperation credible. While these supranational institutions are granted some autonomy, the sovereign member state governments are able to effectively control them. Anticipating that the supranational institutions may use their delegated powers to pursue their own interests, the member states put in place a variety of oversight mechanisms backed by the threat of sanctions. Intergovernmentalism finds nothing surprising about the existence of powerful supranational institutions; it simply emphasizes that these institutions are created by and ultimately serve the interests of the member states.

Intergovernmentalists stumble, however, in the legal arena. The Community's legal order and, in particular, the linkages between the European Court of Justice (ECJ) and national courts, are vital to the enforcement of Community regulation. Yet, as some intergovernmentalists themselves admit, the ECJ's transformation of the Treaty of Rome into a *de facto* constitution and its development of extensive links with national courts cannot be explained as the result of intentional delegation of sovereignty by the member states (Moravcsik 1993, p. 513).[6] The fact that the legal order developed by the ECJ was not foreseen or desired by the member states calls into question the whole notion of member state control of the integration process generally and of policy enforcement specifically. The development of the Community legal order has transformed the EU into far more than a mere international regime, and intergovernmentalist approaches are simply unable to explain this transformation.

Supranationalist perspectives take an entirely different view of the EU. They argue that the EU is far more than an international regime. While it is not a state in any traditional sense, it does constitute a unique body politic in its own right. This "multilevel Euro-polity" surrounds member states, creating constraints and opportunities that influence state preferences and strategies (Marks, Hooghe, and Blank 1996; Kohler-Koch 1996; Jachtenfuchs and Kohler-Koch 1996; Grande 1996; Pierson 1996). While member states may remain the most powerful actors in this polity, they are thoroughly enmeshed in it. Their preferences and strategies can only be understood by taking into account their position within the greater whole.

To account for the development of this multilevel polity, supranationalist scholars offer explanations both of how the sovereign states that were initially in control of the integration process lost control and of why they have difficulty regaining it. They argue that member states may lose control of the integration process primarily for two reasons. First, Community institutions use the autonomy they are granted to pursue their own interests, which often differ from those of the member states. Second, early steps toward integration, which member states take willingly, may produce unintended and undesired consequences. Supranationalists also identify two primary reasons why member states may have difficulty reasserting control over the integration process. The first is political: particular constituencies and interest groups that develop a vested interest in EU policies pressure member states not to reverse them (Pierson 1996, p. 145). The second is institutional: any major institutional redesign requires the unanimous support of the member states. This unanimity requirement is essential to the functioning of the EU. Member states must insulate Community institutions from political interference in order to ensure that they can perform their delegated functions in an independent manner. However, if Community institutions use their autonomy to pursue their own policy goals, member states may find it impossible to agree unanimously on how to rein them in (Scharpf 1988; Weiler 1991; Pierson 1996; Marks, Hooghe, and Blank 1996; Pollack 1997; Alter 1998; Garrett, Kelemen, and Schulz 1998; Tallberg 2000a). Like intergovernmentalists, many supranationalists describe these phenomena using the language of principal-agent theory. However, where intergovernmentalists claim that member state principals are able to exercise control over their supranational agents, supranationalist scholars argue that due to difficulties in monitoring and sanctioning, member states cannot keep their supranational agents under control.

While supranationalists hold that the EU is a polity in its own right, they point out that it lacks some characteristics necessary to be deemed a federal state and therefore resist labeling it or analyzing it as a federal system.

Instead they view the EU as a unique, *sui generis* polity and focus on describing how this system of multilevel governance developed and how it now functions. They present the development of the EU as a path-dependent process, in which each successive step encouraged the next. They point out that in today's Euro-polity (1) decisionmaking is shared by actors at different levels (subnational, national, supranational), (2) collective decisionmaking involves a loss of control for national executives, and (3) domestic and supranational political arenas are interconnected (Marks, Hooghe, and Blank 1996). Some supranationalists speculate on the future development of the Euro-polity. Schmitter (1996a, 1996c) has suggested that the EU might develop into an unprecedented system of "variable geometry," with a variety of centers, each of which is responsible for handling specific policy tasks. States could then choose which common policy regimes to join, thus creating a complex system of overlapping membership.

Analyzing the dynamics of European integration as a whole, this may be the best we can do. Viewing the sum of developments in the internal market, common foreign and security policy, justice and home affairs, social policy, and monetary policy, the EU indeed appears to be a *sui generis* polity moving down an uncharted and unpredictable path. However, supranationalism leaves one wondering why the EU has moved down one particular path and not another. In the sphere of regulatory policy, we can do better than merely say that the EU has developed through a unique, path-dependent process. For in the sphere of regulatory policy, comparative federalism can show that the EU has followed a familiar path of institutional development: the path of regulatory federalism.

The concept of federalism has long been controversial in the study of European integration (Sbragia 1993b; Burgess 1989). Since the founding of the Communities, Euro-federalism was associated with promoters of European integration who hoped that the integration process would lead to the creation of a federal "United States of Europe." When the integration process seemed stalled and hopes for a supranational state faded, the concept of federalism went out of fashion with analysts, most of whom began instead to emphasize the unique institutional characteristics that made the EU a *sui generis* polity. But analysts who reject comparisons of the EU with other federal states have thrown the baby out with the bath water. It is a mistake to conflate the principle of federalism with the federal state, which is but one particular manifestation of that principle (Cappelletti, Seccombe, and Weiler 1986; Elazar 1987). A polity can rely on federal arrangements even if it is not, and will never be, a federal state. Regulatory federalism is one such federal arrangement. The EU already relies on regulatory federalism and much can be learned about the development of regulation in the EU by comparing it to other federal polities.

By comparing the EU's experience with that of other polities that have trodden the path of regulatory federalism, we gain a better understanding of past developments in the EU and of important choices it is likely to face in the future. As Sbragia (1992a, p. 267) puts it, the literature on federalism offers "guideposts to the tensions the Community is most likely to experience even if it does not actually develop into a 'federal-type organization.'" Also, by looking at EU regulation from a comparative perspective, students of the EU will have more to offer to the study of regulation in other political systems. Intergovernmentalists had the right idea when they sought to connect EU studies to the wider world of political science theory. In some issue areas, such as cooperation on policing or defense, viewing the EU as an international regime may still be appropriate. In the area of regulatory policy, however, the EU has come to function more like a federal polity than an international regime. Thus, it is in the realm of comparative federalism that we can find the perspectives necessary to understand the development of regulatory policy in the EU.

The Structure of Regulatory Federalism

Regulatory federalism is an institutional arrangement that divides the public authority to establish and implement regulatory policy between a "federal" government and two or more "state" governments.[7] The following are the basic attributes of a system of regulatory federalism:

1. Two regulators: The polity is composed of two primary levels of government—a federal level and state level. Each has the authority to regulate economic activity, the federal government for the polity as a whole and the state governments for their particular jurisdictions.
2. Common market: The constituent states that together constitute the polity have agreed (in a constitution or a treaty) to establish free interstate commerce.
3. High court adjudication: Both the federal and state governments recognize a high court to be the ultimate arbiter of disputes between them, including disputes over the appropriate division of regulatory authority.

In polities that possess these institutions, regulatory politics will face many of the same fundamental tensions. It is no coincidence that debates in the EU over regulatory competition, the "race to the bottom," the appropriate allocation of regulatory authority and implementation failures sound strikingly familiar to students of federal systems. These debates reflect challenges and choices that all polities that practice regulatory federalism must face.

However, polities that practice regulatory federalism are not alike in all respects. In addition to the *vertical* division of power between federal and state governments common to all federal systems, some systems provide for *horizontal* fragmentation within the federal government. While some polities concentrate federal power in the hands of a single parliamentary majority, others may divide power between the legislative and executive branches, between chambers in a bicameral legislature or parties in a coalition government. More generally, systems that practice regulatory federalism may differ along the following dimension:

4. Structure of federal government: The degree of fragmentation of power within the federal government varies depending on the number of veto players (Tsebelis 1995, 2002) involved in federal policymaking processes. Specifically, the fragmentation of power is positively correlated with the number of veto players.

My central claim is that the *vertical* divisions of power common to all systems of regulatory federalism lead to a similar division of regulatory competences between federal governments and state governments, while differences in *horizontal* divisions within the structure of the federal government explain differences in the discretion granted to states in implementing federal policy. Before presenting this argument in detail, I briefly outline my assumptions regarding the preferences of the primary actors in the politics of regulatory federalism.

Actors and Their Preferences

As noted above, the primary actors in a system of regulatory federalism are the federal government, state governments, and federal courts. In this section, I present a set of assumptions concerning these actors' preferences. I focus on preferences that derive from these actors' institutional self-interests in the context of a system of regulatory federalism.

Federal Government

The federal government seeks to maximize its popular support and the scope of its authority. Its focus on popular support follows from the electoral motivations that drive politicians in democratic polities. Moreover, even political actors who are not directly subject to elections, such as appointed federal bureaucrats, have an interest in gaining popular support for the federal government. They recognize that public support strengthens the moorings of federal institutions and gives them additional leverage in interactions with other levels of government. As a corollary to its preference for maximizing its level of public support, the federal government seeks to promote interstate commerce, which produces efficiency gains that promote growth and thus generally increase the government's popularity.

The federal government's second basic preference is to maximize the scope of its authority. It has an institutional self-interest in increasing the range of policies that it controls. The assumption that federal governments will seek to maximize their authority vis-à-vis lower levels of government is uncontroversial and has led the drafters of federal constitutions to place explicit restrictions on the authority of federal governments. The only limit to this federal drive to self-aggrandizement appears when the expansion of federal competences threatens to decrease the government's popularity. For instance, if by taking control of a new area of regulation the federal government will face significant blame for the costs of that regulation or for regulatory failures, then it is unlikely that the federal government will take on that policy area.

State Governments

State governments are driven by the same basic preferences as the federal government. First, like the federal government, they wish to gain popularity in the eyes of their constituents in order to improve their chances of reelection. As a corollary to their electoral concerns, state governments want to increase economic output. However, unlike the federal government, which is concerned with the polity's overall economic output, state governments are concerned only with output in their state. Therefore, they wish to attract industry to their constituency and to secure access to the markets of other states. More generally, a state government may be willing to pursue policies that benefit its constituents at the expense of its neighbors. Second, state governments want to maintain their autonomy vis-à-vis the federal government. A state government may be willing to transfer regulatory authority to the federal government if doing so enables it to achieve a popular policy objective that it could not achieve independently, or if doing so enables it to shift blame for policy failures. While state governments may be willing to delegate functions to the federal government under such circumstances, they generally seek to resist federal aggrandizement and to maintain a sphere of authority independent of that of the federal government.

Federal Courts

The primary preference of federal courts is to expand the scope of federal law. When federal courts approve federal jurisdiction in a new policy area, they simultaneously establish themselves as the ultimate arbiters of disputes in that policy field, thus expanding their influence (Bzdera 1993). The desire of courts to expand their influence is checked by their need to maintain legitimacy, which rests largely on their reputation as authoritative and independent adjudicators of disputes (Stone Sweet 1999; Burley and Mattli 1993; Garrett, Kelemen, and Schulz 1998). If elected officials frequently ignore, defy, or evade court decisions or propose institutional reforms that would weaken a court, the court's legitimacy as the authoritative voice of the law is diminished.[8] Therefore, in order to prevent threats to its legitimacy, courts prefer to avoid making rulings that elected officials frequently reject. The legitimacy of a court is also grounded in its claim to serve as a neutral, independent voice of the law. Courts therefore prefer to maintain legal consistency by making rulings that uphold the law as established in treaties, constitutions, legislation, or earlier case law. Following well-established precedents and doctrine lends legitimacy to court rulings and provides legal certainty for all parties. In addition to these general preferences, federal courts may have specific policy preferences. Thus, in interpreting constitutional rules or regulatory statutes, they may pursue a particular policy agenda.

The Dynamics of Regulatory Federalism

Two political dynamics influence the development of regulatory federalism. The first dynamic—*the politics of competence*—arises out of the division of power between state governments and the federal government.

Strategic interaction between the two levels of government determines how regulatory competences (policymaking and policy implementation) are divided between them. The politics of competence develops along similar lines in all federal systems: in each instance, it follows a predictable series of stages and reaches a similar outcome.

The second dynamic—*the politics of discretion*—emerges from the nexus of relationships between the branches of the federal government. While the politics of competence is similar in all federal polities, the politics of discretion varies considerably. Where power in the federal government is concentrated, as in the case of parliamentary federal systems, states will be granted wide discretion in exercising their regulatory functions. Where power in the federal government is fragmented, as it is for separation-of-powers federal systems, they will have less discretion.

The Politics of Competence

THE INITIAL STATUS QUO

I assume an initial status quo in which state governments control social regulation.[9] Conflicts over regulatory competence are unlikely to emerge as long as regulation remains a low salience issue. However, if health, safety, and environmental concerns take a more prominent place on the political agenda, then strategic action by the federal government, state governments, and federal courts in pursuit of their underlying preferences sets in motion a dynamic that disturbs the status quo.[10]

INITIAL STATE REACTION

As public concern regarding health, safety, and environmental issues mounts, state governments begin to take regulatory measures to address public demands for protection. The influence of proponents and opponents of social regulation varies across states. Accordingly, some states enact more stringent regulations *(strict states)*, while others adopt more lax regulations *(lax states)*. Differences in regulatory standards cause difficulties for both categories of states. Lax states suffer if strict states bar the import of products that do not meet their regulatory standards. Lax states view such import restrictions as protectionist, nontariff barriers to trade.[11] On the other hand, strict states may complain that the laxity of production process standards in lax states lowers their production costs and gives industries located in their jurisdictions an unfair competitive advantage. Strict states fear that they will have difficulty attracting new industry, that firms located in their jurisdiction may choose to relocate to laxer jurisdictions, and that those that remain will be rendered less competitive, in each case costing them jobs and tax revenues.[12] Strict states are likely to support the establishment of strict federal standards for production processes, in order to raise production costs in lax states. While lax states will oppose federal production process standards, they may be willing to support the establishment of federal product standards to ensure their access to the markets of strict states (Scharpf 1999).

FEDERAL GOVERNMENT ENTERS POLICYMAKING

The federal government sees in this situation an opportunity to expand its competence into a new policy area, gain popular support for addressing an issue of public concern, and increase interstate commerce by eliminating regulatory barriers to trade. Enticed by this three-for-one offer, the federal government begins to issue regulations and establishes federal regulatory institutions. Regulations are set at a relatively high standard because, as mentioned above, the federal government entered this area of regulation in part to gain credit for addressing an area of public concern. If it forced states to lower existing standards, its regulatory intervention would not gain popular support.

The influence of state governments on federal legislation varies depending on the extent to which state governments are directly involved in legislative processes at the federal level. If state governments have a direct say in federal legislative processes, lax states may be able to block federal initiatives in some areas of regulation. However, even in such cases, lax states will support federal involvement in at least some areas of regulatory policymaking.

Opponents of federal regulation may challenge federal competence in the courts. Such challenges, however, are unlikely to succeed. The high federal court that ultimately settles disputes over regulatory competence has an institutional self-interest in seeing the scope of federal law extended, because this enlarges the range of policies over which it is the ultimate arbiter (Bzdera 1993). This self-interest in expanding federal competences is particularly strong during the early development of a federation when the scope of federal competences is particularly limited. In these circumstances, the federal court's interest in expanding federal competences is likely to outweigh any countervailing interest in maintaining a reputation as a neutral arbiter of federalism disputes or in promoting particular policy preferences. The court is therefore likely to support the federal government's justifications for intervening in new areas of social regulation.

At the initial stage of its involvement, the federal government delegates the implementation of federal policies to state governments. While the federal government is likely to allocate some funds to state governments in order both to make federal mandates more palatable and to encourage effective implementation, it is likely to drastically underfund its mandates. The delegation of implementation coupled with underfunding allows federal governments to shift implementation costs to state governments.

ESTABLISHING A NEW EQUILIBRIUM

Leaving implementation of regulations issued by federal authorities in the hands of the states leads to uneven implementation. Just as states initially adopt different levels of regulation, they also take different approaches to implementing federal regulations. As differences in implementation become widely recognized, the federal government comes under increased public pressure to take on a larger role in implementation, both in order to ensure the protection of public health and safety and in order to remove distortions to the common market created by differences in implementation. As a result, the federal government is likely to delve further into the sphere of implementation.

However, the federal government is unlikely to assume a dominant role in policy implementation for two reasons. First, state governments, in particular those with lax implementation practices, may strenuously resist this intrusion, as it threatens to eliminate their remaining regulatory autonomy. Second, taking over implementation would require the federal government to fund a vast regulatory bureaucracy. It greatly prefers instead to shift implementation costs to the states by enacting unfunded (or underfunded) policy mandates (Kincaid 1994a). The prospect of a political conflict with state governments and, in particular, of a dramatic increase in costs deters the federal government from occupying the field of implementation. A division of competences in which the federal government plays an important role in policymaking, while state governments are responsible for most policy implementation, persists (Mashaw and Rose-Ackerman 1984; Watts 1996).

While political battles may continue on the margins, this division of regulatory competences proves relatively stable. State governments may rally against the burdens of unfunded mandates and press for increased involvement in the formulation of federal policies. The federal government may attack state governments for implementation failures. The politics of blame may swing back and forth, but ultimately no fundamental change is likely. The federal government will neither take over implementation completely nor will it retreat from policymaking completely. Finally, both federal and state governments have an incentive to share regulatory authority because it allows each level of government to claim credit for policy successes and to shift blame in the event of policy failures (Weaver 1986).

The Politics of Discretion

The vertical division of power between federal and state governments common to all federal systems produces the pattern described above. These vertical divisions do not, however, explain why in some polities the federal government allows states great discretion in the implementation of federal policies, while in others it allows for little state discretion, issuing detailed regulations with strict, judicially enforceable requirements. The reasons for these differences lie not in the vertical division of power discussed above, but in the horizontal fragmentation of power within the federal government.

The impact of fragmentation on state discretion is counterintuitive. The greater the fragmentation of power in the structure of the federal government, the lower the discretion granted to state governments in implementing federal laws. Where the power of the federal government is highly concentrated, state governments will enjoy wide discretion in implementing federal laws. By contrast, where the power of the federal government is highly fragmented among a number of veto players, state governments will be subject to more stringent controls and enjoy less discretion.

The fragmentation of power is a continuous variable: as the number of veto players increases, the fragmentation of power increases. To highlight the impact of variations in the fragmentation of power, I focus on two ideal types from opposite ends of the continuum: a *fragmented power federal system,* which combines separation of powers and bicameralism, and a *concentrated power federal system,* which combines a Westminster-style parliamentary government and unicameralism. For each of these ideal types, I explore the causal link between the basic structure of the federal government and the degree of state government discretion.

FRAGMENTED POWER FEDERAL SYSTEM

When enacting regulatory statutes, lawmakers seek to guard against two threats to their regulatory program: bureaucratic drift and political drift. Bureaucratic drift involves the administrative bureaucracy's either shirking its responsibilities or pursuing policy objectives at odds with those of the enacting coalition. Political drift concerns the possibility that political opponents who might come to power later could reverse or undermine the policy preferred by the enacting coalition.[13] In political systems where power is fragmented among a number of veto players, a strategy of judicialization offers an attractive means for lawmakers to insulate their policy victories against bureaucratic or political drift.

The first ideal type of federal system combines separation of powers and bicameralism. The separation of powers divides power between the legislature and the executive. Bicameralism adds another degree of fragmentation, by dividing legislative power between two chambers. Passing legislation in a system that combines these institutions requires the agreement of a number of veto players. The difficulty of assembling the coalition needed to pass or amend legislation means that legislation is likely to remain in place, even long after the enacting coalition has lost power.

Recognizing the durability, or "stickiness," of legislation, the enacting coalition drafts legislation in a manner that seeks to insulate the regulatory policies it favors against bureaucratic and political drift. Lawmakers draft statutes that specify in great detail the goals that executive agencies must achieve, the administrative procedures they must follow, and the deadlines they must meet. They provide for extensive judicial review of executive action, ensuring that their allies will have access to the courts to hold the executive accountable for its actions or inactions (Moe 1989, 1991; McCubbins, Noll, and Weingast 1987, 1989, 1999; Horn 1995). Though their objectives differ, both proponents and opponents of regulation may favor detailed, inflexible procedural rules and opportunities for judicial review that provide them the opportunity to monitor and influence the bureaucracy. Proponents of regulation view detailed, action-forcing requirements as grounds for future legal challenges should the executive fail to fulfill its statutory mandate. Opponents will also want the opportunity to challenge bureaucratic actions in court, but for the opposite reason: they want to be able to challenge the bureaucracy for doing too much, too quickly, without considering enough evidence (Moe 1989, 1990; McCubbins, Noll, and Weingast 1987).

This judicialization strategy depends on the willingness of courts to take an active role in the review of administrative actions. The fragmentation of political power in a system with multiple veto players encourages courts to assume such a role. Courts may be willing to challenge the executive branch because they recognize that the difficulty of passing new legislation in the context of separation of powers and bicameralism will prevent the executive from pushing through new legislation to trump court decisions. Knowing that the fragmentation of power insulates them against easy legislative overrides or other forms of punishment, courts may be emboldened to take an active role in challenging executive actions and constraining executive discretion (Shapiro 1981; Ferejohn 1995; Cooter and Ginsburg 1996; Moe and Caldwell 1994). When statutes are drafted with detailed standards, procedures, and deadlines, courts are provided with firm legal backing for such challenges.

While efforts to constrain executive discretion through judicialization occur initially at the federal level, they have an impact on federal–state relations. Federal lawmakers anticipate that a substantial amount of implementation authority will be delegated to state governments. Therefore, in drafting federal statutes, they require that in the event of delegation, state governments adhere to the same detailed, judicially enforceable statutes. Furthermore, federal executive agencies, which are themselves constrained by federal statutes, are pressured to constrain the discretion of states. The causal chain connecting the fragmentation of powers within the federal government to the limits on state discretion is summarized in Figure 1.

CONCENTRATED POWER FEDERAL SYSTEM

In the second ideal type of federal system, the concentration of power within the federal government discourages attempts to insulate policy victories through a judicialization strategy. In Westminster-style parliamentary systems, power is concentrated in the hands of the party or coalition that holds a majority in the lower chamber of parliament. Second chambers, where they exist, wield little power. Executive and legislative powers are effectively fused, so that the same lawmakers that control the legislature also control the executive. This has two important sets of effects. First, unlike in fragmented power systems, lawmakers will not use detailed, action-forcing statutes in an effort to protect against bureaucratic and political drift. In the short term, because the same lawmakers who control legislation also control the executive branch, they need not worry that a hostile executive leadership will undermine their policies. Where political power is concentrated, lawmakers can readily act to rein in an errant bureaucracy. They need not resort to legalistic, inflexible, judicialized means of control. Instead, they can establish incentive structures and more informal control mechanisms to encourage the bureaucracy to pursue their regulatory goals faithfully. Looking to the long run, current lawmakers know that they cannot insulate their policies against future political interference by enacting detailed statutory obligations. Given the fusion of executive and legislative power in parliamentary systems, future governments will be able to enact new legislation with ease, trumping existing laws. Since detailed, inflexible statutes provide no insulation against political drift, current lawmakers prefer vague statutes that permit them a greater degree of flexibility and political control (Moe and Caldwell 1994).

The second, related set of effects concerns the role of the judiciary in the policy process. As noted above, the fusion of executive and legislative power in Westminster-style parliamentary systems makes legislation relatively easy to enact or amend. In this context, courts recognize that if they

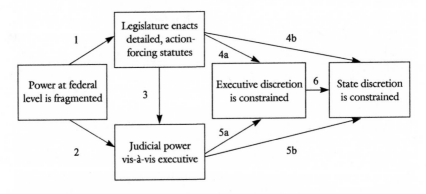

1. Legislature enacts detailed laws to deal with agency problems.
2. Due to fragmentation of power, executive cannot easily overturn judicial interpretation of statutes. Courts do not fear ruling against executive branch.
3. Detailed, action-forcing statutes make violations easier to identify and enforce in court.
4a & 4b. Statutes place detailed requirements on federal executive and, anticipating state implementation, on state governments.
5a & 5b. Judiciary's willingness to rule against executive encourages litigation. Judicial oversight constrains executive discretion.
6. When delegating implementation to states, federal regulators constrain state discretion.

Figure 1   Fragmented power federal system

attempt to rule against executive actions and assert their own interpretation of the law, the executive can easily direct Parliament to pass new legislation overturning the courts' interpretations or undertake other actions
to rein in the courts (Shapiro 1981; Ferejohn 1995). Therefore, courts are
hesitant to question regulations and or general policy decisions made by
the executive in implementing legislative statutes. This judicial deference
to executive discretion is bolstered by the fact that statutes tend to be
vague and contain few specific obligations. Judicial review of executive action focuses on the protection of individual rights in specific cases, generally avoiding more comprehensive review of regulations and policies
(Shapiro 1981; Ferejohn 1995).

While these dynamics stem from the structure of the federal government, they have a powerful effect on federal–state relations. Where lawmakers enact vague statutes and courts defer to the executive, proponents
of regulation cannot pursue a judicialization strategy in order to insulate
their policy victories (Moe and Caldwell 1994; Holland, Morton, and
Galligan 1996; Wilson 1989, pp. 297–300). When implementation of
vague, discretionary federal statutes is delegated to state governments, the
states continue to enjoy a high degree of discretion. The causal chain connecting the concentration of power within the federal government to the
high degree of state discretion is summarized in Figure 2.

Research Design

The theory of regulatory federalism suggests that the politics of competence should develop in all cases following the pattern described above.
Meanwhile, the politics of discretion should vary depending on the structure of the federal government. Case studies were selected to allow for
variance on the concentration of power in the federal government. They
are arrayed in Table 1.

The U.S. federal government is structured along the lines of the first
ideal type, combining separation of powers and bicameralism. The EU's
institutional structure also approximates the first ideal type, dividing
power among a number of veto players (Tsebelis and Garrett 2001). While
the EU's executive (the Commission) is not directly elected, there is a separation of powers between it and the EU's legislative bodies. Within the
EU's legislative branch, power is highly fragmented. Even before the European Parliament became a significant legislative body, there was a high
degree of distrust and fragmentation among member states in the Council

of Ministers. With the increase in power of the European Parliament, the EU now operates with a bicameral legislature in most regulatory policy areas. By contrast, Australia and Canada approximate the second ideal type, as both are Westminster-style parliamentary federal systems. However, power is slightly more fragmented in Australia than in Canada, given the greater power of the Australia's upper house (the Senate). The Federal Republic of Germany falls in the middle of the continuum between the two ideal types. Germany combines parliamentary government with the existence of a powerful upper chamber (the *Bundesrat*).

The theory of regulatory federalism suggests, first, that in each of these polities the federal government should come to play an important role in policymaking, while delegating most implementation to state governments. Second, the theory suggests that the more fragmented the structure of the federal government, the less discretion state governments will have in implementing federal policy. The U.S. states and EU member states should be the most constrained, while Australian states and Cana-

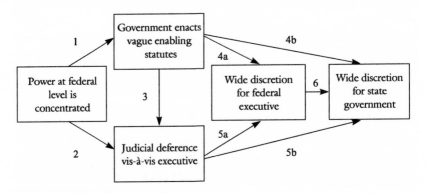

1. Government dominates legislature. Legislature enacts vague enabling statutes.
2. Courts recognize that government can pass new statutes to override judicial decisions. Therefore, courts defer to executive.
3. Where statutes grant executive wide discretion, courts have less legal grounds for forcing executive to take specific actions.
4a & 4b. Vague statutes allow wide executive discretion.
5a & 5b. Little litigation to enforce statutes. Without judicial oversight, there is little constraint on executive discretion.
6. When implementing federal statutes, states have wide discretion.

Figure 2 Concentrated power federal system

Table 1 Placing the cases

	Fragmentation of power in federal government	Judicialization	Discretion of state governments
United States and EU	High	High	Low
Germany	Medium	Medium	Medium
Canada and Australia	Low	Low	High

dian provinces should enjoy the greatest discretion. The German *Länder* should fall in the middle in terms of discretion.

Regulatory Federalism and Regulatory Style

The case studies that follow provide strong support for the theory of regulatory federalism and, in doing so, provide a novel perspective on the EU. The institutional structures of regulatory federalism have had a significant impact on patterns of regulation in all five federal systems in this study. In each case, the federal government has taken on a large role in policymaking while state governments retain control over most implementation. This similarity reminds us that the fact that EU member states control most implementation of EU policies should not necessarily be taken as a sign of the EU's weakness. Rather, it is quite typical of other federal systems. The case studies also support the arguments concerning the politics of discretion presented above. In the fragmented power systems—the United States and the EU—federal lawmakers tend to produce more detailed, rigid statutes and courts take an active role in statutory interpretation and judicial review of administrative action. As a result, the discretion of state governments is limited. In the concentrated power, Westminster-style parliamentary systems—Canada and Australia—federal lawmakers craft more vague, flexible statutes and courts are much less willing to act independently and to limit the discretion of state governments in implementing federal laws. In Germany, courts have played an active role in reviewing administrative action, but only in a narrow range of cases concerning the protection of individual rights. While a number of significant nuances distinguish each case, generally the constraints that federal governments and federal courts place on state discretion vary as anticipated by the theory.

The structure of the EU's federal institutions not only influences state government discretion, it also has a profound impact on the general style of EU regulation. Streeck and Schmitter (1991) noted that policymaking in Brussels resembled that in Washington, D.C. more closely than that in Bonn or Paris. They argued that EU policymaking was driven by U.S.-style pluralism, rather than by corporatist modes of interest group inter-mediation common in Europe. This study highlights another dimension of the similarity between Brussels and Washington. In comparison to tra-ditional national regulatory styles in Europe that granted regulators con-siderable discretion and discouraged recourse to litigation, the EU's approach to regulatory policy is more formal, inflexible, and adversarial (Vogel 1986; Kagan 1997). The similarity in the EU and U.S. regulatory styles is grounded in the similarities of their fragmented federal institu-tional structures. In the long term, the EU's institutional structure is likely to have a profound impact on interest group politics in Europe, in particu-lar by encouraging groups who cannot achieve their ends through tradi-tional means of influence to seek new opportunities in the courtroom.

2 | Environmental Regulation in the EU

Over the past thirty years the European Union (EU) has enacted an enormous body of environmental law. The EU has issued legislation in virtually all areas of environmental policy, including rules concerning drinking water, bathing water, air quality, industrial emissions, waste management, nature protection, and environmental impact assessment. Both the division of competences between the EU and member states and the degree of discretion that member state governments enjoy in implementing Community environmental law have been influenced by the EU's basic federal structures, as anticipated by the model of regulatory federalism. Community institutions have taken over extensive policymaking competence, while policy implementation has remained in the hands of the member states. The gradual shift to this division of competences has followed a pattern strikingly similar to that in the other federal polities I explore in this book. The horizontal fragmentation of power at the EU level has had even more surprising consequences, both encouraging the adoption of detailed laws that limit member state discretion and emboldening the Commission and the European Court of Justice (ECJ) to enforce these laws strictly. While EU institutions are widely held to be weaker actors than the federal governments of well-established federal states, the EU's central institutions already take a more aggressive approach to enforcing Community law requirements vis-à-vis member states than do the federal governments of the parliamentary federations I consider in this study—Canada and Australia. The EU's fragmented institutional structure has encouraged the development of an adversarial, litigious approach to regulatory policy, similar in many respects to that found in the United States.

The EU's institutional structure combines vertical fragmentation of power (between EU institutions and member states) with horizontal fragmentation of power (between institutions at the EU level). In other words, it combines federalism with its own brand of separation of powers. Power at the EU level is divided between legislative, executive, and judicial branches. Comprehensive, detailed analysis of the EU's institutional structure has been carried out elsewhere (Hix 1999), but a brief overview will clarify the basic structure of EU federalism.

The EU has a bicameral legislature with a powerful upper chamber (the Council of Ministers) composed of representatives of member state governments[1] and a weaker, but increasingly powerful, lower house (the European Parliament (EP)) composed of directly elected representatives.[2] The EU has a collegial executive (the College of Commissioners) led by a president and composed of appointees.[3] Commissioners are appointed by the EU's upper chamber (the Council) on a proportionality basis[4] and are subject to a vote of approval by the European Parliament.[5] During its appointed term, the Commission does not rely on the confidence of the legislature to maintain office; the lower chamber does, however, have the power to censure the Commission. The EU's judicial branch is headed by a supreme court, the European Court of Justice, composed of judges selected by the member state governments. The EU has started creating a system of lower federal courts, first with the establishment of the Court of First Instance (CFI) and most recently with provisions for the establishment of specialized judicial panels (Treaty of Nice art. 225a). Also, member state courts are integrated into the EU's judicial system, both through the doctrines of direct effect and supremacy and through the preliminary ruling procedure that allows them to refer cases to EU courts (Alter 1996, 1998, 2001; Stone Sweet 2000, pp. 153–193).

Given its bicameralism, separation of legislative and executive powers, and the independence of its judiciary, power at the EU level is highly fragmented. In Tsebelis's (1995, 2002) terms, the EU is a polity replete with "veto players"; for Lijphart (1999, pp. 42–47), the EU has the characteristics of a consensus democracy. A variety of decisionmaking procedures govern the relationships among the Commission, Council, and Parliament in the legislative process. Prior to 1987, environmental legislation was adopted by a unanimous vote in the Council on a proposal forwarded by the Commission, with the EP playing only a consultative role.[6] Subsequently, treaty revisions in the Single European Act (SEA), the Treaty on European Union (Maastricht), and the Amsterdam Treaty have introduced new decisionmaking procedures—the cooperation procedure, the co-decision procedure, and Amsterdam's reformed co-decision procedure. These procedures replaced unanimous voting in the Council with qualified majority voting and granted increased powers to the European Parliament. Since the adoption of the Amsterdam Treaty, nearly all environmental legislation is made under the reformed co-decision procedure, in which the EP and the Council have essentially equal legislative power.[7] The intricacies of these decisionmaking procedures have been examined elsewhere and need not concern us here (Tsebelis 1994; Garrett 1995; Tsebelis and Garrett 2000, 2001; Crombez 1996; Jacobs, Corbett, and Shackleton 1995; Hix 1999, pp. 84–96; Shackleton 2000). The crucial point is that multiple veto players participate in the EU's legislative procedures, making new legislation difficult to pass and increasing the chance that existing legislation will remain in place. While the move to qualified majority voting has decreased the power of individual member states to block legislation, the accompanying increase in power of the European Parliament has added another layer of complexity and another veto player to the legislative process (Schulz and König 2000; Golub 1999).

As discussed in Chapter 1, the horizontal fragmentation of power at the federal level influences the vertical relationships between the federal government and states. The fragmentation of political power at the federal level encourages the judicialization of regulatory policy, which ultimately works to constrain the discretion of state governments. In this chapter I demonstrate how this dynamic has been at work in EU environmental policy. The fragmentation of power in Brussels has led to the passage of inflexible, action-forcing environmental laws that the Commission has actively enforced against recalcitrant member states. Shielded against political countermeasures by the fragmentation of power in Brussels, the ECJ has proven itself very willing to impose costly rulings on member state governments. For a variety of reasons discussed below, litigation by private parties has played a limited role in the field of EU environmental policy. Nevertheless, it is evident that the structure of the EU has encouraged the emergence of a litigious, judicialized approach to environmental regulation that ultimately places considerable restraints on member state discretion.

The Politics of Competence

The Emergence of EU Environmental Policy

When the Community was established by the Treaty of Rome in 1958, environmental regulation was of little concern in Europe. The treaty made no provision for Community involvement in environmental policy, thus leaving the issue to the member states. For most of the 1960s, environmental policy remained a low-salience issue in which neither the member states nor the Community took great interest. This changed by the end of the decade. As public awareness of environmental problems grew in the late 1960s, environmental policy became a high priority issue in a number of member states. Their regulatory responses differed, with some states, Germany and the Netherlands in particular, opting for more stringent regulation than the others.

The rise of environmental regulation constituted a threat to the functioning of the internal market. Divergences in national environmental standards, in particular in standards for traded goods, threatened to create barriers to trade between member states (Dehousse 1992, p. 385). States with lax standards feared that their stricter neighbors would use environmental standards to protect their domestic markets. Stringent regulators, on the other hand, feared that they would suffer a competitive disadvantage vis-à-vis their laxer neighbors and supported Community-wide harmonization (Majone 1994b; Golub 1996; Hildebrand 1993). Thus, both lax states and stringent states had reasons to support Community involvement in environmental policy. Moreover, they had little reason to fear Community intrusion into this area. At the time, passing any new Community law required a unanimous vote of the member states in the Council of Ministers. Knowing that they could veto measures of which they disapproved, member states accepted the extension of Community jurisdiction to environmental policy (Weiler 1991; Dehousse 1992).

The European Commission and Parliament were eager for the Community to enter the environmental policymaking arena. Environmental policy offered them the "three-for-one" deal described in Chapter 1. First, addressing environmental problems enhanced the Community's legitimacy in the eyes of the environmentally conscious public. The Commission and the MEPs were eager to gain public support for the Community. Second, taking on environmental policy opened up a wide new area of regulatory competence. While the Community's tight budget constraint precluded extensive distributive or redistributive policies (for example, social welfare spending), regulation that had far-reaching impacts across Europe cost the Community very little to enact, because member states had to bear the costs of implementation (Majone 1994b). Finally, setting policy at the European level protected the functioning of the common market by preventing states from using regulations as nontariff barriers to trade within the Community.

The Community adopted its first environmental measure—a directive on the classification, packaging, and labeling of dangerous substances—in 1967.[8] Next, in 1970, the Community enacted two environmental directives concerning motor vehicles, one on noise levels and one on emissions.[9] The Commission and the EP advocated taking more concerted action at the Community level to address mounting environmental concerns. In 1971, the Commission issued a communication suggesting that it was necessary for the Community to adopt an environmental action program.[10]

In October 1972, just four months after the UN-sponsored Conference on the Human Environment had piqued public awareness of environmental problems across Europe, leaders of member states held a summit in Paris. They agreed that a Community environmental policy was necessary and called on the Commission to draw up a plan of action on the environment.[11] Soon thereafter, the Commission presented the First Community Action Programme on the Environment, which set out the basic aims and principles that were to guide Community policymaking.[12] In the ensuing years, the Community issued numerous directives on environmental protection. Many of these involved harmonizing environmental standards for traded goods or placing controls on dangerous substances. For instance, the Community adopted provisions on the sulfur content of fuel oils,[13] the lead content of petrol,[14] noise standards for motorcycles,[15] and restrictions and bans on numerous chemical substances.[16]

Community legislation also addressed environmental quality, nature protection, industrial emissions, and waste management. In 1975, the Community adopted its first environmental quality directives, one on surface waters used as drinking water supplies[17] and another on bathing water.[18] In 1979, it adopted its first nature protection directive on the conservation of wild birds.[19] The most prominent directive on industrial emissions was issued in 1984 and concerned air pollution from industrial plants.[20] The Community adopted its first directive on waste management in 1975,[21] followed three years later by a directive on toxic and dangerous waste.[22] Finally, the Community also issued important procedural requirements, the most significant of which was the 1985 directive on environmental impact assessment.[23] By the mid-1980s, the Community had issued over one hundred Directives and regulations on the environment dealing with the nearly all aspects of environmental policy (Sands 1990; Vogel 1993a, p. 116). In addition to its legislative activities, the Commission made internal organizational changes aimed at elevating the status of environmental policy. Most important, in 1983 it upgraded the Environment and Consumer Protection Service to the full-fledged status of Directorate-General for Environment, Consumer Protection and Nuclear Safety (Hildebrand 1993).

As predicted by the model of regulatory federalism, the ECJ supported the expansion of the Community into the environmental policymaking arena. All Community secondary legislation (that is, directives and regulations) must have a legal basis in the treaties. As the Treaty of Rome made no mention of environmental issues, the Council adopted environmental measures under two general provisions of that treaty. Article 100 empowered the Council to adopt directives to harmonize national laws in order to remove distortions to competition and barriers to trade within the common market. Article 235 empowered the Council to adopt legislation necessary to attain one of the "essential" activities of the Community if the treaty does not elsewhere specifically empower it to do so. The use of Articles 100 and 235 as legal bases for environmental legislation rested on interpretations that easily might have been rejected. However, ECJ rulings approved such interpretations of both articles (Krämer 1990, pp. 3, 54; Bird and Veiga-Pestana 1993, p. 234; Haagsma 1989, pp. 324–325). First, in a 1980 ruling, the ECJ firmly recognized Article 100 as an appropriate legal basis for environmental legislation.[24] Next, in a 1985 decision, the court established that environmental protection was one of the Community's "essential objectives" that could be pursued under Article 235.[25] By approving the Community's role in environmental policy, the ECJ permitted the development of a vast body of law over which it was the ultimate arbiter.

On July 1, 1987, the member states amended the Treaty of Rome with the Single European Act. The new treaty included a section on environmental policy (tit. VII, arts. 130r–t), which, for the first time, provided Community environmental policy with an explicit legal basis. The SEA's environmental provisions served two sets of purposes.[26] On the one hand, they aimed to make the new treaty more acceptable to supporters of strict environmental regulation, most notably Denmark (Haagsma 1989, p. 335). To this end, Article 130r of the SEA outlined the guiding principles and objectives of Community policy and thus entrenched the Community's commitment to environmental policy firmly in the treaty. Also to appease the Danish and other high-standard states, the "opt-up" provision of Article 130t allowed states to maintain or adopt stricter environmental standards where the Community adopted common standards. On the other hand, some member states, the United Kingdom in particular, wanted to use the environmental title as a means to restrain the further expansion of Community environmental policy. They succeeded in inserting restrictive provisions into the title, two of which concerned decision-making procedures and the concept of subsidiarity. However, subsequent ECJ jurisprudence undermined these efforts to restrict the stringency and scope of Community environmental law.

Member states concerned about the expansion and stringency of EU environmental law sought to use the SEA's environmental provisions to ensure that most environmental policy would continue to be subject to unanimity decisionmaking. Changes in decisionmaking procedures were a central element of the SEA. The SEA was the cornerstone of the renewed drive to liberalize the Community's internal market (Moravcsik 1991). Free movement of goods within the common market had long been frustrated by the existence of regulatory barriers to trade, and such impediments increased during the 1970s and 1980s as the member states adopted more health, safety, and environmental regulations at the national level. The Commission had worked to remove these impediments to trade by proposing harmonized Community measures to replace differing national standards. Because of the unanimity requirement, however, negotiations over harmonized standards were lengthy and often unsuccessful (ibid., p. 20). Therefore, in the SEA the member states called for a new approach based on the harmonization of essential health and safety requirements beyond which they would apply "mutual recognition," the principle that member states recognize each other's product standards such that any product legally marketed in one member state would have access to the markets of all the others.[27] Second, in order to speed up decisionmaking processes member states introduced a new decision-making procedure for measures concerned with the completion of the internal market (namely, measures adopted pursuant to Article 100a). The new procedure, termed the "cooperation procedure," replaced the unanimity requirement with qualified majority voting in the Council[28] and gave new agenda-setting powers to the Commission and the Parliament (Garrett 1992; Verhoeve, Bennett, and Wilkinson 1992; Tsebelis 1994).

Lower-standard states, led by the UK, did not want to see this new decisionmaking procedure extended to most environmental policy measures. Member state governments knew that if past trends continued, the vast majority of environmental measures would have been adopted under Article 100 and, therefore, subject to the cooperation procedure (Golub 1994, pp. 26–27). Low-standard states feared that qualified majority voting coupled with increased Commission and EP influence would lead to the adoption of more and stricter environmental regulations.[29] These states saw an opportunity in the SEA's new environmental section (tit. VII, arts. 130r–t). They demanded that legislation introduced under Title VII continue to be made by the traditional decisionmaking rules, which required unanimity in the Council and limited the role of the EP to mere consultation (art. 130s).[30] The low-standard states hoped that most environmental measures would henceforth be taken under Title VII's Article 130s, rather than under Article 100a, and therefore be subject to unanimity voting.

ECJ jurisprudence following the SEA undermined the efforts that had been made to restrict the scope of Community policy. In its landmark *Titanium Dioxide* ruling, the court expanded the extent to which qualified majority voting could be used on environmental measures.[31] The case arose from a dispute between the Commission (supported by the EP) and the Council regarding the appropriate legal basis for a directive on pollution by the titanium dioxide industry. The Commission argued that the directive primarily served to promote the functioning of the common market and should therefore be adopted under Article 100a, which called for the use of the cooperation procedure. The Council countered that the directive was primarily an environmental protection measure and thus should be adopted under Article 130s, which requires unanimity voting. The ECJ sided with the Commission, ruling that the directive's main intent was to improve competitive conditions in the titanium dioxide industry, and that, therefore, the Commission's choice of Article 100a as the legal basis had been correct. This decision sent a message to the Council: it would not easily be able to relegate harmonizing measures to Article 130s where unanimity would be required. Member states had lost their ability to veto environmental legislation in most issue areas and the European Commission and Parliament had won an increased role. The Commission interpreted this ruling broadly and continued to issue most environmental legislation under Article 100a.[32]

Article 130r(4) of the SEA introduced a second set of provisions that some states hoped would limit the expansion of Community competences. The first sentence of the article contained a balancing test commonly known as the "subsidiarity principle." It reads, "The Community shall take action relating to the environment to the extent to which [environmental] objectives . . . can be attained better at Community level than at the level of the individual Member States." British negotiators hoped that this guideline would restrain future Community activity in the field of the environment (Golub 1994). However, the principle of subsidiarity enshrined in the SEA's environmental chapter played little role in constraining the expansion of Community competences. British negotiators did on occasion invoke the principle when opposing proposals in the Council; however, the principle seems to have had little impact on the growth of Community legislation.[33]

In the years following the adoption of the SEA, the Community adopted an increasing number of environmental measures concerning all aspects of environmental policy. None of these measures, nor any previously existing measures, were ever challenged before the ECJ on the grounds that they violated the principle of subsidiarity. Although one can only speculate why member states never brought a case challenging an environmental directive on subsidiarity grounds, it seems likely that they did not anticipate that the ECJ would rule in their favor. In any event, the principle seems to have had little effect on the growth of Community regulation: the Community enacted more environmental legislation between 1989 and 1991 than in the previous twenty years combined (Vogel 1993a, p. 125).

Finally, the second sentence of Article 130r(4) also sought to influence the division of competences. It reads, "Without prejudice to certain measures of a Community nature, the Member States shall finance and implement the other measures [that is, the non-Community measures]." This provision was adopted in response to fears on the part of some member states that the Community was attempting to gain undue influence on their domestic policies through Community funding schemes (Haagsma 1989). By restricting the ability of the EU to use fiscal levers to influence member state compliance, this provision encouraged reliance on judicial approaches to securing enforcement.

The Community Addresses Implementation Failure

As the EU's environmental policymaking competence expanded in the 1970s and early 1980s, policy implementation remained in member state hands, and the Commission made little effort to ensure that Community law was applied in practice. The Treaty of Rome required member states to take necessary measures to implement Community law (art. 5) and required the Commission to oversee this implementation process and ensure that the law was in fact applied (art. 155). However, until the mid-1980s, the Commission generally turned a blind eye to questions of practical application of Community environmental law. The EU also played little role in financing the implementation of Community environmental law.[34] Some member state governments took Community laws lightly, viewing them as "little more than policy intentions or aspirations rather than as distinct legal obligations" (Macrory 1994, p. 4). The absence of strict enforcement facilitated the expansion of the scope of EU environmental legislation. Anticipating that they would not have to comply strictly made it easier for recalcitrant member states to accept new Community environmental regulations (Kelemen 1995; Golub 1996).

Predictably, the Commission's neglect of enforcement led to uneven implementation of Community environmental law, which allowed for distortions to the internal market. Concern regarding the implementation deficit grew, and eventually it became common knowledge that "many European rules are not faithfully implemented, or not implemented at all" (Majone 1995, p. 8). Criticism intensified in 1983 after barrels containing toxic waste from a 1978 accident in Seveso, Italy were lost in transport (Krämer 1995, p. 134). In response to the incident, the European Parliament conducted an enquiry into the implementation of Community legislation. The EP was highly critical of the Commission and called on it to take action to redress the "implementation deficit" (European Parliament 1984).

The Commission responded to these concerns in the late 1980s by taking a more active role in monitoring and enforcement (Macrory 1994, p. 5; Weale et al. 2000, p. 297). It publicly declared this new emphasis on implementation in the Fourth Community Environmental Action Programme.[35] The Commission undertook two major initiatives. First, it increased pressure on member state administrations by instituting regular meetings to discuss implementation problems and by increasing its use of Article 226 (former Article 169) infringement procedure, whereby it could bring member states before the ECJ for failure to implement Community law. Second, it proposed the establishment of a European Environment Agency, which it hoped would play a role in both monitoring and enforcement.

The Article 226 (former Article 169) infringement procedure empowers the Commission to bring infringement proceedings before the ECJ against member states for failure to implement Community law. The Commission exercises wide discretion in employing the infringement procedure. Before the 1980s, the Commission made little use of the procedure in environmental matters or in other areas of Community regulation more generally. Indeed, although the procedure had been in place since the founding of the Community in 1958, 90 percent of all infringement procedures have been commenced since 1978 (Mendrinou 1996). During the 1980s, the Commission dramatically increased its use of the infringement procedure in environmental matters (Collins and Earnshaw 1993). In addition to increasing its use of the procedure, the Commission challenged different types of implementation failures. It earlier had focused only on cases in which a member state failed to take measures to transpose the Community directive into national law. In 1983, the Commission began bringing infringement proceedings in cases in which the state had transposed the directive into national law, but failed to apply it in practice (Macrory 1994, p. 9; Commission 1991).

The Commission coupled its increased use of these formal procedures with increasing efforts to informally pressure member states to improve implementation. In 1990, Commission officials began holding annual bilateral "package meetings" with national authorities to discuss alleged infringements. The Commission's hope was that, backed by the credible threat of instituting infringement proceedings, it could convince states to remedy problems before recourse to such formal measures was necessary.

Despite the Commission's increased efforts, the extent of implementation continued to be criticized widely. One ground for complaints was the Commission's inadequate monitoring capacity. While the Commission could easily detect whether a member state had properly transposed a directive into its national law, it was largely unable to monitor whether the state did an adequate job of applying the law in practice. In order to detect such violations, the Commission relied heavily on the complaints procedure—whereby individuals or organizations could submit complaints regarding suspected member state infringements. The number of environmental complaints received by the Commission increased dramatically in the 1980s, surging from a mere handful in the first few years of the decade to hundreds each year by the decade's end (Commission 1991; Krämer 1995, p. 142). However, reliance on complaints led to systematic biases in the detection of violations. The number of complaints received regarding a member state relates more to the level of public awareness and to traditions of citizen participation in the member state than it does to the actual number of violations that occur (*Economist* 1991; *Financial Times* 1992).

The system's second failing was that it simply overloaded the Commission with complaints. The Commission had very limited enforcement resources in the field of environment. The legal unit of the Directorate General XI (DGXI) had a professional staff of approximately fifteen at this time. Investigating complaints required substantial resources and the Commission faced a mounting backlog. The prospects for expanding the size of the Commission bureaucracy in Brussels were poor given both the limits placed by the Council of Ministers and the European Parliament on increases in the Commission's personnel budget and the more widespread criticisms of the purportedly burgeoning "Eurocracy."

In order to improve its monitoring and implementation capacity, the Commission proposed in January 1989 the establishment of a European Environment Agency (EEA) (Kelemen 1997, 2002; Ladeur 1996). The legal basis for the establishment of the EEA (art. 130(s)) required the unanimous approval of the member states in the Council, some of whom disagreed strongly concerning what powers the agency should be granted. Proponents of strict implementation argued that the EEA should be granted direct monitoring and enforcement powers. For instance, German and Dutch officials favored the establishment of an agency with the power to issue regulations, conduct inspections, and take enforcement actions (Interview, William K. Reilly, former EPA administrator, Stanford, Cal., May 1994; *Financial Times* 1994). Member states that opposed strict centralized enforcement, such as Britain and Spain, succeeded in denying the EEA the authority to conduct inspections and limiting its mandate to the coordination of information gathering activities among the member states; it had no authority to engage in rulemaking, conduct inspections, or take enforcement actions.

The Emerging Balance

By increasing its enforcement activities, the Commission tightened its grip on member state governments. As discussed above, in the early years of Community environmental policy, some member state governments did not view Community environmental laws as strict legal requirements. By the end of the 1980s, after the Commission had intensified its enforcement activities, they could not sustain this view. By that time a large body of environmental regulation was already in force and member states were obliged to implement it.

The member states reacted to this new situation when they negotiated the Maastricht Treaty in 1991. The poorer member states (Spain, Greece, Portugal, and Ireland) demanded that the new treaty include a provision to protect them from the excessive costs of some Community environmental regulations. Maastricht's Article 130s(5) provided that when a Community environmental measure "involves costs deemed disproportionate for the public authorities of a Member State," the Council shall provide for temporary derogations and/or financial support from the Cohesion Fund. The member states agreed on the details of the Cohesion Fund at the Edinburgh Summit in December 1992: the fund would supply 15.1 billion ECUs spread over the next six years to fund infrastructure and environmental projects in the four "Cohesion" states—Spain, Greece, Portugal, and Ireland (Allen 1996, p. 219). In addition to the money provided by the Cohesion Fund, the Community allocated an increasing portion of its existing Structural Funds to environmental protection projects (Krämer 1995, p. 130; Johnson and Corcelle 1995, p. 353). Thus, along with the provision that they could request temporary derogations from meeting EU law requirements, poorer member states succeeded in securing additional Community funding.[36]

The British approach in Maastricht was different. As was the case in the SEA, British efforts focused on the principle of subsidiarity. Whereas the principle of subsidiarity in the SEA had only applied to the environmental sector, the Maastricht Treaty elevated it to the status of a general principle of Community law.[37] The British hoped that with this higher status, the subsidiarity principle might finally serve to rein in Community competences. After the ratification of Maastricht, the British instigated an attempt to roll back a number of existing EU environmental directives. At the Edinburgh summit in 1992, the UK presented a list of existing Community legislation that it argued violated the principle of subsidiarity and should be returned to national governments. The British attack on Community regulation met with little success, however. While they did pressure the Commission into withdrawing some pending proposals (Golub 1994), they failed to gain the support of other EU members necessary to return established areas of Community regulation to the member state level. While the pace of new environmental legislation slowed somewhat in the 1990s, this is attributable to the fact that the EU had already adopted legislation covering most major areas of environmental policy.

As anticipated by the model of regulatory federalism, the EU has taken on a great deal of policymaking competence, while member states retain responsibility for implementation. In the years since Maastricht, even opponents of Community level regulation who had sought to roll back EU involvement have accepted that the Community will not beat a large-scale retreat from environmental policymaking. In the 1997 Amsterdam Treaty, no major efforts were made to roll back existing environmental policy; quite to the contrary, Article 175 (former Article 130s) of the Amsterdam Treaty extended the use of co-decision procedure to environmental policymaking.[38] On the other hand, implementation remains firmly in the hands of the member state governments. The EEA has increased the EU's monitoring capacity and EU funding for the implementation of Community law has increased substantially, but there is little prospect of the EU taking on a more substantial, direct role in implementation. Even erstwhile supporters of extending the EEA's mandate to include rulemaking, inspection, and enforcement functions no longer support such reforms.[39]

With the Community's competences in most areas of environmental policymaking well established, the Commission now focuses primarily on improving the implementation of Community law by member state administrations. The Commission has promoted the development of a network of member state environmental authorities, the IMPEL Network (European Union Network for the Implementation and Enforcement of Environmental Law) (Duncan 2000). Working with IMPEL and through the EU's regular legislative channels, the Commission is seeking to establish common, minimum criteria for environmental inspections. To date, these efforts have taken the form only of nonbinding recommendations, such as a set of voluntary mimimum criteria for inspections developed by IMPEL and a joint recommendation of the Council and European Parliament.[40] The EU's more coercive efforts to improve implementation by member states have relied on enforcement actions taken by the Commission (pursuant to Articles 226 and 228) and on the promotion of decentralized enforcement by private parties before national courts. In the next section, I examine how these enforcement efforts have constrained member state discretion.

The Politics of Discretion

After an initial period of laxity, the EU turned to a coercive approach to the enforcement of EU environmental law. Both the level of detail in Community legislation and the strictness of enforcement place great constraints on EU member states. As subsequent chapters demonstrate, EU members states have less discretion in the implementation of Community environmental law than the constituent states in some other federations (Canada and Australia, for example) do in implementing their federal environmental laws.

The EU's fragmented power structure has had an important impact on both the level of detail in EU environmental laws and the EU's approach to enforcing them. The separation of executive and legislative power and the lack of trust among the Commission, Council, and EP, and among member states within the Council, have encouraged the enactment of legislation that often specifies in great detail goals member states must achieve, deadlines they must meet, and procedures they must follow. The fragmentation of power has also emboldened the ECJ to engage in aggressive judicial review of national administrations.

The enforcement of EU environmental policy has relied largely on centralized enforcement actions taken by the Commission against member states. In contrast to the United States, where the federal government is prohibited from commandeering state administrations, the EU relies almost exclusively on this practice (Halberstam 2001). Member states are legally obligated to implement EU environmental directives and regulations, and the Commission has acted aggressively to bring enforcement actions in cases of nonimplementation. The Commission's efforts have been limited by its severe resource constraints, however, and in many instances member states have been able to avoid implementing Community law in practice. While private parties have served as watchdogs of Community law, notifying the Commission of violations, they have played but a limited role in enforcement litigation, given the restrictive standing requirements of many member state legal systems and the ECJ, coupled with other structural impediments to interest group litigation. A number of recent developments promise to increase the effectiveness of both centralized and decentralized enforcement in the EU. The Commission has gained new legal tools that bolster its enforcement power, and efforts are underway to increase the role of private parties in enforcement. As private parties bring more litigation and as the Commission intensifies its efforts, member states are likely to lose more and more discretion in the application of Community environmental law.

The Prevalence of Detailed Directives

Much of EU environmental legislation contains very detailed requirements, including emissions limits, ambient levels of pollution, sampling and testing methods, reporting requirements, deadlines, and various procedural rules (Rehbinder and Stewart 1985). One measure of the prevalence of detail in Community environmental law is the erosion of the distinction between the two primary forms of Community legislation—directives and regulations. Well over 90 percent of EU environmental legislation is issued in the form of directives. In principle, directives are flexible instruments that are binding on member states with respect to the objective to be achieved, but that leave national authorities free to choose how and in what form to implement them. After the Community adopts a directive, member states must, within a fixed period, transpose it into national law in a manner that accords with their national legal system. The second form of Community legislation—the regulation—is intended to be less flexible. Regulations need not be transposed into national legislation; they are binding in their entirety and directly applicable in member states.

One might assume that since directives are the primary form of Community legislation in the environmental arena, member states would enjoy wide discretion in implementation. Some environmental directives do contain vague language and grant member states wide discretion (Dillon 1999). However, most environmental directives are highly detailed, often specifying precisely the actions that must be taken. As in other areas of Community law, directives and regulations are often indistinguishable (Prechal 1995, pp. 15–18, 109–113). Rehbinder and Stewart (1985, pp. 137–138) highlight the frequency of such "regulation-type" directives, explaining that "In many areas of environmental policy, the Community has not followed the mandate of Art. 189(3) of the EEC Treaty to fix only the results to be achieved and to leave Member States the choice of form and methods. Instead, it has issued Directives which comprehensively regulate the environmental area concerned, thus leaving Member States no discretion."

The Community's tendency to produce detailed legislation has resisted efforts at reform. The Commission's White Paper on the Completion of the Internal Market announced a "new approach" to regulation (Commission 1985; Pelkmans 1995). As discussed above, the Community was to limit its harmonization efforts to essential health and safety requirements, beyond which the principle of mutual recognition of standards would apply. While the new approach may have yielded simpler regulations in some areas of Community policy, this has not been the case generally in regard to environmental regulations (Pelkmans 1995; Interview, European Commission, November 29, 1996). In response to demands from some member states for greater discretion, the EU has introduced new framework directives that promise to give members more flexibility and has promoted the adoption of "new" policy instruments such as voluntary agreements and various economic instruments (Golub 1998;

Rittberger and Richardson 2001; Jordan, Wurzel, and Zito 2001). Nevertheless, on the whole Community environmental law remains highly detailed. While much of the existing EU environmental legislation was amended during the 1990s, its strict, nondiscretionary approach was left in place (Jordan, Wurzel, and Zito 2001). Despite rhetoric to the contrary, most of the new pollution control measures adopted by the EU in the 1990s continue to take an inflexible, command-and-control approach (Rittberger and Richardson 2001). In comparative terms, the specificity of substantive and procedural requirements in EU environmental law by far exceeds that of the Westminster-style federal systems (Canada and Australia) examined in Chapter 5.

The EU's fragmented power structure encourages the high degree of detail in its environmental legislation. The Parliament views strict, detailed laws as a tool to constrain the member states and to encourage the Commission to take enforcement actions. The Parliament is a strong advocate of EU environmental policy. It does not trust the member states to implement Community law effectively and recognizes that the Commission may come under political pressure not to prosecute member states for infringements.[41] The presence of detailed provisions and deadlines makes it easier for the Commission to identify infringements and encourages it to initiate proceedings against noncompliant states. Recognizing that it will come under pressure from the Parliament to ensure that member states implement Community law, the Commission also views detail as a useful tool (Dehousse 1992, p. 392).

While there are clear reasons for the Parliament and Commission to advocate detailed laws, it may appear more surprising that member state governments in the Council, who play such a powerful role in EU legislative processes, would allow for such detailed provisions that can only serve to constrain them. The explanation, simply put, is that member states distrust one another. When member states collectively produce legislation working through the Council of Ministers, they act as political principals. However, member states individually play the role of bureaucratic agents, because they are responsible for implementing EU policies (Kelemen 2000; Franchino 2001). When acting collectively in the Council, the member states recognize that individual governments may have incentives to shirk on their commitments. Majone (1995, pp. 11–12) summarizes the impact of such distrust as follows: "Regulatory complexity is in part another manifestation of the cascading effect of mutual distrust. Doubting the commitment of other governments to seriously implement European rules, and being usually unfamiliar with different national styles of admin-istration, national representatives often insist on spelling out mutual obligations in the greatest possible detail." In particular, member states that support high standards of compliance fear that laxer members will not implement environmental directives effectively and want to make it easier for the Commission and interested parties to challenge member states for nonimplementation in the courts.[42] More generally, this same distrust encourages the member states to hand the ECJ powerful enforcement tools in order to police one another.

Litigation and Enforcement

Just as the fragmentation of power within the EU's federal institutions has encouraged the passage of detailed, inflexible laws, so too has it encouraged the emergence of an adversarial, litigious approach to the enforcement of EU environmental law. The fragmentation of power in the EU insulates the ECJ against political attacks and thus emboldens it to actively review the exercise of executive discretion by the member states in their role as the implementers of Community law. The multiple veto points in the EU's legislative process make new legislation difficult to pass (Dehousse 1992, p. 391; Tsebelis 1994; Tsebelis and Garrett 2001). The ECJ recognizes that if it rules that a member state has failed to properly implement a piece of EU legislation, it is extremely unlikely that the government in question will rally sufficient support to pass new legislation overturning the ECJ ruling, or to punish the ECJ in some other manner (Garrett, Kelemen, and Schulz 1998; Alter 1998; Pollack 1997). More generally, the fragmentation of legislative power at the EU level encourages the ECJ to make expansive constitutional and statutory interpretations (Weiler 1991; Cooter and Drexl 1994; Bednar, Ferejohn, and Garrett 1996; Pollack 1997; Alter 1998; Tsebelis and Garrett 2001).

The Commission has used the EU's infringement procedure to great effect, winning hundreds of cases before the ECJ against member states for failures to implement Community environmental law and most often securing compliance with these rulings. Recently, an environmental infringement case brought against Greece led to the first ever imposition on a member state of penalty payments for failure to implement Community law.[43] Despite the many successes of the infringement procedure, however, this centralized approach to enforcement has proven inadequate to ensure consistent compliance with Community environmental law. Therefore, the Commission has begun promoting a decentralized approach to enforcement relying on litigation by private parties before national courts, which may then refer cases to the ECJ via the Article 234 (former Article 177) preliminary ruling procedure. This decentralized approach to enforcement has played a powerful role in constraining member state discretion in other EU policy areas, but to date has played little role in environmental policy. In the following sections, I analyze the development of both the centralized and decentralized approaches to judicial enforcement in the EU.

Centralized Enforcement

The primary tool used by the Commission to enforce Community environmental law is the Article 226 (former Article 169) infringement procedure. Formally, the infringement procedure consists of three stages. First, upon detecting a violation of Community law, the Commission must send the member state in question a letter of formal notice. Next, it issues a "reasoned opinion" that states in detail the arguments it will use when referring the case to the ECJ. Finally, at its discretion, the Commission may refer the case to the ECJ. If the ECJ finds the member state to be in noncompliance, the state is required to make changes necessary to come into compliance with Community law.[44]

In practice, the infringement procedure is a flexible political tool. While it is legally obliged to open infringement proceedings if it detects a violation, in practice the Commission has discretion (Krämer 1996). As a high-ranking official in the environmental directorate (DGXI) put it, "Deciding when to bring a case is an art" (Interview, European Commission—DGXI, November 29, 1996). Discretion continues after the proceedings have commenced. No legally binding procedural rules govern the Commission's use of the infringement procedure, and Commission decisions on opening or continuing with infringement proceedings cannot be challenged by third parties.

Before the ratification of the Maastricht Treaty, the infringement procedure relied exclusively on the threat of public shaming to convince member states to comply with the law. Being the subject of an infringement proceeding compromises a member state's reputation as a law-abiding member of the Community. The cost to a member's reputation is particularly high if an infringement case ends with the ECJ ruling against the state (Garrett and Weingast 1993). While this name-and-shame technique proved effective in most cases, there were numerous instances in which member states chose to ignore adverse ECJ rulings in infringement cases. In those cases the Commission's only recourse was to initiate a second case (under Article 228 (former Article 171)) denouncing the member state for ignoring the previous court decision. Even then, some states failed to comply after a second ECJ ruling. The Maastricht Treaty strengthened the infringement procedure by amending Article 228 (former Article 171) to allow the ECJ to impose penalty payments on member states who fail to comply with ECJ rulings in infringement cases.

Since the mid-1980s, when the Commission adopted a more aggressive approach to enforcement, it has used the infringement procedure to pressure member states into compliance with considerable success. The Commission initiates hundreds of infringement proceedings for suspected breaches of Community environmental law every year (Commission 1996a, 1999c, 2000b). Most cases are resolved before reaching the ECJ, with the Commission's becoming satisfied that the member state has come into compliance and dropping its infringement case. However, aggregate data on the effectiveness of the infringement procedure are somewhat unreliable, because there are undoubtedly many cases that the Commission chooses to drop or delay for political reasons. For instance, the Commission may drop or delay a case as a concession to a member state in exchange for cooperation in negotiations on a related issue, or the Commission may be hesitant to pursue a case if it anticipates that the member state will refuse to comply even after an ECJ ruling. Whatever the actual reason, both the government in question and the Commission have the incentive to claim that a proceeding was dropped because the member state had come into compliance, as this explanation presents the member state as a faithful implementer of the law and presents the Commission as a powerful enforcement body.

Nevertheless, a close examination of infringement cases shows that the Commission has successfully enforced EU environmental policy, even when doing so imposed substantial costs on recalcitrant member states. ECJ decisions have severely restricted the discretion of member states in implementing Community environmental law, even in cases in which the directives in question appear to afford them wide discretion. For instance, in infringement cases involving the implementation of the 1979 directive on the protection of wild birds, the ECJ has restricted a member state's discretion considerably.[45] The directive calls on member states to establish special protection areas for migratory birds and other species listed in an annex to the directive. By leaving the designation of these protection areas up to individual member states, the directive would seem to afford them wide discretion in implementation. However, in a 1993 ruling, the court found that Spain had violated the directive by failing to designate a specific marsh—the *Marismas de Santona*—as a special protection area.[46] The ECJ explained that the area constituted an important ecosystem for numerous migratory birds and species listed in the annex to the directive and, as such, should have been classified as a protected area.[47] Dissatisfied with the measures taken by the Spanish government to implement the ECJs ruling, the Commission later initiated Article 228 proceedings against Spain. Finally, in 1999 after the Commission was satisfied by additional measures taken by the Spanish government to restore the site and prevent future deterioration, the Commission dropped its Article 228 case (Commission 2000b, pp. 74–75).

In recent years, numerous other infringement cases involving the wild birds directive have severely constrained member state discretion in designating special protection areas (Commission 2000b, pp. 73–76). In a ruling against the Netherlands, the ECJ summarized its interpretation of the scope of member state discretion, explaining that, "while the Member States have a certain *margin of discretion* in the choice of SPAs [Special Protection Areas], the classification of those areas is nevertheless subject to certain ornithological criteria determined by the Directive. . . . Consequently, Member States are obliged to classify as SPAs all the sites which, applying ornithological criteria, appear to be the most suitable for conservation of the species [listed in Annex I to the Directive]."[48]

The ECJ has developed a similar case law with regard to infringements of the directive concerning bathing water.[49] The directive establishes limit values for waters used by recreational swimmers. It appears to provide member states with wide discretion by allowing them to designate when the number of swimmers using an area is large enough that the directive should apply. In one well-known case, the Commission challenged the British government's implementation of that directive, charging that it had not achieved the required levels of water quality at beaches in Blackpool and Southport. The British government held that it was unclear whether these beaches fell under the scope of the directive, claiming that while people used these beach areas, few actually swam.[50] The ECJ ruled for the Commission, arguing that given the presence of numerous swimmers, lifeguards, toilets, and changing stalls, it was evident that the areas should be classified as bathing waters.[51] In response to the ruling, the UK made considerable investments to clean the bathing waters in question. These efforts did not, however, satisfy the Commission. In a January 2000 press release, the Commission explained, "While substantial clean-up investments appear to have been made since, recent monitoring results show that beaches around Blackpool continue to breach the standards set [by the directive]" (Commission 2000h). As a result, the Commission initiated a second, related infringement action against the UK, and won another ECJ judgment finding the UK in breach of the bathing water directive.[52]

ECJ rulings have restricted the discretion of member states not only in regard to the substantive requirements of directives, but also in regard to procedural issues. The court has consistently held that when directives contain rights or obligations for individuals, member states must transpose them into national law using binding legal instruments. They cannot merely issue administrative guidelines or other nonbinding instruments. For instance, in its famous *TA Luft* ruling, the court ruled that Germany's practice of implementing a Community air-quality directive on sulfur dioxide and suspended particulates by issuing a nonbinding "technical guideline" *(Technische Anleitung)* for administrators was inadequate.[53] Germany emphasized that it was simply following its standard administrative practice and that, in any case, the air-quality standards set out in the directive had been met. Nonetheless, the Court sided with the Commission, holding that member states must implement Community directives by adopting measures "with unquestionable binding force, or with the specificity, precision and clarity required . . . to satisfy the requirement of legal certainty."[54]

The ECJ's case law has led to a reduction of the use of administrative circulars as a means of policy implementation throughout the Community. More generally, the Commission has recently commenced a series of infringement cases against member states for violations of procedural requirements, such as reporting requirements associated with water pollution and waste disposal directives and procedural aspects of the environmental impact assessment directive (Commission 2000b).

In the most recent escalation of its crackdown on noncompliance, the Commission has begun to request that the ECJ fine member states that fail to comply with ECJ rulings in infringement cases. In the Maastricht Treaty, the member states revised Article 171 to empower the Commission to make such requests, but this provision was not put to use until January 1997, after the Commission agreed to a formula for calculating the amount of daily penalties to be imposed (*Agence Europe* 1997a). Depending on the gravity of the violation and the size of the member state in question, penalty payments were to vary between 500 and 791,293 ECUs (now Euros) per day. Three weeks after agreeing to the fining formula, the Commission brought five cases that included requests that the ECJ impose penalty payments on member states.[55] Each case involved implementation failures in Community environmental policy. Subsequently, the Commission has initiated dozens more Article 228 (former Article 171) cases against member states. The threat of penalty payments seems to have had a substantial impact, pressuring member states that had long resisted pressure from the Commission and ECJ to come into compliance rapidly (Commission 2000c; Interviews, German and Italian Permanent Representations, Brussels, January 1997).

On July 4, 2000, the ECJ delivered its first ruling on such a case and imposed the EU's first ever penalty payments on a member state for failure to implement Community law. The decision involved Greece's failure to implement EU waste management directives in relation to waste disposal in the Kouroupitos River, in the Chania area in Crete. The Commission first began investigating the case in 1987 after receiving a complaint regarding uncontrolled waste disposal into the river. In 1991 the Commission brought a case against Greece, charging that it had failed to implement provisions of Community waste management directives.[56] In 1992, the ECJ ruled against Greece, finding that it had failed to fulfill its legal obligation under the directives by not establishing waste disposal plans for the area in question and not taking measures to ensure that waste from the area was disposed of without endangering human health or the environment.[57] After Greece failed to notify the Commission of any measures taken to comply with the ECJ ruling, the Commission pressed the Greek government to comply. Although Greece did take steps to reduce the amount of toxic and dangerous waste dumped in the river, it failed to adopt and implement a comprehensive waste disposal plan for the area of Chania. Dissatisfied with Greece's efforts, the Commission brought a second case against Greece in 1997 for failure to comply with the ECJ's 1992 ruling.[58] The Commission asked the ECJ to apply the new provisions of Article 228 (former Article 171) and impose penalty payments on Greece in the amount of 24,600 euros per day from the date of its second judgment. In its decision of July 4, 2000, the ECJ found against Greece on two of the three substantive issues raised in the case, and ordered it to pay 20,000 euros per day until it came into compliance with the 1992 judgment. The daily penalty of 20,000 euros ran until February 26, 2001, when the EU confirmed the closure of the waste dump and receipt of a waste management plan for the region in question. In all, Greece was fined 4.8 million euros, which it paid to the Commission (*Ends Environment Daily* 2001).

While the Commission very often succeeds in using the infringement procedure to secure compliance with Community law, it remains clear that the Commission's enforcement efforts suffer from fundamental deficiencies that limit its effectiveness. First, the Commission has difficulty identifying infringements. The Commission divides noncompliance into three categories; nontransposition,[59] incorrect transposition,[60] and nonapplication in practice. The Commission has little difficulty identifying nontransposition. In the early 1980s it standardized the monitoring of nontransposition and now automatically initiates proceedings against member states who fail to give notice of transposition measures within the prescribed time period (Commission 1982). The Commission has more difficulty in identifying incorrect transposition. Determining the adequacy of measures adopted by a member state in order to fulfill obligations imposed by a directive may require a lengthy analysis of national implementing legislation. Moreover, in order to avoid being cited for incorrect transposition, some member states have adopted a policy of "copy over"—simply copying the text of a directive into national law verbatim (Macrory 1994). The Commission has the greatest problems, however, in identifying failure to apply Community law in practice. The practical implementation of many directives, for instance those concerning water quality, waste management, and industrial emissions, are difficult to detect. The Commission does not have the authority to conduct on-site inspections of implementation, but must rely primarily on individuals and associations using the EU's complaints procedure to serve as its eyes and ears in the member states.[61]

Complaints from private parties regarding suspected infringements greatly expand the Commission's monitoring capacity; however, they do not resolve other problems related to the Commission's scarcity of staff and resources. The small professional staff the legal unit of the environmental directorate (DGXI) is overwhelmed by complaints regarding infringements (IMPEL 2000, p. 32). Investigating suspected infringements is a laborious process. If the Commission decides to pursue a case, the series of informal discussions with the member state administration and the formal stages of the infringement procedure can stretch out over several years. The average length of time between the Commission's decision to initiate an infringement procedure on an environmental matter and the actual judgment by the ECJ is nearly five years (Krämer 1996; IMPEL 2000, p. 162). The procedure fails to provide the private parties that bring complaints with any form of legal certainty. Infringement procedures are not subject to judicial or administrative review. Private parties that notify the Commission of an infringement have neither the right to be notified of the status of their complaint nor the right to challenge the Commission should it choose not to pursue the case (Krämer 1996; Macrory 1992, 1994; Rehbinder and Stewart 1985).[62]

The threat of fines is likely to make infringement procedures a more effective tool. Nonetheless, the Commission's other problems remain. While steps have been taken to improve monitoring, the Commission's understaffing problem persists. Opposition to any substantial expansion in the size of the Commission bureaucracy is simply too stark to be overcome in the foreseeable future. Chronically overburdened, the Commission recognizes that it cannot hope to enforce EU law effectively from Brussels. This recognition has led the Commission to take steps to encourage decentralized enforcement by private parties before national courts.

Decentralized Enforcement

National courts are an integral part of the Community legal order. Insofar as they apply Community law in their decisions, they can be viewed as lower courts in a Community legal system that culminates in the European Court of Justice. The ECJ hears only a small fraction of the total number of enforcement actions brought throughout the Community, while the vast majority of judicial enforcement of Community law takes place strictly before national courts. When Community directives are transposed into national law on time and properly, they are indistinguishable from laws that originated strictly from the national parliament. National courts enforce these laws just as they would any other national laws (Siedentopf and Ziller 1988, p. 179). Every time a national court makes a judgment enforcing a national law that derived originally from Community law, it is in effect acting as an enforcer of Community law.

The situation for individuals is more problematic if their government has failed to transpose a Community directive into national law on time or has failed to transpose it correctly. In such cases, individuals cannot rely on national provisions to protect their rights under Community law. The ECJ first addressed this problem in its landmark *Van Gend* ruling that established the doctrine of direct effect of European law.[63] Direct effect holds that Community laws do not simply impose duties on governments, but actually create rights for individuals that they can uphold before their national courts. Subsequent ECJ case law clarified the conditions under which a provision of Community law has direct effect: it must be clear and unambiguous, unconditional, and not dependent on further action being taken by Community or national authorities.[64]

The doctrine of direct effect was developed largely in order to improve the implementation of Community law. The ECJ specifically acknowledged the importance of decentralized enforcement by private parties in *Van Gend*, stating that "the vigilance of individuals concerned to protect their rights amounts to an effective supervision in addition to the supervision entrusted by Articles 169 and 170 to the diligence of the Commission and the Member States." In conjunction with the doctrine of the supremacy of Community law, direct effect allows individuals to benefit from their rights under Community law in the event of noncompliance.[65] The ECJ has ruled that a great number of EU environmental directives satisfy the conditions for direct effect (Riechenberg 1999), including directives concerning product standards,[66] minimum environmental-quality standards for air and drinking water,[67] and procedural requirements in environmental policymaking.[68]

Cases brought by private parties before national courts to enforce Community law can reach the ECJ via the preliminary ruling procedure (art. 234 (former art. 177)), which provides that where a national court finds that a ruling hinges on the interpretation of Community law, it may refer the question to the ECJ. The national court orders a stay in its proceedings while its referral to the ECJ is pending. After the ECJ has replied, the national court then applies the ECJ's "preliminary ruling" to the case at hand and makes a judgment. Overall, more than half the cases that reach the ECJ are requests from national courts for preliminary rulings. In some areas of Community law, individual plaintiffs have used the preliminary ruling procedure with great effect; for instance, women's rights advocates in the UK have enjoyed great success using the procedure to secure the implementation of the Community's requirements concerning the equal treatment of the sexes (Alter and Vargas 2000; Caporaso and Jupille 2001; Harlow 1999; Stone Sweet and Caporaso 1998).

To date, the preliminary ruling procedure has not played a significant role in Community environmental law. From 1976 to 1996 the ECJ made preliminary rulings in only thirty-six environmental cases (Cichowski

1998, p. 396).[69] Though the pace of referrals from national courts accelerated in the late 1990s and has begun to play an important role in areas such as nature conservation policy (Cichowski 2001), overall the impact of the preliminary ruling procedure on EU environmental policy remains limited.

There are a number of reasons why the ECJ has issued relatively few preliminary rulings in cases having to do with environmental law. First, most environmental regulations concern matters of diffuse public interest. For this reason, coupled with the fact that litigation is costly, private parties often lack the individual incentive to commence legal action to secure enforcement. Second, even when they wish to initiate litigation, environmental advocates may be denied standing before national courts. National legal systems, not Community law, determine rules of legal standing before national courts.[70] Most member states limit standing to plaintiffs who can prove a direct and concrete interest in a case, and national rules concerning standing for interest associations vary widely (IMPEL 2000; Afilalo 1999). While some member states—for example, Sweden, Denmark, the Netherlands, and Italy—permit associations such as environmental nongovernmental organizations (NGOs) to bring cases in the public interest, most others limit standing to parties who can claim to have suffered a personal harm due to the administration's action or inaction (for instance individuals whose health suffers due to pollution). Other differences in the scope of judicial review are also significant. The types of administrative decisions that are subject to judicial review vary among member states. In some states, such as Germany, only individual decisions are subject to review, whereas in others general decisions on standards and programs may be challenged.

Recent Commission initiatives and developments in European law promise to create new incentives and opportunities for private parties to initiate litigation before national courts concerning environmental matters. In the mid-1990s, the Commission and the European Parliament began pressuring member states to harmonize their national rules on access of private parties to national courts (Commission 1996a; European Parliament 1996, 1997a). In 1998, the EU member states and the EU itself signed the Aarhus Convention on access to information, public participation in decisionmaking, and access to justice in environmental matters.[71] The Aarhus Convention includes a set of commitments concerning access to justice in environmental policymaking. Though these provisions are rather vague, the Commission and member state environmental inspectorates have interpreted them to demand that environmental NGOs have at least some opportunity to challenge administrative decisions in the public interest (IMPEL 2000, pp. 16, 160–163). The majority of member states continue to oppose the outright harmonization of procedures relating to access to justice. However, most have expressed support for the establishment of some minimum criteria on access to justice and debate concerning the harmonization of such criteria is ongoing.

One impediment to the establishment of such minimal standards, particularly concerning standing for environmental interest associations, is the ongoing reluctance of the Commission and the ECJ to grant such groups standing to challenge Commission decisions. On several occasions, individuals and environmental NGOs have attempted to challenge Commission decisions affecting the environment.[72] However, the ECJ has consistently denied these plaintiffs standing, arguing that they are not directly and individually concerned with the decisions in question (Krämer 1996). Most recently, in *Stichting Greenpeace Council (Greenpeace International) v. Commission*,[73] the ECJ denied standing to a group of appellants including Greenpeace International, two local environmental organizations, and sixteen local residents in a case challenging the Commission's funding of the construction of two power plants in the Canary Islands. The appellants claimed that the Community's environmental impact assessment directive had been violated in the decision to construct the plants, and that their rights to participation in the assessment process had been violated.[74] ECJ denied them standing, maintaining that they did not meet the direct and individual concern requirements and refusing to recognize any distinct standing for environmental associations to protect diffuse public interests. In other areas of Community law where the ECJ has created pressure for the harmonization of member state legal procedures, it has typically done so by relying on norms of Community law as a baseline for such harmonized standards. As long as the ECJ persists in denying environmental plaintiffs standing, it will deter efforts to identify minimal, common standards for access to justice throughout the EU.

In other respects, however, ECJ jurisprudence has greatly increased the likelihood of decentralized, environmental litigation. The ECJ's case law concerning the principle of state liability has created the potential for environmental plaintiffs to sue member states for damages they suffer due to the nonimplementation of environmental law. In *Francovich*,[75] the ECJ established a new principle of Community law: member states can be held liable for damages suffered by individuals as a result of the state's failure to implement Community law. *Francovich* established three criteria necessary for state liability claims in cases of nonimplementation of a directive: (1) the directive must confer rights on individuals, (2) the content of those rights must be identifiable in the directive, and (3) there must be a causal link between the failure of the member state to fulfill its obligations and the damage suffered by the individual. In subsequent case law, the court added that the breach of the directive must be "sufficiently serious" in order to warrant liability claims.[76]

To date, there are no known cases of the application of the *Francovich* state liability principle to environmental matters.[77] However, considering the criteria for state liability, it is likely that individuals will in the future bring claims for damages relating to environmental directives (Lefevere 1996). Concerning the first two *Francovich* criteria, the ECJ has ruled on a number of occasions that environmental directives create rights for individuals that are identifiable in the directive. The third criteria—demonstrating causality—presents the greatest difficulty for those wishing to claim damages due to violations of environmental directives. It is often difficult to demonstrate a link between a specific violation of an environmental directive and a harm suffered. While causality is often difficult to prove, one can anticipate cases of illness caused by toxic spills or water pollution where individuals could demonstrate causality. Moreover, the mere anticipation of the possibility of such suits is likely to have an impact on states' implementation practices (Alter and Vargas 2000). Finally, beyond these general principles of member state liability, the Commission is pushing for the adoption of EU legislation specifically addressing environmental liability. The Commission issued the White Paper on Environmental Liability in 2000 proposing a framework directive that would establish liability rules for various forms of environmental damage (Commission 2000e).

Taken together, these legal developments suggest that the stage is set for a rapid increase in the role of decentralized litigation brought by private parties in the implementation of EU environmental law. A number of EU environmental directives create rights that individuals and associations can invoke before national courts. In addition to the many directives establishing rights to clean air and water and safe products, EU legislation establishing procedural rights is likely to encourage extensive litigation. For instance, the directive concerning environmental impact assessments, gives individuals the right to be consulted in those assessments.[78] Private parties have started to defend their rights under this directive, challenging member state impact assessment practices before national courts.[79] The directive on freedom of access to environmental information[80] gives individuals the right to access to information on the environment held by public administrations.[81] This measure will encourage litigation both by increasing the information available to would-be litigants and by itself creating a potential basis for litigation when member state administrations refuse access to information (Telephone interviews, Stichting Natuur en Milieu, Utrecht, the Netherlands, December 1996). Commission initiatives and the signing of the Aarhus Convention are increasing pressure on member states to increase access to justice for individuals and interest groups in environmental matters. Finally, the development of the ECJ's state liability doctrine, coupled with the potential adoption of Community legislation on environmental liability, will increase the incentive for litigants to bring cases.

Conclusion

The EU has established a powerful role in environmental policymaking, enacting legislation in all major areas of environmental protection. The expansion of EU policymaking competences has followed the pattern anticipated in Chapter 1. As in the other polities in this study, a division of competences has emerged in which the EU plays a dominant role in policymaking, while member states control most implementation and enforcement. Indeed, although EU funding for environmental programs has increased in recent years, essentially EU environmental policy relies on compelling member states to implement unfunded mandates.

The EU has developed a highly adversarial, litigious approach to enforcement that places great constraints on member state discretion. Insofar as the EU has no power to prosecute polluters directly, its enforcement capacity is limited.[82] However, the Commission clearly takes the most aggressive stance of any federal government in this study in enforcing member state compliance with EU law. The ECJ has not simply condemned member states for gross implementation failures, such as the failure to transpose directives into national law, it has interpreted many environmental directives in a manner that greatly constrains member state discretion in implementation. Recently, the Commission and ECJ set the precedent of fining a member state for nonimplementation.

The one respect in which EU environmental policymaking has not become thoroughly judicialized is in the realm of litigation by private parties. As of yet, the ECJ has not opened wide its courtroom doors to environmental litigants bringing cases in the public interest, and many national systems maintain restrictive rules on legal standing that impede such litigation. However, recent inititiatives to expand access to justice and establish Community rules concerning environmental liability, coupled with the development of the state liability principle, promise to stimulate more litigation by private parties. Ultimately, litigation by private parties is likely to place even greater constraints on member state discretion than enforcement actions brought by the Commission.

3 | Environmental Regulation in the United States

Wary of the tyranny that can result from the concentration of power, the framers of the U.S. Constitution set out to establish a system of government that would fragment public power through the separation of powers, a system of checks and balances, and federalism. They succeeded in producing a federal government in which power is highly fragmented, and the subsequent development of U.S. federal institutions have enhanced this fragmentation. The framers anticipated that the separation of powers would help safeguard states' rights by making it difficult for political forces at the federal level to coalesce in order to infringe on state powers and by encouraging the development of an independent judiciary that could police the federal bargain (Madison 1987, no. 51; Bednar, Eskridge, and Ferejohn 2001). However, the development of environmental regulation in the United States demonstrates that the combination of fragmentation of power at the federal level with federalism has had unintended and counterintuitive consequences. As in other federal systems in this study, the U.S. federal government has taken on a powerful role in environmental policymaking, while delegating most policy implementation to state governments. At the same time, however, it has placed greater constraints on the discretion of state governments than have other federal governments. The fragmentation of power in the U.S. federal government has encouraged the enactment of detailed, inflexible regulations, the emergence of active judicial review of administrative action, and, ultimately, the development of an adversarial, litigious approach to enforcement that severely constrains state government discretion in implementing federal laws.

The U.S. Constitution divides government authority among three branches: the legislature, the executive, and the judiciary. The executive is controlled by a popularly elected president and does not rely on the confidence of the legislature. Legislative power is divided between two power-ful, directly elected chambers, the House and Senate. The judicial branch is headed by a Supreme Court, whose justices enjoy lifetime tenure. While the Constitution divides legislative, executive, and judicial functions of government among the branches, it also empowers the branches to place checks on each other's exercise of these powers. For instance, the execu-tive can place a check on Congress by vetoing legislation, both the presi-dent and the Senate determine the composition of the Supreme Court through the nomination and confirmation process, and the Court can check the actions of Congress and the executive branch through its pow-ers of constitutional and statutory review. The president, senators, and representatives in the House are all elected by different constituencies and serve different terms of office. Differences in the sources of electoral sup-port and/or legitimacy of these institutions provide the actors who oc-cupy positions in them with different incentives that may encourage them to pursue different policies (Madison 1987, no. 39; Mayhew 1974).

The fragmentation of power within the U.S. federal government has had a profound impact on environmental regulation. The separation of legislative and executive power has encouraged Congress to draft detailed environmental statutes aimed at limiting executive discretion. The frag-mentation of political power has also safeguarded judicial independence and encouraged courts to play an active role in the regulatory process. These dynamics have also limited the discretion of state governments in implementing federal laws. When federal officials delegate implementation to state governments, they burden them with the same inflexible statutory requirements and the same legalistic approach to enforcement. In the 1990s, a backlash by state government officials coupled with a series of Su-preme Court decisions aimed at protecting state autonomy reduced the degree to which the federal government can limit state discretion. In com-parative terms, however, U.S. states remain highly constrained.

Given this system of fragmented power, analyzing the development of environmental regulation in the United States yields important lessons for the European Union (EU). Although the EU's institutional structure dif-fers in many ways from that of the United States, the two systems share ba-sic features that have encouraged the development of similar regulatory styles. Both demonstrate how the fragmentation of federal power can en-courage a legalistic approach to enforcement that constrains state discre-tion. Comparison of the two suggests that while the U.S. federal govern-ment continues to place greater constraints on state governments than does the EU, this difference stems not simply from the greater powers and resources of the U.S. government, but also importantly from the greater frequency of decentralized enforcement of federal law by private parties in the United States. This development of decentralized enforcement in U.S. environmental policy provides insight into how such enforcement by private parties may develop in the EU, should the EU continue increasing opportunities and incentives for enforcement litigation.

The Politics of Competence

The Emergence of Federal Policymaking

Like the other federal constitutions examined in this study, the U.S. Constitution originally made no mention of environmental policy. Under the Tenth Amendment, the authority to make environmental policy, like other powers not granted to the federal government in the Constitution, remained in the hands of the states. For most of U.S. history, pollution problems were of low political salience and neither state nor federal officials took concerted action to address them. Many local governments issued antipollution laws, such as smoke abatement ordinances, aimed at protecting public health, but these were generally very poorly enforced (Percival 1995, p. 1148; Jones 1975, pp. 21–25). In cases where major pollution problems caused serious public health threats, state health officials occasionally took legal action against polluters under common law principles such as public nuisance and negligence. States occasionally came into conflict with one another over interstate pollution, as for instance when Missouri sued Illinois to stop Chicago from dumping raw sewage that flowed into the Mississippi (*Missouri v. Illinois,* 180 U.S. 208 (1901)) or when New York sued New Jersey to stop the dumping of sewage into the New York Bay (*New York v. New Jersey,* 256 U.S. 296 (1921)).[1] In the late 1940s and 1950s, a few states enacted statutes concerning pollution, but none could be said to have adopted comprehensive environmental policies.[2]

Although the federal government had played a significant role in conservation policy from the turn of the twentieth century,[3] it did not become involved in contemporary pollution control issues until it took action regarding water and air pollution in the late 1940s and 1950s.[4] Federal involvement during this period was limited to conducting research and, most important, providing funding to assist state and local pollution control programs.[5] State governments supported these funding initiatives; indeed, they lobbied for them. Funding for projects such as wastewater treatment facilities provided ample opportunities for pork barrel politics. Most significant is the fact that federal dollars came with few strings attached; the federal government left setting standards in state hands and did little to control their implementation efforts (Moe 1989, pp. 306–310; Ingram and Mann 1978, pp. 131–162; Davies and Davies 1975).

States used their ample discretion during this period to tailor their regulatory programs to meet the demands of local interests. In most states, polluting industries predominated and environmental protection efforts lagged. In the area of water pollution, federal spending on research and sewage treatment construction grants did not succeed in controlling pollution, as was amply demonstrated by rivers so filled with pollutants that they caught fire (Hodas 1995, p. 1554). In the area of air pollution, states did not respond to federal calls to action. The federal government had funded research and state pollution control programs beginning in 1955, but most states did little to control air pollution.[6] California and New York did adopt strict measures creating impediments to trade in automobiles and high-sulfur coal, (Elliot, Ackerman, and Millian 1985, pp. 330–338). The federal government slightly expanded its regulation of air quality in 1963, 1965, and 1967, largely in order to discourage the restrictions to trade in automobiles and coal that might be caused by divergent state regulations.[7] The automobile industry itself supported the enactment of uniform national standards in order to avoid facing divergent state requirements (Elliot, Ackerman, and Millian 1985).

The Air Quality Act of 1967 was the most significant legislation among these enactments. The act established the National Air Pollution Control Administration within HEW and required that states set air-quality standards and submit implementation plans to the federal government for approval. With the exception of automobile emissions standards, which the act empowered the federal government to establish, the Air Quality Act left standard setting, implementation, and enforcement in state hands. It merely demanded that states set some standard and devise a feasible implementation program. While states such as California, Pennsylvania, and New York took an active role in addressing air pollution problems, most states were slow to comply with the federal call to action. By the end of 1970, only twenty-one states had submitted implementation plans under the 1967 act and none had been approved by the federal government (Ingram and Mann 1978, p. 133; Melnick 1983, p. 26).

In the early 1960s, just as the ineffectiveness of state pollution control efforts was becoming increasingly apparent, public concern regarding environmental issues began to increase. The publication of Rachel Carson's *Silent Spring* in 1962, followed by a series of highly publicized pollution incidents, focused attention on environmental issues. In the wake of these events, public concern regarding environmental issues grew dramatically between 1965 and 1970 (Dunlap 1989, pp. 95–101; Jones 1975, pp. 137–155). Increasing public outcries surrounding such environmental catastrophes as the 1969 Santa Barbara oil spill and the participation of an estimated 20 million Americans in the Earth Day activities on April 22, 1970 ushered environmental issues onto the national stage.

The federal government responded decisively. The executive and legislative branches raced to demonstrate their commitment to environmental protection, with rivals in the House, Senate, and White House competing to claim credit as the strongest defenders of the environment (Moe 1989; Jones 1975, pp. 175–210). In 1969, Congress passed the National Environmental Policy Act (NEPA), which required the federal government to conduct environmental impact assessments for all major federal actions. More landmark legislation was soon to follow. Unprecedented increases in the federal role in air and water pollution came first, with the Clean Air Act Amendments of 1970,[8] the Federal Water Pollution Control Act Amendments of 1972,[9] and the Safe Drinking Water Act of 1974.[10] Federal regulation of chemicals and toxic substances followed, with the Federal Environmental Pesticide Control Act of 1972,[11] the Toxic Substances Control Act of 1976,[12] and the Resource Conservation and Recovery Act of 1976 (RCRA).[13]

President Nixon quickly jumped on the bandwagon. He declared himself an environmentalist and, as his first official act of 1970, signed the NEPA into law. Later that year he orchestrated a major bureaucratic reorganization in order to create the Environmental Protection Agency (EPA).[14] He transferred federal employees dealing with pollution control in the Departments of Agriculture and the Interior and the HEW to the EPA, which would play a key role in implementing the new federal environmental laws on the congressional docket and would report directly to the president.[15] Together, these legislative and bureaucratic developments established a major federal role in environmental regulation.

Although the U.S. federal government had no explicit remit to enact environmental policy, it had little reason to worry about constitutional challenges to its environmental initiatives.[16] The Constitution's Commerce Clause (art. 1, para. 8) grants Congress the power to regulate interstate commerce. The Supreme Court interpreted this clause broadly; indeed, the Court had not struck down a single federal regulation claiming to promote interstate commerce since the New Deal.[17] Given this wide interpretation, advocates of federal involvement could easily sustain the claim that federal environmental regulations served to promote interstate commerce.[18]

Federal Involvement in Implementation and Enforcement

Before 1970, the enforcement of environmental policy in the United States had been conducted almost exclusively by state governments.[19] The establishment of the EPA, however, along with the federal environmental statutes of the early 1970s, provided for a powerful federal role in environmental policy implementation and enforcement. In particular, the EPA was empowered to issue heavy fines against polluters and to take over enforcement responsibilities from laggard states (Davies and Davies 1975, p. 205; McCubbins, Noll, and Weingast 1989, p. 448; Humphrey and Paddock 1990). The federal government increased its enforcement efforts throughout the 1970s and placed great pressure on states to intensify their own efforts, but it never seriously threatened to strip states of their role as the primary implementers of federal law.

The EPA quickly signaled its willingness to take on polluters, bringing five times as many enforcement actions during its first two months as all its predecessor bodies had done in any comparable period (Vogel 1986, p. 178). The EPA grew significantly in subsequent years. In 1973, it had a budget of approximately $500 million and a staff of 8,200. By 1980, the budget reached $1.3 billion and the staff 10,600. By 1992, the budget topped $6.5 billion[20] and the agency employed more than 18,000 people, two-thirds of whom worked in one of the EPA's ten regional offices spread across the United States (Rosenbaum 1994, p. 126; Vig and Kraft 1994, p. 16).

With the growth of the EPA, the U.S. federal government came to play a powerful role in the direct implementation and enforcement of environmental policy. Nevertheless, the U.S. federal government never developed the capacity to totally assume control over the implementation of federal regulations, opting instead to delegate most responsibility for implementation to the states. Cases of "complete preemption," in which the federal government occupies a field of regulation and prevents states from playing any role in standard setting, implementation, or enforcement, are extremely rare. The two major instances of complete federal preemption in environmental regulation are motor vehicle emissions[21] and, in some respects, toxic substances.[22] Instead of complete preemption, the federal government typically relies on a "partial preemption" approach, setting minimum environmental standards and goals but allowing states to design and implement their own laws and programs aimed at achieving these objectives, subject to federal approval.[23] Only in the rare cases of complete preemption does the federal government set ceilings on state environmental standards.

Regulations concerning air and water pollution, pesticides, and hazardous wastes all rely on variants of the partial preemption approach, which was first introduced in the Clean Air Act Amendments of 1970. The amendments called on the federal government to set national air quality standards, but asked states to enact and enforce emissions limits adequate to meet these standards (Melnick 1983, p. 46). States were expected to submit a SIP to the EPA, detailing their plans for implementation and enforcement.[24] If the state failed to submit an adequate plan, the EPA could propose a plan for the state.[25] After EPA approval of a SIP, enforcement would be left primarily in the hands of the state government, with the EPA playing only a limited oversight role.

The federal government's oversight role under the Clean Air Act and other environmental statutes empowers the EPA to bring direct enforcement actions against polluters if it is not satisfied by state government efforts.[26] The EPA may initiate an action where a state has failed to do so. Under certain circumstances, the EPA may engage in a practice known as "overfilling," in which an action is brought against a polluter who is already subject to a state enforcement action. Over the course of the 1970s, environmental statutes provided the federal government with greater powers of direct enforcement. For instance, under the Federal Water Pollution Prevention and Control Act of 1972, after a state had been granted primacy in implementation and enforcement, the EPA could still bring a direct enforcement action against a polluter in the state without notifying that state in advance.[27] The Resource Conservation and Recovery Act of 1976 granted the EPA wide-ranging enforcement powers, including the authority to assess civil penalties, issue compliance orders, revoke permits, and initiate criminal investigations.[28] The Clean Air Act Amendments of 1977 increased the EPA's enforcement power by enabling it to assess civil penalties against polluters for past violations of SIPs (Melnick 1983, pp. 189–190).

As I have already noted, while the federal government made notable increases in its implementation and enforcement activities, it never sought to establish a dominant role in implementation and enforcement. Instead, the federal government preferred to delegate most responsibility for implementation and enforcement to state governments. As discussed in Chapter 1, this approach enabled the federal government to claim credit for addressing public concerns over environmental issues, while passing on much of the cost of implementation to the states. But a variety of federal environmental statutes provided that, after the delegation of primacy in enforcement to a state, the EPA could take back responsibility for implementation and enforcement if it found that a state was systematically failing to enforce the statute. However, the EPA has never opted to do so (Humphrey and Paddock 1990, p. 44). The agency has little incentive to preempt state implementation. First, were the EPA to completely take over implementation in a state, it would have to bear the cost of establishing and staffing a statewide enforcement program. Second, such preemption would ignite major conflict with state environmental officials, on whose cooperation the EPA depends for so many of its programs. Finally, nothing would stop the state government from later submitting a new state implementation plan and taking back primary responsibility from the EPA, leaving the EPA's newly established structures redundant (Pfander 1996). Both the EPA and state governments recognize these incentives and understand that the threat of EPA takeover is not credible.

Establishing a New Equilibrium

By the end of the 1970s, the division of regulatory competences between the federal government and the states was well established. The federal government would play a dominant role in policymaking, establishing minimum federal standards in a variety of areas. Most implementation and enforcement would be left to the states, with the federal government playing an important oversight role. This division of competences withstood President Reagan's promised devolution revolution, and persists to this day. While the Reagan administration did not succeed in rolling back federal environmental regulation and devolving regulatory authority back to the states, major funding cuts during the Reagan years reduced support to the states for the implementation of federal environmental laws. As the financial burden of federal environmental laws increased, states complained more vociferously about "unfunded mandates" and demanded an increased voice in federal policymaking. This mobilization by state governments has pressured the EPA to take a more flexible approach in its interactions with states; however, the basic division of competences established in the 1970s persists.

Reagan entered office promising to roll back the mass of regulation that he claimed was suffocating the U.S. economy, and environmental regulation was one of his primary targets. In his first two years in office, Reagan signed into law legislation aimed at reducing government regulation, including the Paperwork Reduction Act of 1980, the Regulatory Flexibility Act of 1980, and State and Local Cost Estimate Act of 1981. He also signed Executive Order 12,291 that required federal agencies and departments, including the EPA, to justify major rules with cost–benefit analyses. These analyses would be submitted to the Office of Management and Budget in the White House, which could approve them or demand revisions.[29]

In addition to these general provisions, President Reagan attacked federal environmental regulation through changes in staffing changes and funding cuts. Early in his administration, Reagan left important posts in the EPA unfilled. When he appointed an EPA administrator after six months in office, he selected Anne Gorsuch, someone known to oppose federal regulation. He appointed another well-known anti-environmentalist, James Watt, to head the Department of Interior. Reagan also cut the EPA budget, reduced the staff, and eliminated a number of offices, including the Office of Enforcement (Vig and Kraft 1994, p. 17).

While Reagan did reduce EPA scrutiny of state implementation efforts and did eliminate some minor regulations, no major pieces of environmental legislation were repealed during his administration. The fragmentation of power built into the structure of U.S. government served to prevent such a roll back, as Democrats in Congress could block legislation aimed at reducing the federal role in environmental protection. Reagan's regulatory relief initiatives were outweighed by the new regulatory requirements enacted during his administration, allowing the overall regulatory burden to increase (Rose-Ackermann 1990, p. 289; 1992, pp. 159, 162; Kincaid 1994a, p. 46). The number of statutory mandates calling for state implementation passed in the 1980s exceeded that in any previous decade (Conlan, Riggle, and Schwarz 1995, p. 25; ACIR 1984, 1993). Environmental mandates enacted in the 1980s under Reagan (and later Bush Sr.) included rules concerning underground storage tanks, asbestos removal from schools, and toxic wastes. In addition to new statutes, existing statutes on hazardous waste disposal and water quality were reauthorized and strengthened.[30]

While the number of statutory mandates and the costs to states of implementing them increased, federal funds did not. Federal support for many regulatory programs was cut significantly. Measured in constant dollars, aid to states for implementing federal statutes was lower in 1990 than in 1980 (Conlan, Riggle, and Schwarz 1995, p. 26). Between 1979 and 1988, federal funding for state air pollution control programs fell by 54 percent and funding for state water pollution control programs fell by 68 percent (Ringquist 1993, p. 62). In the absence of federal support, states were pressured to increase funding and staff for environmental protection. Most states made significant increases throughout the 1980s and 1990s. In 1982, federal grants funded approximately 70 percent of spending on state environmental programs, while states themselves provided only 30 percent (Pfander 1996, p. 88). By 2000, these figures had reversed, with states providing approximately 67 percent of the funding for their programs and the federal government providing only 33 percent (Brown 2001). Collectively, the states have nearly four times the staff of the EPA and conduct the overwhelming majority of environmental inspections (Council of State Governments 1996; Pfander 1996).

States have not assumed the burdens of financing federal regulation quietly. As the cost to states of implementing federal mandates increased, they demanded both an increased role in policymaking and greater flexibility. From 1991 to 1993, state and local officials mounted a campaign against federal mandates culminating in nationwide protest in October 1993 called "National Unfunded Mandates Day" (Conlan, Riggle, and Schwarz 1995, p. 26) Environmental mandates were widely regarded as the most costly ones. President Clinton responded to these concerns by issuing an executive order to restrain administrative mandates (Kincaid 1994a, p. 45). In 1995, Congress passed and Clinton signed into law the Unfunded Mandate Reform Act (UMRA), which makes it more difficult for Congress to issue unfunded mandates.[31] For instance, the act allows a member of Congress to block consideration of unfunded mandates unless overruled by a majority. However, the act does not totally ban unfunded federal mandates. It does not apply to certain categories of mandates, such as civil rights mandates, and it allows existing mandates to remain in place.

In the area of environmental protection, the EPA has responded to state complaints about the burden of federal mandates by establishing new cooperative institutions. In 1993, the EPA set up the State/EPA Capacity Steering Committee (SECSA) and called on it to make proposals to increase cooperation between the federal and state governments.[32] This initiative led to the establishment of the National Environmental Performance Partnership System (NEPPS) in 1995. Under this system, individual states and their respective EPA regional offices sign performance partnership agreements (PPAs) concerning environmental goals and indicators, program assessment and oversight, and public outreach and involvement. In essence, a state agrees to collect data on specific environmental indicators, to provide regular self-assessment reports, and to engage in certain monitoring activities. In return, the federal government agrees to give a state greater flexibility in implementing policy and to reduce its oversight of the state's day-to-day enforcement activities, in particular if the state shows improvements on the agreed-upon environmental indicators. This flexibility may also apply to federal grants; as part of an agreement, the federal government may offer performance partnership grants (PPGs) that, in contrast to traditional, narrowly targeted grants, allow state commissioners to shift federal funds among environmental programs as needs dictate. The first states to sign such agreements were Utah, Illinois, Delaware, Colorado, New Jersey, and Oklahoma. Today, over three dozen states have such agreements at some stage of development.

While the EPA was setting up institutions to promote cooperation with states, the states were organizing themselves as well. In 1993, the states established a new institution to increase their influence on federal-level environmental policymaking. During a meeting in Phoenix in December 1993, representatives of twenty state governments established the Environmental Council of the States (ECOS) to serve as a forum for dialogue among state environmental agencies and to lobby Congress and the EPA on their behalf. Since May 1995, the permanent headquarters and staff of ECOS have been located in Washington, D.C. EPA quickly brought ECOS into the policy process, agreeing in 1997 to work with the council to develop common performance measures for the EPA and states to use in the NEPPS program (EPA 1997a).

Just how much influence state officials will manage to gain over U.S. federal policymaking with the creation of institutions such as NEPPS and ECOS remains to be seen. State government officials have formed a number of institutions aimed at increasing their influence over various spheres of federal policymaking and some have proven successful.[33] Generally, however, the track record of such bodies is weak. For instance, institutions such as the National Governor's Association and the National Conference of State Legislatures have had limited success in promoting state interests in federal policymaking arenas. In any case, the establishment of the NEPPS and ECOS in the United States has striking parallels with developments in Australia and Canada discussed in Chapter 5. In all three, the state governments have established such intergovernmental institutions to make up for their lack of direct representation in federal legislative processes and increase their influence over federal policymaking.[34] This suggests that the division of competences common to all federal systems, in which states are responsible for most of the implementation of federal environmental laws, leads state governments to demand direct influence over federal policymaking.

The evolution of the division of competences in the United States followed the pattern anticipated by the model of regulatory federalism in Chapter 1. Growing public concern with environmental issues coupled with the potential for distortions to trade caused by divergent state environmental regulations led the federal government to assume a role in environmental policymaking. Although the U.S. federal government has taken on a more active role in direct implementation and enforcement than any other polity explored in this book, it still leaves implementation and enforcement primarily in the hands of the states. As in other polities, the burden of federal mandates on state governments has only increased over time.

The Politics of Discretion

Comparative studies of regulatory policymaking in a variety of policy areas suggest that policy implementation and enforcement in the United States is unusually legalistic, litigious, and costly (Kagan and Axelrad 1997; Kagan 2001). Federal environmental statutes and regulations in the United States contain many detailed, action-forcing requirements that spell out how federal agencies and states are to implement them (Kagan and Axelrod 1997, p. 150; Holland 1996, pp. 159–184; Davies and Davies 1975, p. 206; Moe 1989, 1990; McCubbins, Noll, and Weingast, 1987, p. 263; Bardach and Kagan 1982; Vogel 1986). Conflicts concerning the implementation of these statutes do not end in the halls of Congress or the Oval Office. They often end up in court, and such litigation has played a central role both in shaping general environmental policy measures and in influencing enforcement in specific cases (Melnick 1983, pp. 1–2; Holland 1996, p. 168). Federal and state courts actively enforce many of these requirements, both against polluters and against the federal and state agencies that are responsible for implementing them. Litigation constrains the discretion of environmental regulators, at both the federal and state level. Anticipating that their actions may be challenged in court, officials are pressured to adhere to the procedures and requirements prescribed by the law (Bardach and Kagan 1982). Some observers value this pattern of policymaking because of the added safeguards that judicial involvement provides (Rose-Ackerman 1995; Wenner 1994), while others view it as an "American disease" (Stewart 1993a) characterized by excessive costs, delays, and adversarialism (Vogel 1986; Melnick 1983; Kagan 1997).

Action-Forcing Environmental Statutes

Federal environmental regulation emerged alongside other forms of social regulation including consumer protection and occupational safety and health regulation in the context of what Cass Sunstein (1990) has termed the "rights revolution." Adopting an approach and rhetoric borrowed from the civil rights legislation of the 1960s, advocates of these social regulations sought to create federally protected "rights" for individuals, such as rights to clean air and water and rights to participate in environmental decisionmaking processes (Sunstein 1990; Rose-Ackerman 1992; Melnick 1993, 1996; Derthick 1999; Vogel 1981; Kincaid 1994a; Epp 1998). The structure of regulatory federalism in the U.S. separation-of-powers system shaped the development of this rights revolution. In 1970, when for the first time advocates of federal environmental regulation in Congress were in a position to pass sweeping new legislation, they did not trust executive agencies or states to implement these statutes faithfully. As described above, the legislature's distrust of the executive is programmed into the separation-of-powers federal system of government. This inherent distrust was heightened at the time many new social regulations were enacted because Democrats controlled both houses of Congress while Republicans controlled the executive. Moreover, environmental advocates were influenced by new academic literature that argued that regulatory agencies were often "captured" by the very industries they were intended to regulate (Lowi 1969; Noll 1971; Stewart 1975). Environmental advocates also distrusted state governments, particularly in light of those governments' previous efforts to protect the environment. Anticipating that state governments would conduct most of the actual implementation of the new federal rules, they had a clear incentive to control their discretion.

In drafting regulatory statutes, environmental advocates in Congress sought to ensure that the EPA and other federal and state agencies would implement the statutes as intended by the legislative majority. They recognized that due to the difficulty of putting together coalitions powerful enough to pass major legislation in the U.S. system, any legislation they enacted would likely remain in place for some time (Holland 1996, pp. 159–184; Davies and Davies 1975, p. 206; Moe 1990; McCubbins, Noll, and Weingast, 1987, p. 263). Therefore, in order to limit executive discretion, they enacted statutes full of "action-forcing" requirements that specified in considerable detail the standards that implementing agencies must achieve, the deadlines they must meet, and the procedures they must follow (Bryner 1987, pp. 94–98; Moe 1989, p. 313; Melnick 1983, 1996; Lazarus 1991). Statutes such as the Clean Air Act, the Clean Water Act, and the Toxic Substances Control Act list specific substances to be regulated by the EPA and states. Environmental statutes also require implementing agencies to follow rulemaking procedures more detailed than those required by the Administrative Procedures Act. Such procedures include conducting oral hearings following a specific timetable, considering petitions regarding rules, providing detailed explanations with documentary support, of the reasons particular decisions were made, and considering the views of a variety of interests. Some of these additional procedures were included to empower environmental advocates, others to appease regulated industries, and still others to satisfy demands made by federal courts. Environmental statutes also contain many strict deadlines: by 1988, Congress had demanded that the EPA meet eight hundred statutory deadlines (Rosenbaum 1994, p. 132).

The role of detail in legislation was intimately linked to the role of courts. Drafters of environmental regulation put detailed statutory requirements in place so that if implementing agencies or states failed to meet such requirements they could be brought before federal courts and forced to do so. To promote recourse to the courts, many statutes explicitly called for the use of litigation as a means of enforcement. For instance, in addition to providing for EPA suits against polluters, the Clean Air Act Amendments of 1970 provided that citizens could bring enforcement actions "against anyone who is alleged to be in violation of the act" and "against a government agency for failing to perform its duty under the act."[35] Nearly every federal environmental statute adopted subsequently has included similar "citizen suit" provisions.[36] Congress's aim in enacting these provisions was to "motivate governmental agencies to be more active" in implementing federal statutes.[37]

The inclination of Congress to write detailed regulations that require the EPA and states to meet specific requirements and deadlines has proven persistent. For instance, the Clean Air Act Amendments of 1970, which at the time of their passage were remarkable for their detail and stringency, took up a total of fifty pages. The 1977 amendments expanded to two hundred pages, and the 1990 amendments came in at a voluminous eight hundred pages. The latter required the EPA to write 55 major new regulations within two years and to write standards for 189 different toxic pollutants, each according to a prescribed schedule.[38] The 1990 amendments also gave the EPA power to seek civil penalties against polluters and made it easier for environmental organizations to bring suits by instituting a permitting system similar to the one that had existed under the Clean Water Act (Wenner 1994, p. 149). Congress has continued to include strict timetables despite the EPA's repeated failures to meet statutory deadlines.[39]

Litigation and Enforcement

Just as the fragmentation of power rooted in the structure of U.S. government encouraged the passage of detailed, inflexible statutes, so too has it encouraged a litigious approach to enforcement. Knowing that the fragmentation of power insulates them against easy legislative overrides or other forms of punishment, courts may play an active role in challenging executive actions and limiting executive discretion (Cooter and Ginsburg 1996; Moe and Caldwell 1994; Ferejohn 1995). When Congress enacted environmental statutes in the early 1970s that invited courts to play an increased role in the regulatory process, courts accepted the invitation with zeal. This in turn incited a boom in enforcement-related litigation that ultimately placed great constraints on state government discretion.

The U.S. federal government has relied on both centralized and decentralized approaches to enforcement. Centralized enforcement has focused on direct litigation against polluters and the use of fiscal levers to pressure state governments to act. For reasons to be discussed below, the United States has not followed the EU's approach of bringing litigation against state governments themselves. The federal government has also relied heavily on decentralized enforcement, empowering individuals and environmental organizations to act as private attorneys general enforcing federal law. During the 1980s and 1990s, Supreme Court jurisprudence limited the federal government's use of both centralized and decentralized approaches to enforcement of environmental law. Nevertheless, in comparison to the courts of other federal systems in this study, U.S. courts continue to show less deference to administrative agencies and, therefore, litigation continues to play a more significant role in the regulatory process.

In the 1960s and 1970s, federal courts increased their involvement in environmental regulation on a number of fronts. Both political conditions and the policy preferences of many federal judges at this time encouraged this marked increase in active judicial review.[40] The political divisions surrounding environmental and other new social regulations, coupled with Congress's explicit invitation, convinced the courts that they could engage in active judicial review without fear of political reprisals that might undermine their legitimacy. The executive branch might resent the judiciary's intrusion, but without the support of Congress, the executive could neither pass new statutes to overturn judicial interpretations nor take other actions to punish the courts. Moreover, many judges were in agreement with the academic literature that argued that many public agencies had been "captured" by regulated industries. These judges were motivated to use their powers of judicial review aggressively to police the behavior of public agencies (Melnick 1983, p. 12; Stewart 1975). In the 1960s, lower federal courts interpreted the Administrative Procedures Act's standing *(locus standi)* requirements in such a way as to enable environmental advocates to bring legal actions against public agencies and against polluters.[41] The Supreme Court upheld this approach in the 1970s, allowing environmental nongovernmental organizations (NGOs) to sue on behalf of their members and providing an expansive interpretation of the types of injuries that justified standing.[42] Courts also demanded that administrative agencies take into account the views of a variety of groups and provide reasons for their decisions.[43] They began to routinely overturn decisions made by administrators and in some cases forced the EPA to initiate new programs. Throughout the 1960s, federal courts were also increasingly distrustful of state governments, many of which were associated with racist policies and opposed progressive federal initiatives more generally. As early as 1960 the Supreme Court revealed its distrust of state and local governments and opened the doors of federal courts to litigants who wished to challenge the actions of state governments.[44]

Judicial supervision of federal and state regulatory agencies diminished somewhat after the late 1970s as the Supreme Court made landmark decisions that limited judicial control over administrative discretion.[45] While these decisions tempered the activism of most lower U.S. federal courts, they by no means stopped extensive judicial intervention. Courts in the United States remain far more active in their review of executive action than their counterparts in other federal polities, and they continue to review and remand many rulemaking decisions with great frequency (Rose-Ackerman 1995, pp. 151–152; Wenner 1994, p. 152).[46]

In the United States, both centralized enforcement by the EPA and decentralized enforcement by private litigants have played an important role in pressuring states to implement federal environmental policy. The federal government has brought pressure to bear on states both with litigation and with fiscal tools such as cross-cutting sanctions. Private litigants have generated further pressure by suing both polluters and implementing agencies.

Whereas the European Union issues directives that member states are required to implement, the U.S. federal government cannot compel a state to administer a federal program. The Supreme Court has reaffirmed this in its recent jurisprudence on the "anti-commandeering" principle.[47] In *New York v. United States,* the Court struck down a section of the Low-Level Radioactive Wastes Policy Amendment Act of 1985[48] that gave states a choice between regulating low-level radioactive waste in a manner determined by Congress or taking ownership of the waste and assuming liability for it. The Court held that this "take-title" provision violated the Tenth Amendment of the U.S. Constitution because it "commandeered" the state governments for the purpose of implementing a federal program. The Court explained that while the federal government may pressure states to implement federal programs, for instance by providing funds to states that do so and denying them to states that do not, it may not directly compel states to administer a federal program.[49] Rather, federal statutes must leave it to the states to decide whether to assume an implementation role or leave implementation to the federal government.

Even before *New York v. United States,* the federal government chose not to sue states for their failure to implement federal environmental mandates adequately. Such suits would have raised troubling questions for the federal government. Most federal environmental programs delegate primacy in enforcement to state governments, with the proviso that the EPA may assume primacy in enforcement if it detects a systematic pattern of nonenforcement on the part of the state government. Like all federal polities, the U.S. federal government prefers that states maintain primacy in implementation and enforcement. If the federal government were to prove in court that a state was systematically failing to enforce a federal statute, it would increase pressure on the EPA to take over primacy in enforcement in the state (Humphrey and Paddock 1990, p. 44). Not wanting to assume this role, the federal government relies on other instruments to pressure state governments into implementing federal statutes.

There are two instruments or "levers" available to the U.S. federal government, but not to he European Commission, for securing compliance.[50] First, the federal government prosecutes polluters directly. Even after a state implementation plan is approved and a state assumes primacy in enforcement, the EPA retains the right to bring enforcement actions directly against polluters. The EPA can assess administrative penalties, initiate cases seeking civil penalties, and, in the case of some statutes, seek criminal penalties and jail time. The EPA has brought tens of thousands of administrative enforcement actions and thousands of civil actions that have forced polluters to pay hundreds of billions of dollars in fines. In addition, many enforcement actions have led to criminal sanctions. Between 1983 and 1991, 790 individuals and corporations were charged with environmental crimes and 191 corporations and 387 individuals convicted, leading to over $34 million in fines paid and over 158 years in jail served (Gaynor et al. 1991). Since the Pollution Prosecution Act of 1990[51] strengthened its criminal enforcement powers, the EPA has intensified its criminal prosecution efforts considerably. In 2000 alone, the agency's criminal enforcement program charged 360 defendants and federal courts imposed 146 years of criminal sentences and $122 million in criminal fines (EPA 2001). Altogether in 2000, the EPA initiated "6,027 civil judicial, criminal and administrative enforcement actions requiring polluters to pay 2.6 billion in injunctive relief . . . and $224.6 million in civil and criminal penalties" (ibid.).

These federal enforcement actions against polluters place significant pressure on states. The federal government often brings enforcement actions where states have already initiated an enforcement action against the polluter in question. With this practice, known as "overfiling," the federal government seeks to ensure that the state government does not take a soft line with the polluter (Humphrey and Paddock 1990, p. 13). State governments resent this interference, as it indicates to regulated industries that the state is not in control of its own regulatory agenda and thus compromises it credibility in negotiations (Telephone Interview, Environmental Council of the States (ECOS), Washington D.C., March 23, 1998). In other cases, the federal government brings enforcement actions where states have failed to do so. Again, these actions damage state government credibility, by pointing out its implementation failures. The threat of federal intervention gives states an incentive to pursue enforcement actions on their own. Even state governments that oppose strict environmental regulation generally prefer that their own environmental agencies, rather than the EPA, handle enforcement against polluters.

Fiscal tools are the second set of levers that the federal government uses to induce states to choose to implement federal programs (ACIR 1984; Kincaid 1994a, 1996). Conditional grants-in-aid are one such tool. Congress can attach conditions to federal grants-in-aid to states that require states to regulate in specified ways in order to receive funds. For instance, in order to receive funds under the Resource Conservation and Recovery Act and the Clean Air Act, state enforcement programs have to meet federal targets regarding the number of inspections conducted and the number of enforcement actions taken (Humphrey and Paddock 1990, p. 20). Congress may also impose "cross-cutting" requirements that apply to all recipients of federal funds. For instance, under the National Environmental Policy Act, whenever state officials plan to take an action that is supported by federal funding, they must file an environmental impact statement (Lester 1990, p. 84). Finally, Congress may use powerful "crossover" sanctions, allowing it to withhold federal funds for specified programs to punish states for violations of other regulatory programs. For instance, the Clean Air Act Amendments of 1977 require the federal government to withhold highway grants to states that refuse to comply with the act.

Litigation brought by environmental organizations has played a vital role in the implementation and enforcement of federal statutes. As mentioned above, since the early 1970s Congress has enacted environmental statutes with citizen suit provisions that encourage private parties (such as environmental organizations) to enforce federal law. Some statutes allow courts to order defendants to pay the legal fees of successful plaintiffs.[52] Thus, at least in the case of successful suits, litigation can be partially self-financing.[53] Four major statutes—the Clean Air Act, the Clean Water Act, Superfund, and the Resource Conservation and Recovery Act—allow plaintiffs to sue violators for civil penalties.[54] Decentralized enforcement has been used to pressure federal and state implementing agencies to fulfill their mandates as well as to sanction polluters themselves.

With Congress and the courts opening up access to the courtroom in the early 1970s, environmental groups increased their use of litigation as a strategy to influence environmental policy.[55] Groups such as the Natural

Resources Defense Council, Environmental Action, and the Sierra Club Legal Defense Fund were founded during the early 1970s with the explicit aim of bringing lawsuits. The use of litigation started slowly. Between 1970 and 1980, eighty-five citizen-suit cases were decided by federal courts of appeals (Bryner 1987, p. 116). Most such suits focused on the EPA's failure to properly implement statutes. Some suits also charged the federal government with violating the National Environmental Policy Act by failing to follow appropriate procedures in preparing an environmental impact statement (EIS) for a federal project.[56] Some suits brought by environmental organizations led to significant policy victories, forcing the EPA and state environment agencies to initiate new programs. For instance, a federal court decision pressured the EPA to initiate a program to prevent significant deterioration of air quality in areas that already met national standards (*Sierra Club v. Ruckelshaus,* 344 F. Supp. 253 (D.D.C. 1972)). Another decision forced the EPA to initiate a program to reduce smog in cities by implementing transportation control plans (*Natural Resources Defense Council v. EPA,* 475 F.2d 968 (D.C. Cir. 1973)). Other decisions forced the EPA to initiate programs to control specific pollutants, not explicitly required by statute *(Natural Resources Defense Council v. Train,* 545 F.2d 320 (2d Cir. 1976); *Environmental Defense Fund v. Ruckelshaus,* 3 Envt'l L. Rep. 20173 (1973)). Few enforcement actions were brought against polluters as environmental groups left these difficult cases to the EPA.[57]

Environmental litigation shot upward in the 1980s. As President Reagan sought to relax enforcement, environmental organizations fought back by instigating more lawsuits. For instance, environmental groups initiated only 20 percent of the water pollution enforcement cases in the 1970s, but they initiated nearly 50 percent of the cases during the Reagan and Bush Sr. administrations (Wenner 1994, p. 152). By 1987, environmental organizations had brought hundreds of citizen suits. Most suits were brought under the Clean Water Act and the Resource Conservation and Recovery Act (Kibel and Klinski 1994, p. 68). Detecting violations of discharge permits issued under the Clean Water Act was relatively easy, as polluters had to produce frequent monitoring reports that were open to the public.

In the 1990s, the Supreme Court jurisprudence regarding standing (Susan Rose-Ackerman 1995: 136; Kibel and Klinski 1994; Phillips 2000) and regarding the sovereign immunity of state governments (Araiza 2000; Jackson 2000) placed new restrictions on the ability of private parties to act as the enforcers of federal law. The Supreme Court modified its position on standing for environmental groups in three important cases: *Lujan v. National Wildlife Federation*, 110 S. Ct. 3177 (1990) *(Lujan I)*; *Lujan v. Defenders of Wildlife*, 112 S. Ct. 2130 (1992) *(Lujan II)*; and *The Steel Co., Chicago Steel and Pickling Co. v. Citizens for a Better Environment*, 523 S. Ct. 83 (1998). In *Lujan I*, the National Wildlife Federation challenged a decision by a federal agency (the Bureau of Land Management) to reclassify some lands in order to open them to mining. The federation claimed that members of their organization used land in the vicinity of the area in question, and would suffer as a result of mining. The Court denied the National Wildlife Federation standing, explaining that because the group had not specified exactly which lands their members used, their claim of injury was too tenuous.

In *Lujan II*, members of Defenders of Wildlife disputed a regulation issued by the secretary of interior that limited the scope of the Endangered Species Act[58] to the United States and the high seas. The act requires agencies to consult with the secretary of interior regarding the impact of activities on endangered species, but the regulation in question established that this requirement did not apply when U.S. agencies took actions in foreign countries. Individual members of Defenders of Wildlife who had visited Sri Lanka sought to challenge U.S.-funded development project there that they claimed would likely destroy the habitat of endangered species.

The Endangered Species Act contains a well-known "any person" citizen-suit provision, which provides that anyone can gain standing to bring suits to ensure that the act is enforced. However, in *Lujan II* the Court found a way around this provision by "constitutionalizing" the issue.[59] It ruled that the members of Defenders of Wildlife did not have standing because they did not suffer an injury sufficient to warrant standing under the Constitution's Article III "injury-in-fact" test, which requires that an injury be actual or imminent. By invoking this constitutional requirement, the Court effectively trumped the laxer standing requirement provided under the Endangered Species Act's citizen-suit provision. Similarly, in *Steel Company* the Court denied standing to Citizens for a Better Environment based on Article III's "redressability" requirement. The case involved a suit alleging that the company had failed to provide timely reports of discharges as required by the Emergency Planning and Community Right-to-Know Act of 1986 (EPCRA). Though the company eventually provided the reports, Citizens for a Better Environment nevertheless requested that the company be fined for violating the statute. The Court held that the payment of such fines would not redress any harm the plaintiff had suffered, and that because their grievance was not redressable, they lacked standing under Article III.[60]

While the precedents set in *Lujan I, Lujan II,* and *Steel Co.* clearly bode poorly for groups with tenuous injury claims who might try to bring litigation under the citizen-suit provisions of various environmental statutes,[61] they have by no means shut the courtroom door entirely. More recently, the Supreme Court has granted standing to an environmental group in an enforcement action under the Clean Water Act (*Friends of the Earth, Inc. v. Laidlaw Environmental Services, Inc.,* 120 S. Ct. 693 (2000), and has begun clarifying the conditions under which the government can delegate enforcement tasks to private parties (*Vermont Agency of Natural Resources v. United States ex rel. Stevens,* 120 S. Ct. 1858 (2000); see Gilles 2001). More generally, federal circuit and district courts continue to find grounds for standing for environmental groups in many cases.[62]

The Supreme Court's recent case law on the doctrine of sovereign immunity also diminishes the ability of private parties to serve as enforcers of federal law. The comparison with the EU is striking in this regard: while the European Court of Justice has been developing a doctrine of member state liability for the nonimplementation of Community law, the U.S. Supreme Court has been doing just the opposite, shielding state governments against liability claims. In a series of recent decisions including *Seminole Tribe v. Florida,* 517 U.S. 44 (1996); *College Sav. Bank v. Florida Prepaid Postsecondary Educ. Expense Bd.,* 119 S. Ct. 2219 (1999); *Florida Prepaid Postsecondary Educ. Expense Bd. v. College Sav. Bank,* 119 S. Ct. 2199 (1999); and *Alden v. Maine,* 119 S. Ct. 2240 (1999), the Supreme Court has made it nearly impossible for private parties to seek retrospective relief (that is, damage awards) from state governments for violations of federal law in federal or state courts (Araiza 2000; Jackson 2000).

Taken together, the Court's recent jurisprudence on commandeering, standing, and sovereign immunity can be seen as part of an attempt to increase state autonomy and reduce public interest litigation. The anti-commandeering cases reduce the federal government's ability to pressure states into compliance. In this respect, they make it necessary for the federal government to rely on decentralized enforcement. However, the standing cases deter litigation aimed at enforcing federal laws, particularly litigation brought by environmental organizations, and the sovereign immunity cases shield states against damage claims should they fail to implement federal law. Together, these legal principles promise to increase the discretion of state governments in implementing federal law.

If the Supreme Court continues to restrict standing for environmental plaintiffs, the politics of discretion in the United States may begin to look more like that in Germany, where courts play a more limited role and litigation focuses on cases in which individuals have suffered personal damages due to violations of environmental laws. If federal agencies and states are less concerned about potential lawsuits by environmental advocates for failure to fulfill statutory obligations, they will be more likely to deal with regulated industries in a flexible manner and less likely to resort to litigation themselves. However, such incentives will take time to filter through the system. In any case, litigiousness will not soon disappear from U.S. policymaking. Environmental litigants have proven themselves to be strategic actors, who search out new ways to use the legal system to pursue their policy objectives.

Conclusion

The division of regulatory competences between the federal and state governments in the United States developed in accord with the pattern described in Chapter 1. In response to mounting public concern with environmental issues and the potential for distortions to trade caused by divergent state level regulations, the U.S. federal government established for itself a powerful role in environmental policymaking. Subsequently, it developed an extensive role in the implementation and enforcement of environmental law, a role more powerful than that played by other federal governments in this study. Nevertheless, like those other polities, the United States continues to delegate most implementation and enforcement functions to state governments and relies heavily on underfunded and unfunded mandates. The basic structures of American separation-of-powers federalism have encouraged the development of an inflexible, litigious approach to environmental regulation that has greatly constrained state discretion. The particular constellation of political interests that existed during the so-called rights revolution of the late 1960s and early 1970s intensified this policy style. Subsequently, the political backlash by state and local governments against federal mandates, coupled with Supreme Court jurisprudence sympathetic to state autonomy concerns and antipathetic to environmental public interest litigation, has tempered this style to some degree. Nevertheless, when compared to the other federal polities in this study, the U.S. approach to enforcement remains by far the most inflexible, adversarial, and litigious.

Comparing the politics of discretion in the United States with that in the other federal systems yields two findings of particular interest for the European Union. First, the litigious pattern of policymaking and the resulting constraints on state discretion are rooted in the basic institutional structure of the U.S. federal government. The fragmentation of power in the separation-of-powers system encourages proponents of regulation in Congress to draft detailed environmental statutes to constrain executive discretion. The same fragmentation encourages Congress to invite the federal courts to increase their involvement in enforcement and gives courts the insulation they need to accept this invitation. The willingness of courts to intervene in the regulatory process in turn incites a flood of enforcement litigation that serves to constrain both federal and state regulators. In recent years, increasing judicial deference to executive agencies and increasing judicial protections for state autonomy, coupled with efforts of federal regulators to adopt a more flexible approach, have permitted some increase in the discretion of state regulators. Nevertheless, in comparative terms the U.S. approach to environmental enforcement remains inflexible and litigious, and states remain highly constrained by federal mandates. Given the similarities in the institutional structures of EU and U.S. federalism, these developments suggest that the EU's tendency to impose detailed, judicially enforced mandates on member states will persist.

Second, the U.S. experience highlights the importance of decentralized enforcement in environmental law. Even the EPA, with a staff of over eighteen thousand and powerful fiscal levers, cannot ensure uniform implementation and enforcement of federal environmental laws by state governments. The federal government's coercive powers are ultimately limited by its desire to leave states in control of most implementation and enforcement. Given these limits, decentralized enforcement of federal law by private parties has played a vital role in pressuring recalcitrant states to enforce federal requirements. The same can be expected in the EU, should it succeed in expanding opportunities for access to justice across the member states.

4 | Environmental Regulation in Germany

On the surface, the pattern of environmental regulation in Germany bears many similarities to the U.S. pattern: the federal government issues statutes on most environmental policy issues, states *(Länder)* control most implementation, regulations are highly detailed, and environmental litigation is common. Closer analysis, however, reveals that regulatory politics in Germany differ in important respects from the U.S. model. Most important for our purposes is that, though German courts do play an active role in the regulatory process, they engage in a more limited form of judicial review and ultimately do less to constrain state discretion than do their counterparts in the United States. The patterns of regulatory federalism found in Germany stem from the basic institutional structures of the German federal government, where the concentration of power falls on the continuum between the two ideal types depicted in Chapter 1. As a result, the politics of discretion in Germany falls between the patterns depicted in the two models, allowing *Länder* governments more discretion than the *fragmented power federal system* and less discretion than the *concentrated power federal system*. The causal pathways linking institutional structures and the politics of regulatory federalism differ in some respects from those in either of the ideal-type models but are nonetheless consistent with the underlying theory.

One crucial respect in which the German case differs from the others in this study is that as a result of the development of the European Union's (EU) role in environmental regulation, Germany has in effect become a federal system within a larger federal regulatory system. In order to grasp both the internal dynamics of the German system and the impact that EU membership has had on that system, I begin by analyzing the dynamics of regulatory federalism in Germany as they emerged from the 1950s through the 1980s and later examine the impact that the growing regulatory role of the EU in the 1980s and 1990s had on the German polity.

The structure of the German federal government provides for a greater fragmentation of power than the Canadian and Australian systems, but it is less than fragmentation that is found in the United States or the EU. Power is more concentrated in Germany than in the EU or the U.S. separation-of-powers model because the German parliamentary system fuses together control of the first chamber of Parliament (the *Bundestag*) with control of the executive. However, power is more concentrated than in the Westminster-style parliamentary federalism model because of the extensive power of the second chamber (the *Bundesrat*) and because of the constitutionally entrenched powers of the judiciary.

Germany's constitution, the Basic Law *(Grundgesetz)*, enshrines the principle of separation of powers among the legislature, executive, and judiciary (Basic Law art. 20(2)). In practice, however, legislative and executive powers are partially fused. As in most parliamentary systems, the chief executive—the chancellor—is the leader of the strongest party in the lower house of Parliament (the *Bundestag*). The chancellor selects the cabinet ministers, sets the general direction of government policy, and is the *de facto* head of state.[1] While in principle the *Bundestag* controls the chancellor through its power to oversee the government and replace it at any time, in practice the situation is reversed.[2] The chancellor and his cabinet (collectively referred to as "the government") are drawn from the leadership of parties who have formed a majority coalition in the *Bundestag*. The government controls the legislative agenda of the *Bundestag* and most legislation originates in federal ministries.[3]

The government does not control all legislative power, however, as it does not control the powerful second chamber of Parliament. The *Bundesrat* is structured much more like the EU's Council of Ministers than like the U.S. Senate. Members of the *Bundesrat* are not politicians elected to serve at the federal level but rather are representatives of the sixteen *Länder* governments, and they directly represent the institutional interests of their governments at the federal level.[4] The consent of the *Bundesrat* is required for all regulations that are to be implemented by the *Länder* and also for many statutes. Since the mid-1950s, between 50 and 60 percent of all federal laws have required *Bundesrat* approval (*Bundesrat* 1995, p. 33). Thus, the second chamber of Parliament is a powerful force in many policy areas, including environmental regulation. Conflict with the *Bundestag* is most common when the *Bundesrat* is dominated by a different majority (party or coalition of parties) than the majority that controls the government, as has been the case for substantial periods (Scharpf 1995; Leonardy 1994). Conflict occurs, however, even when the same party or coalition controls both houses of Parliament, because members of the *Bundesrat* act to protect *Länder* interests that often conflict with those of the federal government (Adelberger 1999, p. 4).

The judiciary plays a powerful role in the German political system. In the wake of the Nazi era, the drafters of the Federal Republic's Basic Law placed a particular emphasis on the need for politically independent courts to protect the rights of individuals against the government.[5] Article 19(4) of the Basic Law provides that any person whose rights have been violated by any public authority shall have recourse to the courts.[6] This constitutional guarantee is supplemented by a provision that individuals may file constitutional complaints before the Federal Constitutional Court *(Bundesverfassungsgericht)* concerning violations of their individual rights after exhausting all other legal remedies.[7] Over the years, German courts have widely interpreted the rights that individuals can claim against the state (Currie 1994, p. 165; Greve 1989, p. 239).

The Federal Constitutional Court sits at the pinnacle of the German judiciary. Beneath it, the judiciary is divided into a system of five specialized supreme courts at the federal level and corresponding lower courts at the state level. With the exception of judges on the Constitutional Court, who are appointed for twelve-year, nonrenewable terms of office, all judges are appointed for life.[8] Administrative courts handle most environmental matters.[9] There are three tiers in the administrative court system.[10] The Federal Administrative Court *(Bundesverwaltungsgericht)* hears appeals from lower administrative courts. Its members are selected by a committee chaired by the federal minister of justice and composed of state ministers of justice and equal number of members of the *Bundestag*. Similar arrangements exist at the state level for appointments to the state administrative courts. Administrative Courts of Appeal (*Oberverwaltungsgericht* or *Verwaltungsgerichtshof*) are state-level courts of appeal. They also serve as courts of first instance for some categories of cases (see discussion below). Finally, the lowest administrative courts, which hear most cases in the first instance, are known simply as Administrative Courts *(Verwaltungsgerichte)* (Jarass and DiMento 1993, p. 49).

The Politics of Competence

The Emergence of Federal Competence

The politics of competence in Germany differs in one major respect from that in the other federal systems in this study. Other polities had to resolve two questions: first, how would federal and state governments divide legislative authority, and second, how would they divide the authority to implement legislation. In Germany, the second question was never at issue. The Basic Law enshrines the principle that, except in a narrow range of specified areas, the *Länder* are to serve as the implementers of federal legislation (Basic Law arts. 83–87)(Benz 1991).[11] The federal government never took steps to expand its involvement in implementation and enforcement, and the politics of competence focused exclusively on how the federal and *Länder* governments would divide legislative authority.

When the Basic Law was adopted in 1949, its lists of respective federal and *Länder* competences made no explicit mention of environmental protection (Basic Law arts. 73–75). The only related areas in which the federal government had a specific legislative competence were land-use planning and water management, where the federal government had the power to issue framework legislation (Basic Law art. 75(1.4)). All areas of regulation not explicitly conferred on the federal government in the Basic Law remained *Länder* competences (Basic Law art. 70).

In the years following World War II, as Germany faced the momentous task of reconstruction, environmental protection was not a political concern. The controls that did exist were local and followed a pattern established in nineteenth-century Prussia when local officials in trade offices *(Gewerbeaufsichtsämter)* had made some effort to regulate industrial facilities in order to reduce air pollution (Weale 1992, pp. 150–160; Kloepfer 1994, pp. 39–46). For instance, in the area of air pollution, local authorities had some power to force polluters to curtail emissions if it could be proven that their particular emissions were damaging public health. Local standards for air and water pollution control varied substantially during this period (Weale 1992, p. 162).

Environmental issues first gained attention in the 1950s in North Rhine Westphalia, a *Land* that suffered from severe air pollution problems due to the concentration of heavy industry (Boehmer-Christiansen and Skea 1991, p. 161; Héritier et al. 1994; Weale 1992, p. 163). Pressure for federal action mounted during the 1950s. In 1959, the federal government adopted the Federal Air Purity Act (*Luftreinhaltegesetz* (LRG)) under its constitutional power to regulate economic affairs (Basic Law art. 74(11)). The new act followed the approach of the laws that had been in force since the nineteenth century, requiring industrial plants to obtain permits for pollution. But the new law went further in that it extended the number of plants that required permits, established ambient air-quality standards, and made it easier for local officials to demand that firms reduce emissions.

Finally, the act required new sources to be equipped with "best available technology" *(Stand der Technik)*, although this was later qualified such that only technologies available at reasonable costs were required.

The environmental movement in Germany spread slowly during the 1950s, and environmental groups began calling for a new, more stringent approach to pollution control. The environment became an issue in the 1961 federal elections, and later that year the government set up a Federal Health Ministry with responsibility for air-pollution policy. The ministry developed a new set of technical directives that specified licensing procedures for industrial plants and detailed air-quality standards for five pollutants (Weale 1992, p. 163). The true watershed in German environmental policy, however, came in the late 1960s and early 1970s when a mounting wave of public concern induced the federal government to take a number of environmental policy initiatives. Public concern with environmental issues grew during the late 1960s, with citizen action groups concerned with environmental protection forming in communities throughout Germany. These groups organized nationally in 1972 by founding the Federation of Citizens Groups for Environmental Protection (*Bundesverband Bürgerinitiativen Umweltschutz* (BBU)).[12] A number of ecological crises, such as the poisoning of fish in the Rhine River in 1969 as a result of toxic waste dumping, attracted national attention during this period (Weale 1992, p. 164). In 1969, a new, reform-oriented coalition government comprising the SPD and the FDP took power. Recognizing the mounting popularity of environmental protection policies and noting the successes of environmentalists in the United States, the new government took a series of environmental initiatives (Boehmer-Christiansen and Skea 1991, p. 103; Wilhelm 1992, pp. 19–21).[13]

In 1971, the government issued the first federal environmental program establishing the principles of federal policy and setting out a number of goals (Héritier et al. 1994, p. 160). The government also pushed through three amendments to the Basic Law in order to expand federal environmental competences. First, in 1969, the federation was empowered to issue legislation regarding nature conservation (Basic Law art. 75(3)). This amendment gave the federal government only the power to issue framework laws *(Rahmengesetzgebung)*: it could issue legislation establishing general principles and goals, but could not issue detailed regulations. Second, a 1971 amendment made animal and plant protection measures subject to concurrent legislation by the federal government and the *Länder* (Basic Law art. 74(20)). Third, a 1972 amendment added waste disposal, air pollution control, and noise abatement as areas of concurrent federal–state legislative competence (Basic Law art. 74(24)). The two latter amendments enabled the federal government to issue both general framework legislation and detailed regulations and administrative rules (Rehbinder 1989, p. 8). The third amendment was particularly important, as it opened up the way for a more comprehensive approach to air pollution control at the federal level.[14]

With its power to act in the environmental arena established by these constitutional amendments, the German federal government created new institutions and enacted important new legislation. In 1974, the government created the Federal Environment Agency (*Umweltbundesamt* (UBA)), which was called on to assist government ministries by conducting research on environmental conditions, helping draft legislation, reporting on developments in science and technology, and informing the public about environmental issues (Boehmer-Christiansen and Skea 1991, pp. 108, 163; Rose-Ackerman 1995, pp. 62–63). Legislation enacted in this period included the 1971 Petrol Lead Law (*Benzinbleigesetz* (BzBlG)), the 1972 Waste Disposal Act (*Abfall-beseitigungsgesetz* (AbfG)), the 1972 DDT Law *(DDT-Gesetz)*, and the 1974 Federal Air Pollution Control Act[15] (*Bundes-Immissionsschutzgesetz* (BImSchG)).[16] The landmark Federal Air Pollution Control Act ended the need for a public health justification for abatement measures and held that air pollution control should protect fauna, flora, water, and soil as well. It provided for integrated control of all environmental requirements at industrial facilities, including air and noise pollution, and extended beyond industrial facilities to potentially cover all sources of air pollution. The act also gave the federal government the power to issue binding regulations *(Verordnungen)* and associated technical guidelines *(Technische Anleitungen)* (Jarass and Dimento 1993, p. 63).

The federal government met with more resistance in trying to expand its competences in areas of water pollution control and nature conservation. The *Länder* governments used their power in the *Bundesrat* to deny the federal government full legislative competence in these areas, forcing it to rely only on its competence to adopt framework legislation (Wilhelm 1992, pp. 28–29). In 1976 the federal legislature passed amendments to the Water Resources Act (*Wasserhaushaltsgesetz* (WHG)) and enacted a new Waste Water Charges Act (*Abwasserabgabengesetz* (AbwAG)) in order to address water pollution issues.[17] The same year, it adopted the Federal Nature Conservation Act (*Bundesnaturschutzgesetz* (BNatSchG)). In addition to these specific statutes, the federal legislature added a section on environment to the criminal and civil codes.[18]

The Expansion of Federal Competence

The model of regulatory federalism presented in Chapter 1 anticipates that the initial federal move to establish legislative competence is followed by complaints about uneven implementation and later by an effort on the part of the federal government to assume a role in implementation and enforcement. As explained above, however, in Germany the Basic Law severely limited the potential for any federal expansion into these areas by requiring that the *Länder* play the primary role in implementation and enforcement of federal legislation. Though this division of responsibilities is a deeply entrenched principle of German constitutional law, a constitutional amendment might have overcome this restriction. However, constitutional amendments require a two-thirds majority in both the *Bundestag* and the *Bundesrat* (Basic Law art. 79), and given the preference of *Länder* governments to retain control over implementation within their jurisdictions, support in the *Bundesrat* would not have been forthcoming. Therefore, when complaints regarding nonimplementation and calls for more regulation became prevalent, the federal government could expand its regulatory activities, but could not take on a significant role in implementation and enforcement.

Complaints regarding uneven enforcement surfaced soon after the federal government issued environmental legislation. In 1974, a high-level advisory council to the federal government, the Advisory Council of Environmental Experts *(Der Rat von Sachverständigen für Umweltfragen)* issued a report finding a considerable "enforcement deficit." The federal government acknowledged the existence of an enforcement deficit, while *Länder* governments denied it, at least officially (Rehbinder 1976, pp. 373–374; Mayntz and Scharpf 1975; Boehmer-Christiansen and Skea 1991, p. 178; Rose-Ackerman 1995, p. 167; Kloepfer 1994, p. 105). Despite such reports of uneven enforcement, the federal government made no significant effort generally to increase its involvement in enforcement, and took on implementation functions in only a few areas. The federal government assumed its most direct role in the screening of new chemicals, which is conducted by the Federal Health Agency *(Bundesgesundheitsamt)*.[19] It also took on a more direct role in the approval and construction of nuclear power plants, interstate highways, and airports (Jarass and Dimento 1993, p. 54; Rehbinder 1989, p. 9; Schlemminger and Wissel 1996, pp. 33–35).

Environmental issues continued to attract great public concern in Germany throughout the 1980s. In the early years of that decade, concern over "forest death" *(Waldsterben)* caused by acid rain was the most prominent issue. The Chernobyl nuclear disaster provided another focus for public concern after 1986. Membership in environmental organizations swelled during this period (Blühorn 1995), as the public grew increasingly dissatisfied with the government's handling of environmental policy. Perhaps the clearest manifestation of the public's concern was the emergence of the Green Party in the 1970s and their entrance onto the national stage in the 1980 election, when they won 1.5 percent of the vote. Once established, they acted to maintain public attention to environmental issues. The Greens benefited from concern surrounding forest death in the early 1980s and improved their vote share to 5.6 percent in the 1983 election, thus breaking the 5 percent threshold necessary to gain seats in the *Bundestag*. The Greens's vote share jumped to 8.3 percent in the 1987 election.[20]

The federal government reacted to continuing public concern for the environment by taking a number of regulatory initiatives, most prominently concerning forest death. In 1983, the government enacted the Large Combustion Plants Regulation (*Gross-feuerungsanlagenverordnung* (13.BimSchV)). The regulation, which was adopted under the framework of the Federal Air Pollution Control Act, set exact limits on a range of pollutants for different categories of industrial plants and set deadlines for the achievement of standards (Boehmer-Christiansen and Skea 1991; Weale 1992, p. 168). Also in 1983, the technical guideline on air pollution prevention *(TA Luft)* was amended to allow *Länder* to enforce limits on ambient pollution levels. In 1985 the government revised the Federal Air Pollution Control Act to make it easier for enforcement officials to demand that plants apply state of the art technologies. In 1986, the government again revised *TA Luft*, setting even tougher emission standards for combustion plants (Boehmer-Christiansen and Skea 1991, pp. 171–172).

Federal regulation of water pollution and waste management also expanded. In 1986, the legislature amended the Water Resources Act (WHG) to tighten the technical standards for effluent controls, especially toxics. In 1986 the government adopted the Waste Avoidance and Waste Management Act (*Abfallgesetz* (AbfG)), which established a permitting system for waste treatment and disposal sites and a system for tracking dangerous wastes (Winter 1994, pp. 44–48; Schleminger and Wissel 1996, pp. 411–455). Pursuant to this act, the government adopted the Regulation on the Avoidance of Packaging Waste (*Verpackungsverord-nung* (VerpakV)) in 1991. This controversial regulation established a strict recycling system that required product distributors either to accept returned packaging or to pay into a private system, named the *Duales System Deutschland,* that would pick up packaging from households and then transport it to recycling centers. Also, in 1990 the legislature adopted an important law of general applicability, the Environmental Liability Act (*Umwelthaftungsgesetz* (UmweltHG)), which facilitated suits against polluters by reducing the threshold necessary to establish causation and providing for strict, joint, and several liability (Jarass and Dimento 1993, p. 65).

EU Membership and the Politics of Competence

The model of regulatory federalism explains the dynamics of regulation within any given federal system, and thus far I have treated Germany as an independent case study. From the 1980s onward, however, the German case cannot be examined without viewing it in the context of the EU. Germany is a federal state within the larger federal regulatory system of the EU. Before the 1980s, EU regulations placed few restrictions on Germany, as it already met or exceeded the environmental standards set at the EU level. Indeed, many EU regulations were modeled after German regulations (Héritier et al. 1994). But from the mid-1980s onward, a number of EU directives and regulations introduced important new requirements into German law and promoted a further centralization of regulatory policymaking.

As in many other policy areas, the increasing role of the EU in environmental policy encouraged the shift of legislative competence within Germany from the *Länder* to the federal level.[21] The EU holds the federal government, not the *Länder,* responsible for failures to implement EU law. This gives the federal government a powerful incentive to centralize policymaking, and most EU laws are transposed into German law as federal regulations or guidelines.[22] EU directives not only introduced new substantive requirements into German federal law, some directives also mandated the introduction of procedural measures that took an approach far different from the traditional policy style in Germany, and imposed new obligations on the *Länder* (Héritier et al. 1994; Knill and Lenschow

1998, 2000; Börzel 1998; Kimber 2000). EU directives on environmental impact assessment[23] and freedom of information on the environment[24] are two prominent examples. To transpose the EU impact assessment directive, the German government enacted federal legislation establishing uniform procedures for environmental impact assessments and established an extensive list of the types of projects for which assessments were required.[25] To transpose the EU freedom of information directive, the German government enacted federal legislation requiring both environmental authorities and regulated entities across Germany to release information that had previously been inaccessible to the public.[26]

The shift in legislative competence from the national to the EU level reduced the influence of German *Länder* on the legislative process. In policymaking at the national level, the *Länder* could defend their interests through their position in the *Bundesrat*. But at the EU level, only the federal government was directly represented at the bargaining table in Brussels, and *Länder* governments often had difficulty monitoring policy developments closely (Interviews, Permanent Representation of Germany to the EU, Brussels, April 3, 1998; Permanent Representation of the State of Hesse to the EU, Brussels, April 6, 1998). Thus, with the shift in legislative authority to the EU level, German *Länder* governments, which enjoyed such a powerful position in the domestic legislative process, eventually found themselves in a position similar to state governments in the United States, Canada, and Australia, which had less direct involvement in legislative processes. Beginning in the late 1980s, the *Länder* sought to defend against the threat that the shift in authority to Brussels posed to their role in regulatory policymaking (Hrbek 1999, p. 219; Schneider 1999, pp. 70, 74–79; Adelberger 1999, p. 11). In 1992, the *Länder* secured an amendment to the Basic Law that provides that the *Bundesrat* shall be involved in decisionmaking at the EU level insofar as it would be involved in corresponding processes domestically (Basic Law art. 23(4)) (Gress 1996, p. 64). In practice, this means that the *Bundesrat* designates representatives to accompany federal government representatives in the working groups of the EU Council of Ministers. Some *Länder* also sought to roll back federal involvement in some policy areas by invoking the principle of subsidiarity, but these attempts failed to win the support of a majority of *Länder* in the *Bundesrat* (Schneider 1999, p. 77; Adelberger 1999, p. 13).

The development in Germany of the politics of competence generally reflects a pattern similar to that anticipated by the model of regulatory federalism and observed in the other polities I explore in this book. The one significant difference in the German case was caused by the constitutional provision that *Länder* are generally responsible for the implementation of federal laws. Because of this constitutional rule, the federal government never made a serious effort to expand its role in implementation and enforcement. Nonetheless, the division of regulatory competences that emerged in Germany is similar to that found in the other polities. Most lawmaking has been centralized to the federal or European Union level, while state governments retain very little exclusive legislative competence. Implementation, on the other hand, remains a responsibility of *Land* governments. Domestically, German *Länder* had a powerful influence over federal legislation through their presence in the *Bundesrat*. After this influence was undermined by the shift of policymaking from Bonn to Brussels, German *Länder* demanded and won an increased influence on EU policymaking processes.

The Politics of Discretion

In Chapter 1, I hypothesized that the concentration of power within the structure of a federal government determines the degree of discretion that states enjoy in implementing federal law. Where power at the federal level is fragmented, states are more constrained in their implementation of federal law. By contrast, where power is more concentrated, states enjoy greater discretion in implementation. I spelled out the causal connections between concentration of power and state discretion in two ideal-type models—one a fragmented power system combining separation of powers and bicameralism, and the other a concentrated power system characterized by Westminster-style parliamentary government. The structure of German government falls between these two ideal types in terms of the concentration of power. Power is more concentrated in Germany than in the separation-of-powers model because the German parliamentary system fuses together control of the *Bundestag* with control of the executive. However, power is less concentrated than in a Westminster system because of the extensive power of the *Bundesrat* and because of the constitutionally entrenched powers of the judiciary.

The politics of competence in Germany differs in important respects from the patterns reflected in the two ideal-type federal systems. Nevertheless, the German politics of competence supports the underlying hypothesis in Chapter 1 that greater fragmentation of power at the federal level leads to lower discretion for state governments in implementation. Just as the degree of fragmentation in the structure of the German federal government falls between the two ideal-type models, so too does the politics of discretion in Germany. First, courts play a more active role in regulation in Germany than they do in the Westminster-style model, but a lesser role than they do in the separation-of-powers model. Second, the nature and role of detail in German environmental law differs from that in either of the ideal types. Detail is not used by the legislature to control the administration, as it is in the United States. German legislative statutes are generally quite vague. Nevertheless, the federal bureaucracy, with the consent of *Land* governments in the *Bundesrat,* issues numerous, highly detailed regulations and administrative guidelines that specify precisely how state and local officials are to implement any given environmental statute.

The role of detail in German federal regulations is linked to the practice of judicial review. Only persons (individuals or legal "persons") whose individual rights are violated by an administrative act can gain standing to challenge the act before the administrative courts.[27] As a result, litigation focuses almost exclusively on specific licensing decisions, such as those concerning the operation of new industrial facilities, which affect the legally protected interests of regulated firms and local residents. Judicial rulings regarding individual cases can have a precedent-setting effect (Scharpf 1970). If the government were to adopt vague regulations, court decisions determining whether an administrator had applied the law correctly in a specific case could set a precedent that would bind other administrators in future cases. Anticipating that implementation in specific cases will be challenged, the government issues detailed implementing measures in an attempt to shield regulators against such judicial interference. When plaintiffs argue that an administrative action violated their individual rights, the administration can point to the detailed requirements of the implementing regulation and maintain that they simply followed the letter of the law.

The remainder of this section examines these causal linkages in more detail, showing how the institutional structure of German federalism influences the politics of competence.

Vague Statutes, Detailed Implementing Measures

As mentioned above, detail plays a very different role in German environmental law than it does in the United States. In U.S. environmental law, federal legislators include detailed requirements in legislation in an effort to ensure that federal and state administrative agencies implement statutes according to congressional intent. Legislators encourage courts to review administrative rulemaking and implementation and to enforce the detailed requirements set out in the statutes. By contrast, in Germany, the legislature does not use detail primarily as a tool with which to control the executive. The legislative process is dominated by executives, with the federal executive dominating the *Bundestag* and state executives making up the membership of the *Bundesrat*. Federal and state executives in Germany choose to place detailed requirements in regulations for a far different reason than do American lawmakers. In the German case, detail is used primarily to minimize judicial interference in the implementation process. Also, as in the EU case, state governments seek to use detailed regulations to ensure that other state governments will face a similar regulatory burden.

German environmental statutes establish the general principles and goals of federal policy, but leave the specification of standards and implementation requirements to the administration (Rose-Ackerman 1995, p. 58; Jarass and DiMento 1993, pp. 53, 69; Halberstam 2001; Von Annegret 1991, p. 255). Statutes contain no deadlines specifying when the administration must issue implementing regulations. They also contain few requirements regarding the procedures that the administration must follow when issuing implementing regulations. Indeed, although the administration typically issues many implementing regulations pursuant to any given environmental statute, it is not specifically required to do so. In some cases, the relevant ministry may choose to implement some provisions of a statute by reaching an agreement with industry, rather than by issuing formal regulations (Rose-Ackerman 1995, p. 69). For instance, the government implemented the Law on Detergents (*Wasch–und Reinigungsmittelgesetz* (WRMG §9)) not by issuing a regulation, but simply by accepting an industry plan to address the issue as sufficient.

In contrast to environmental statutes themselves, the regulations and administrative guidelines produced by the federal administration in order to implement statutes are highly detailed (Jarass and DiMento 1993, p. 69). The first type of legal instrument employed by the administration is the regulation *(Verordnung)*. Regulations are directly binding on all individuals and legal persons. The second legal instrument is the administrative directive *(Verwaltungsvorschrift)*. These directives are binding only on the state authorities that are required to implement them, not on polluters themselves. The federal government must obtain the approval of the *Bundesrat* before it can issue any regulation or any directive that the *Länder* are to implement.[28] One important category of administrative directives are known as technical guidelines (*Technische Anleitungen* (TAs)). TAs specify in considerable detail the technical standards that *Länder* authorities are to apply in implementing federal laws.

This hierarchy of legal instruments is well illustrated in the area of air pollution control. The Federal Air Pollution Control Act (BImSchG) is a piece of framework legislation that defines the principles of pollution control, such as precautionary action and the reliance on requiring use of state-of-the-art emissions reduction technologies. The act empowers the federal government to issue both regulations and administrative directives (Boehmer-Christiansen and Skea 1991, p. 171). The government has adopted a number of regulations under this legislation, including the regulation on large combustion plants *(Grossfeuerungsanlagenverordnung)* adopted in 1983. Most of the detailed requirements of air pollution control policy are set out in TAs. Most famously, the technical guideline on air pollution prevention (*Technische Anleitung zur Reinhaltung der Luft*, or *TA Luft*) specifies in great detail the technical standards that regulators are to require of individual polluting facilities and the ambient air-quality standards that must be met.[29]

Air pollution control is typical of other areas of regulation in this respect. For instance, a technical guideline against noise pollution *(TA Lärm)* was adopted under the Federal Emission Protection Act. Book-length technical guidelines on hazardous waste *(TA Sonderabfall)* and household waste *(TA Siedlungsabfall)* have been adopted under the Waste Avoidance and Waste Management Act (AbfG) (Jarass and DiMento 1993, p. 69; Rose-Ackerman 1995, p. 187).

While regulations, administrative directives, and technical guidelines are replete with extremely detailed technical standards, they contain very few procedural requirements. Detail focuses on substantive issues, not procedural ones (Rehbinder 1976, p. 376; Nolte 1994, p. 204). General provisions of administrative law do require that notice and comment periods be available to parties whose interests might be affected by a particular bureaucratic action.[30] In addition, some environmental statutes require the administration to hold a hearing open to concerned parties before it issues new regulations or guidelines.[31] However, these requirements are relatively informal; official records of the hearings are not kept and the government is not obliged to provide reasons for its decisions. Only licensing and planning procedures contain more detailed procedural rules, requiring the administration to notify the public, hold hearings open to concerned parties, and offer a statement of reasons along with any decision (Greve 1989, p. 205; Rose-Ackerman 1995, p. 82).

The focus on substantive rather than procedural detail makes sense when one considers that executives draft regulations in an effort to protect themselves against subsequent litigation. Creating detailed procedural requirements might expand causes of action for potential litigants, enabling them to challenge a decision on the grounds that the administration violated a procedural rule. By contrast, the substantive details in German regulations and technical guidelines serve as defense mechanisms. By specifying in detail the technical standards that the administration is to apply when licensing various categories of industrial facilities, the regulations and guidelines limit room for judicial interpretation (Weale 1992, p. 166). If regulated industries or environmental advocates challenge an administrative decision as a violation of their individual rights, administrators can defend their decision by arguing that they treated the particular case in question according to the substantive requirements set out in the administrative guideline. Although technical guidelines are not directly binding on polluters, courts generally treat them as binding laws and defer to administrative decisions that are based on them (Schlemminger and Wissel 1996, pp. 37–39; Rose-Ackerman 1995, p. 78).

The Nature of Judicial Review

Judicial review of the public administration in Germany focuses on the protection of individual rights. German administrative courts only review implementation in specific cases, when it affects the rights of individuals. Unlike U.S. or EU courts, German administrative courts do not hear cases challenging general patterns of implementation or challenging implementing measures (that is, regulations or technical guidelines) before they are applied in specific cases. Groups and individuals can defend their private rights, but cannot act as "private attorneys general" suing the government to defend the public interest. Therefore, most cases involve challenges brought by local residents or regulated firms against administrative licensing decisions (see discussion below).[32]

This pattern of judicial intervention has two sources. First, the Basic Law establishes and protects the role of administrative courts in protecting individual rights. (Basic Law art. 19(4)) Second, although courts have attempted to extend their power of review to cover other matters, they have been prevented from doing so by political resistance from the other branches of the federal government. The Basic Law places a strong emphasis on the role of the courts in protecting individual rights.[33] In the late 1950s, the government attempted to restrict judicial review in a subtle fashion, by enacting statutes that limited the scope of judicial review and increased administrative discretion. However, the Federal Constitutional Court declared such statutes invalid, defending the guarantee of judicial protection of individual rights.[34] The government could, of course, try to pass a constitutional amendment limiting judicial review. The German constitution can be amended more easily than the U.S. Constitution or the EU treaties.[35] Indeed, political pressures have led to numerous amendments to the Basic Law in some areas, such as the division of legislative competences. However, an attempt to restrict the role of the courts in the protection of individual rights would be viewed as an attack on one of the most fundamental, sacrosanct principles established in the Basic Law. In Germany, the guarantee of judicial protection of individual rights against abuse by the administration is viewed as a basic right. It is difficult to imagine circumstances under which any political actor would be motivated to openly attack this judicial protection by proposing a constitutional amendment.

While the government is unable to limit the role of courts in protecting individual rights, it has prevented administrative courts from extending the scope of their review beyond individual rights claims. Conflict over the reach of judicial review emerged particularly in the context of environmental legislation. Beginning in the 1950s, suits by local residents challenging administrative decisions to issue licenses or building or operating permits for industrial facilities became common (Greve 1989, p. 209). Residents often argued that the operation of the facilities unfairly devalued their property. As public concern regarding environmental issues mounted, the number of such cases increased through the 1960s and early 1970s. The lower administrative courts sensed the clear public support for their intervention (Greve 1989, p. 223).

By the mid-1970s there was a clear trend toward increasing judicial oversight of the administration, and courts loosened standing requirements for environmental plaintiffs. For instance, traditionally only local residents who could claim that their individual rights were affected by a licensing decision had standing to sue. In the 1970s, courts loosened this requirement by holding that the "neighborhood" of a plant or other polluting facility could extend up to seventy kilometers (Von Oertzen 1983, p. 270; Greve 1989, p. 211). The widest expansion of judicial review took place in the context of nuclear reactor licensing, where courts routinely challenged administrators' assessments of reactor safety issues (Greve 1989, p. 225; Nolte 1994, p. 204).

While judicial activism in the environmental arena pleased environmental advocates, it was certainly not welcomed by the government. Judicial review slowed down many construction projects significantly. In particular, judicial intervention in nuclear plant licensing procedures threatened to undermine the government's energy policy. The federal government openly considered transferring the licensing of nuclear power plants from the administration to the legislature in order to cut administrative courts out of the process (Greve 1989, p. 224). The government never took this step, but did enact another important court-curbing measure instead.

The legislature correctly observed that judicial intervention in environmental matters was being spearheaded by young activist judges in the lowest-level administrative courts (the administrative trial courts). These judges saw judicial review as a means to both expand judicial power and to realize their personal policy preferences. So, the legislature passed a law that stipulated that appeals against administrative decisions concerning large industrial facilities—including nuclear reactors, incinerators, highways, and airports—could no longer be taken to administrative trial courts.[36] Such appeals would have to bypass the lower courts and go directly to administrative appeals courts. This law sent a signal to young activist judges on the administrative trial courts, and to judges throughout the judicial system, that active judicial intervention was to be reined in. At the same time, the law removed one step in the judicial review process, thus speeding up the appeals and the licensing process more generally (Greve 1989, p. 225). The legislature enacted other court curbing measures as well, such as the limits on judicial review of administrative action it placed in a federal law concerning land use regulation.[37]

Higher courts understood the threat that the judicial activism of the administrative trial courts in environmental regulation posed to the legitimacy of the administrative court system. The highest administrative court, the Federal Administrative Court *(Bundesverwaltungsgericht)*, overruled lower court interpretations and declared that the nuclear power law and of the Federal Emissions Protection Act did not intend to "protect" individual rights.[38] The Federal Constitutional Court made decisions supporting the constitutionality of the government's nuclear power program and curtailing judicial review (Greve 1989, p. 212).

In response to pressure from the government and the restraint demonstrated by the high courts, courts throughout the system restrained themselves from the early 1980s onward. They began to limit the access of environmental litigants to the courtroom by raising standing requirements, and also limited the scope of their review of administrative action (Jarass and DiMento 1993, p. 57). While the political backlash against the administrative trial courts prevented them from expanding the scope of their review, their constitutionally guaranteed role in protecting the rights of individuals against abuse by the administration remained intact.

Enforcement

In Germany, centralized enforcement by the federal government has played a minimal role in pressuring *Länder* to implement federal environmental law. Decentralized enforcement by private litigants has played a stronger role, but has been limited to cases involving violations of individual rights. Informal normative mechanisms operating through a variety of policy networks have served to constrain the discretion of *Länder* governments in implementing federal law. However, increasing criticism from the EU about *Länder* implementation failures, discussed below, raises questions about just how constraining such informal mechanisms actually are.

The federal government in Germany does very little to enforce federal environmental laws. Implementation and enforcement are responsibilities of the *Länder,* and the federal government has few formal tools to ensure that the *Länder* do an adequate job implementing federal law. Articles 84 and 85 of the Basic Law establish the legal mechanisms by which the federal government might force the *Länder* into compliance when they are charged with implementing federal law. These articles provide that the federal government may regulate the organization and procedures of state agencies, may issue administrative regulations, and may even issue instructions for actions in particular cases. Finally, Article 37, the federal coercion *(Bundeszwang)* article, provides that where a *Land* fails to fulfill federal obligations the federal government may take "necessary measures" to enforce compliance. However, the federal government has never taken such coercive measures as bringing enforcement cases against *Land* governments (Currie 1994, p. 68; Page 1997, p. 540). The absence of such coercive measures stems not simply from the fact that the *Länder* have a perfect implementation record, but from weaknesses in the federal government's monitoring and enforcement mechanisms. First, coercive actions against a *Land* require the consent of the *Länder* in the *Bundesrat,* putting *Länder* in a strong position to block such action. Second, monitoring of compliance is also left to the *Länder*. There has never been any national environmental inspectorate. The Federal Ministry for Environment, Protection of Nature and Nuclear Safety (*Bundesministerium für Umwelt, Naturschutz und Reaktorsicherheit* (BMU)) drafts legislation, but does not monitor its enforcement.[39] The Federal Environment Agency (*Umweltbundesamt* (UBA)) conducts research and formulates policy advice, but does not engage in monitoring or enforcement. Outside the legal arena, the federal government's other enforcement "levers" are weak as well. Fiscal levers are weak because, in most cases, the Basic Law bars the federal government from attaching conditions to grants made to the *Länder* (Currie 1994, pp. 57–58, 83–84; Rose-Ackerman 1995, p. 47).[40]

Despite the weakness of formal control mechanisms, the federal government does employ informal mechanisms to pressure *Länder* regarding enforcement. The most important informal means available to promote uniformity of implementation stem from the bi-annual Conference of Environmental Ministers *(Umweltministerkonferenz)* and the various, permanent federal–state working groups *(Bund-Länder Arbeitskreise)* (Rehbinder 1989, p. 9; Jarass and Dimento 1993, p. 55; Héritier et al. 1994, p. 52; Müller-Brandeck-Boquet 1993, pp. 106–110). The working groups bring together technical experts from both levels of government to discuss implementation and enforcement. Recommendations from these committees have a strong influence on the regulations and statutes eventually adopted at the federal level. Most important, *Länder* singled out for poor implementation can be subject to extreme normative pressure from their counterparts. While many scholars of German federalism view these informal mechanisms, backed by widely held norms of federal comity *(Bundestreue)*, as extremely constraining (Lehmbruch 1989; Klatt 1987), the track record of the *Länder* in implementing federal environmental law raises doubts about the strength of these informal, normative constraints. Weaknesses in the enforcement of environmental law by the *Länder* are well-known (Mayntz et al. 1978; Von Annegret 1991; Müller-Brandeck-Boquet 1993), and recently the EU has highlighted both the failure of the *Länder* to comply with EU environmental law and the failure of the German federal government to force them to do so.

Litigation brought by private parties has played a central role in the implementation and enforcement of German environmental policy. However, environmental litigation has focused on a narrow range of cases. With rare exceptions, private plaintiffs cannot act as "private attorneys general" bringing cases in the public interest, as they have in the United States.[41] They cannot challenge the administration for failures in its general pattern of implementation. German courts also refuse to hear challenges based solely on the administration's violation of procedural rules. Plaintiffs can only bring cases where they can claim a substantive violation of their individual rights. As a result of this restriction, nearly all environmental litigation in Germany has been brought by local residents challenging administrative decisions to license large industrial facilities in their vicinity.[42]

Administrative decisions regarding the licensing of power plants (coal-fired and nuclear), major industrial facilities, and infrastructure projects have generated thousands of lawsuits before administrative courts. Opponents of projects rarely prevail in the courtroom. Nevertheless, these cases constituted a powerful tool and were successful both in delaying projects, thereby raising their costs, and in raising public awareness about potential environmental impacts. Court challenges to nuclear power plant construction contributed to the end of new plant construction (Rose-Ackerman 1995, p. 88). Since 1976, the federal government and some *Länder* have introduced provisions on such mass proceedings in order to enable courts to manage the deluge. In essence, these procedures allow courts to group together what are essentially identical lawsuits and issue rulings that apply to all of them.

Environmental advocates in Germany have focused their litigation on these "individual rights" cases, because they provide the only real means of access to the courts. Many environmental organizations would have preferred to follow the practice of American environmental organizations that bring cases in the "public interest," challenging general implementing measures or practices. German environmental advocates have repeatedly called on the federal government to grant environmental groups standing to sue in the public interest (Rehbinder 1976). The clamor of such proposals was loudest in the debate over the Nature Protection Act *(Bundesnaturschutzgesetz)*, where it was claimed that standing for environmental groups was particularly important in nature conservation policy, since individuals would have difficulty gaining standing in nature conservation cases on "individual rights" grounds. For instance, if a public administrator decided to permit the construction of a road in a national park, environmental advocates could not gain standing to challenge the decision in court, because the decision would not affect their private property rights (Greve 1989, p. 202).

While some members of Parliament were in favor of granting standing to environmental groups, the government never backed the idea. The reason is simple. Foreseeing that granting standing to environmental groups would lead to increased judicial oversight of the administration, the government preferred to keep courts out of the regulatory process as much as possible in order to maintain administrative discretion. Moreover, the government could see that the issues at stake extended beyond environmental policy: if they granted standing to environmental groups, other interest associations would surely push for group standing. As Greve (1989, p. 228) puts it, "legal barriers to collective litigation . . . were purposefully designed, and consciously maintained, so as to keep organized interests out of court." In order to partially appease environmentalists, the government included a provision in the Federal Nature Protection Act (*Bundesnaturschutzgesetz* (BnatSchG)) that permits approved environmental groups to participate in administrative proceedings. However, in order to prevent unwanted litigation, the act did not grant these groups standing to bring challenges in the administrative courts after the administration has made a decision.[43] Some *Länder* that wanted to demonstrate their commitment to the environmentalist cause did enact additional provisions that granted standing to groups that had participated in administrative proceedings.[44] Administrative courts could have permitted extensive public interest litigation under these statutes, and some administrative trial courts did so. However, as mentioned above, higher administrative courts understood that *Länder* governments did not want them to encourage widespread interest group litigation. They foresaw that if they did so, governments would attack them for being "activist" and could easily enact court-curbing measures. Therefore, administrative appeals courts established a narrow interpretation of environmental group standing. In Hessen, for example, courts dismissed every lawsuit brought by environmental groups under Hessen's nature protection statute (Greve 1989, p. 216).

Restrictions on group standing, however, have not completely shut citizens groups out of the judicial review process. Citizens groups have found an alternative route to gain standing: they often buy land in the proximity of an industrial facility so that the group, as a legal entity, can claim a personal interest in the licensing decision. Courts have permitted such claims (Rose-Ackerman 1995, p. 89; Greve 1989, p. 209). Nonetheless, in such cases, groups can only raise claims regarding their property, not regarding the implications of the project for the public interest. Also, in some cases, environmental groups may participate from behind the scenes, by lending their support to a person with land in the vicinity of the project who has a right to standing.

Another restriction on the scope of judicial review in Germany, in comparison to the United States, is the weakness of review of administrative procedures. German courts generally do not recognize claims made by plaintiffs solely regarding violations of their procedural rights (Greve 1989, p. 206; Rose-Ackerman 1995, pp. 90, 196; Jarass and Dimento 1993, p. 67; Nolte 1994). Although some statutes and some implementing regulations contain procedural rules (see above), courts very rarely overturn administrative decisions merely because the administration violated these rules. Plaintiffs can only bring cases on procedural grounds if they claim that the administration's violation of procedures affected the outcome of the decision. If a court finds that procedural errors did not affect the outcome of the decision, it will allow the decision to stand. If, on the other hand, a court finds that errors did affect the outcome, it may rule the decision null and void, call for a slight change, or demand that the aggrieved parties be compensated (Rose-Ackerman 1995, p. 91). By contrast, in the United States, if the administration violates one of the Administrative Procedures Act's rulemaking procedures (for example, mandatory public notice and comment period or the publication of a statement of reasons for decision), then federal courts may, and often do, invalidate the rule on purely procedural grounds.

EU Membership and the Politics of Discretion

The institutional structure of the German polity underlies the politics of discretion described above. However, as the EU has come to play a stronger role in environmental policymaking, the EU's own institutional structure has gained much greater influence on regulation in Germany. To understand recent patterns of environmental regulation in Germany, German domestic structures must be viewed within the larger institutional framework of the EU. In important respects, the EU places greater constraints on the implementation of EU law by the member states than the German federal government traditionally placed on the *Länder*. Therefore, EU requirements have actually led to a decrease in discretion for the *Länder*.

While the German government has long included detailed technical standards in its implementing regulations and guidelines, EU directives have forced it to adopt additional requirements. Traditionally, German environmental law did not place an emphasis on procedural issues. EU directives, by contrast, often include detailed procedural requirements. A number of the cases that the Commission has brought against Germany have concerned such procedural issues. The Commission's insistence that member states adhere to procedural requirements has frustrated government officials in Germany, who object to being brought before the European Court of Justice (ECJ) for procedural violations when they are nonetheless achieving the substantive aims of the law (Interviews, Permanent Representation of Germany to the EU, Brussels, April 3, 1998; Permanent Representation of the State of Hessen to the EU, Brussels, April 6, 1998).

As noted in Chapter 2, conflict between the EU and Germany has emerged over Germany's use of administrative circulars, technical guidelines, and other nonbinding instruments as tools of implementation (Schwarze 1996, pp. 126–130). Opposing the use of such instruments because they are not legally binding, the Commission brought a case before the ECJ challenging Germany's use of an administrative guideline *(TA Luft)* to implement an EU directive on air quality. The ECJ ruled for the Commission, holding that the administrative guideline did not provide the necessary "legal certainty" to constitute a sufficient means by which to implement EU law.[45] The Commission has brought a number of other successful infringement actions against Germany in cases where Germany attempted to use nonbinding instruments to implement EU legislation.[46] *Länder* implementation failures regarding the EU directive on environmental impact assessment have been the source of numerous complaints to the Commission and have sparked infringement procedures against Germany (Wessels and Rometsch 1996, p. 96).[47]

EU directives, backed by ECJ decisions, have also forced the German government to introduce deadlines into its regulations. Traditionally, German regulations had not contained action-forcing deadlines. Their presence in EU directives has encouraged the federal government to centralize more authority, because such deadlines must be met nationwide. The failure of any *Land* to implement an EU directive on time can result in an infringement action being brought against the federal government. In one such case concerning Germany's failure to implement the Drinking Water Directive,[48] the ECJ held that the directive required Germany to introduce formal requirements forcing the *Länder* to notify the Commission of derogations under the directive within the prescribed deadlines. The ECJ emphasized that the German federal government could not rely on general, constitutional principles of the *Länder's* loyalty to the federation *(bundesfreundlichen Verhalten or Bundestreue)*, but had to require the *Länder* to meet specific deadlines.[49] Similarly, in a case involving the Urban Waste Water Treatment Directive,[50] Germany attempted to justify its delays in implementation by noting that the *Länder* had regulatory competence in this area. In keeping with its case law in this area, the ECJ rejected this argument and insisted that the German federal government must ensure that the *Länder* meet the deadlines set out in the directive.[51]

Finally, some EU directives have introduced detailed substantive and procedural requirements into areas of German environmental law that had historically been subject to only loose controls. For instance, water pollution control had been one of the least detailed areas of German environmental law. German regulations concerning nitrate levels in drinking water and bathing water have all become far more detailed in light of EU requirements. Also the EU waste directive set out detailed requirements regarding the regulation of landfills, where *Länder* had previously enjoyed great discretion. After the German federal government failed to force the *Länder* to draw up detailed plans for the disposal of dangerous waste as required by the directive on toxic and dangerous waste, the Commission brought an infringement action against Germany. The ECJ ruled against Germany, noting that while Germany had "very largely fulfilled that obligation," the failure of particular *Länder* (most notably North Rhine–Westphalia and Baden-Württemberg) to issue and notify waste disposal plans within the prescribed deadline constituted a violation of the directive.[52] Thus, the German federal government was held accountable for the failures of particular *Länder.*

EU enforcement actions bring pressure to bear on German *Länder.* Where the German federal government traditionally relied on informal means to press the *Länder* to implement federal laws effectively, the Commission regularly employs the more formal, adversarial infringement procedure (art. 226, former art. 169). While the Commission can only bring cases against the German federal government, it is clear to all parties involved when the implementation failure is actually attributable to one or more *Länder.* If the German federal government comes under pressure from Brussels, then it in turn pressures *Land* government officials to redress the implementation problem (Interview, German Permanent Representation to the EU, April 3, 1998).

Conclusion

In Germany, as in the other federal polities examined in this book, the federal government plays a powerful role in issuing environmental legislation, but leaves implementation in the hands of state governments. Germany's membership in the EU has contributed to the shift in legislative power from the states to the federal government within Germany. Traditionally, the federal government did little to pressure the *Länder* to implement federal laws. Private litigants had limited opportunities to enforce federal statutes, as the structure of German government limited the role of courts in the regulatory process to cases concerning individual rights. This limitation prompted environmental litigants seeking to influence state and local governments to focus on a narrow range of cases involving specific licensing decisions. In recent years, pressure from the EU has caused the German federal government to place more constraints on German *Länder* in their implementation of environmental law. EU laws have also created new causes for action for private parties wishing to bring cases before German courts.

5 | Environmental Regulation in Australia and Canada

As federal systems, both Australia and Canada have had to face the same issues as the other polities explored in this book concerning the relationships between federal and state governments in matters of environmental regulation. In Australia and Canada, however, these intergovernmental relationships are framed within Westminster-style parliamentary governments at the federal level. This system of government provides for a much higher concentration of power within the federal government than do the governmental structures of the other polities examined thus far.[1] The combination of federalism and parliamentary government has channeled the development of environmental regulation in the direction anticipated in the model of regulatory federalism presented in Chapter 1. In both cases, the division of jurisdictional competences developed along similar lines. Following the stages outlined in Chapter 1, the federal governments took on significant policymaking competences, while ultimately leaving implementation in states hands. The politics of discretion also developed as anticipated in the parliamentary federal systems. In each instance, Parliament has produced vague legislation that grants federal and state executives wide discretion. Courts, with a few noteworthy but isolated exceptions, have not acted to limit this discretion. As a result of discretionary legislation and judicial deference, litigation has not become a routine part of the regulatory process, as neither federal officials nor private litigants have made frequent use of litigation as a means to enforce policy. State governments enjoy wide discretion in implementing federal laws.

In the Westminster model of parliamentary government, power is concentrated in the hands of the party—or coalition of parties—that holds a majority in the lower house of Parliament. The majority party or coalition forms a cabinet of ministers (the government) that controls the executive branch, thus fusing control of the legislature with control of the executive.

In theory, Parliament is sovereign and government ministers are held accountable by Parliament for the actions of their ministries. In practice, party discipline leads to the government's dominating the legislature.

Westminster-style parliamentary systems typically have weak upper houses (Lijphart 1984). Canada fits this mold; the Canadian Senate is composed of appointees rather than elected officials and exercises no substantial power. Australia departs somewhat from the Westminster model insofar as power is less concentrated. this is because the Australian Senate is a significant, independent political player; all legislation must win the Senate's approval.[2] Governments often adjust bills so that they will be acceptable to the Senate majority. While the Senate has certainly had some influence on environmental legislation, it has consistently allowed governments to enact the vague, discretionary statutes they prefer. Both major parties have a preference for strong executive-led government and have, therefore, refrained from placing detailed, action-forcing requirements in legislation (Lynch and Galligan 1996, p. 208).[3]

Parliamentary government in Australia and Canada has had important implications for the role of the judiciary. In parliamentary systems, courts tend to grant wide discretion to the executive in its implementation of legislative acts (Shapiro 1981; Ferejohn 1995). This judicial behavior is not merely a product of traditional attitudes on the part of judges or of their acceptance of the theory of parliamentary sovereignty. Such traditions of judicial deference indeed exist, but they have concrete institutional underpinnings. Because of the fusion of executive and legislative power in parliamentary systems, the government can easily persuade Parliament to pass new legislation. Courts are hesitant to review regulations or general policy decisions made by the executive in implementing legislative acts, because they recognize that if they attempt to rule against executive actions and assert their own interpretation of the law, the executive can easily direct Parliament to pass new legislation overturning the court's interpretation.

This structural reality has discouraged the judicialization of regulatory policymaking in both Australia and Canada. Given the reluctance of courts to constrain executive discretion, proponents of regulation do not attempt to cement their legislative victories by enacting court-enforceable requirements. In the case of each polity, while the federal government has established a wide-ranging policymaking competence in the environmental arena, it has avoided enacting strict, court-enforceable measures. Instead, the federal government has tended to enact general, framework legislation with few detailed requirements that might be enforceable in court. Environmental groups have on occasion initiated litigation to challenge the exercise of executive discretion; however, such challenges have met with little success. Moreover, the federal governments of Canada and Australia have rarely taken legal action against states to force the implementation of environmental regulations, and, on the whole, have taken a less coercive approach to enforcement than have other federal governments in this study, including that of the European Union (EU).

While the overall development of environmental regulation in Canada and Australia fits the patterns predicted by the theory of regulatory federalism, it does reveal a few unanticipated nuances. First, the scope of federal environmental policymaking in these two cases has been more limited than that in the other polities in this study. While the Canadian and Australian federal governments did assert their authority to play a role in environmental policymaking, they did not adopt federal regulations in as wide a range of policy areas as did the other federal governments considered here, including the EU. Second, both nations experienced a gradual increase in the role of the courts. While judicial activism in Canada and Australia has not approached the level of that in the United States or Germany, courts over time have taken on a greater role in regulation. In Canada, the role of courts was increased with the introduction of the Charter of Rights and Freedoms in 1982. Australia introduced no such bill of rights, but did establish new mechanisms for judicial review of administrative action in the late 1970s. These developments increased the role of courts to some extent, but judicial activism in environmental regulation has remained limited in both cases, due to the institutional checks on courts identified above.

A third nuance is that states in both Canada and Australia have demanded, and won, an increased role in policymaking at the national level. During the 1970s and 1980s, the federal governments in both nations encroached on state jurisdiction. Some states resisted federal intrusion, but given the support of the courts for federal jurisdiction, recalcitrant states were eventually forced to concede that they could not maintain exclusive jurisdiction over environmental issues. In the 1990s, however, another shift occurred. Both federal governments recognized that they could only implement policy with the cooperation of state governments. In order to elicit that cooperation, states have been granted an increased role in policymaking at the national level by delegating policymaking competence to new "intergovernmental" decisionmaking bodies that sit outside the regular parliamentary structure. These bodies are composed of representatives of state governments and the federal government. Policymaking in these forums resembles the sort of intergovernmental bargaining that goes on in the EU's Council of Ministers. Coupling this observation with one mentioned above regarding enforcement of environmental regulations suggests that the divide between the "domestic" politics of Australia and Canada and the "intergovernmental" politics of the EU is illusory. Increasingly, policymaking in Australia and Canada is conducted in intergovernmental forums, while the federal governments in those countries actually take a less coercive approach to enforcement than do the central institutions of the EU.

Environmental Regulation in Australia

The Politics of Competence

Like other constitutions examined in this study, the Australian Commonwealth Constitution of 1901 makes no specific mention of environmental issues. Like the U.S. Constitution, the Australian Constitution confers a limited number of powers (enumerated in §§51 and 52) on the commonwealth government and leaves all residual powers to the state governments (§107). As none of the commonwealth's enumerated powers relate specifically to the environment, environmental regulation has remained, by default, in the hands of state governments.[4] Moreover, the constitution explicitly left ownership of public lands in the hands of state governments.[5]

THE EMERGENCE OF COMMONWEALTH POLICYMAKING

Public concern over environmental issues was limited during the first six decades of the Australian federation. A number of nature conservation groups did press for the protection of Australia's indigenous flora and fauna early in the century. These groups tended to focus on local land use decisions and brought their pressure to bear on state and local governments.[6] The few groups that focused on pollution problems concentrated exclusively on local issues of urban sanitation (Hutton and Connors 1999, pp. 70–80). In this context, there was little jurisdictional conflict between the commonwealth and the states regarding environmental competences. States created a number of parks, and enacted a limited amount of legislation concerning the protection of species and the control of urban water and air pollution. The commonwealth government took almost no action in regard to the environment.

During the late 1960s, paralleling trends in other industrialized countries, public concern regarding the state of the environment grew in Australia. Some of the same environmental catastrophes that raised awareness in North America and Europe, such as the 1968 Torrey Canyon oil tanker wreck off the English coast and the 1969 Santa Barbara oil spill, also attracted attention in Australia (Hutton and Connors 1999, p. 103). In the early 1970s, environmental issues came to the forefront of the Australian national political agenda with a dispute over the fate of Lake Pedder in Tasmania. The lake was to be submerged as part of a Gordon River hydroelectric scheme, a plan that enjoyed the strong backing of the Tasmanian state government. Conservationists turned to the commonwealth government, asking that it intervene to stop the project. Some Lake Pedder supporters hoped that with the victory of Labor in the 1972 election, the commonwealth might take action. However, the Commonwealth Labor government, under Gough Whitlam, offered inducements to the Tasmanian state government to preserve Lake Pedder, but refused to intervene more directly. Conservationists ultimately lost their battle, and Lake Pedder was submerged in 1972.

The dispute over Lake Pedder raised the political salience of environmental issues. And, as anticipated by the model of regulatory federalism, following this increase in issue salience the federal government recognized that it could gain public support for environmental policymaking at the federal level. Thus the Whitlam government began issuing commonwealth environmental statutes, including the Environment Protection (Impact of Proposals) Act of 1974 (hereafter the Impact of Proposals Act), the Australian National Parks and Wildlife Conservation Act of 1975, and the Australian Heritage Commission Act of 1975 (Kellow 1996, pp. 135–156). In addition to issuing legislation, the government made institutional changes. In 1972, it reshuffled the portfolios in the cabinet to create a separate minister for environment.[7] Also in 1972, in order to improve administrative consultation between the commonwealth and states, the commonwealth established the Australian Environment Council (AEC), which brought together the commonwealth's environment minister and the state environment ministers for regular meetings. Two years later, the commonwealth established another council, the Council of Nature Conservation Ministers (CONCOM) (Bates 1992, p. 43).

While state governments in Australia were not totally opposed to a commonwealth role in environmental protection, they did want to maintain control over development and resource management decisions. When the commonwealth began to take coercive actions against states in these areas under the new environmental statutes, industrial interests and state governments challenged the constitutional bases of the laws before the Australian High Court. However, like other high courts in systems of regulatory federalism, the Australian High Court had an incentive to see the commonwealth government establish competence in environmental matters.

In a pair of landmark cases, the High Court upheld the commonwealth's authority to act regarding the environment under a number of constitutional powers.[8] The first legal challenge to commonwealth competence came in 1976, when the commonwealth took its first coercive action against a state in the field of environmental regulation. The dispute concerned the mining of sand on Fraser Island in Queensland. The conflict surrounding Fraser Island had its roots in the early 1960s, when conservationists had first opposed plans to mine mineral sands on the island, which was the largest sand island in the world. When mining on the island began in 1975 with the support of the Queensland government, conservationists turned to the commonwealth for help. They convinced Environment Minister Moss Cass to conduct a public inquiry into the impact of the sand mining operations under the 1974 Environment (Impact of Proposals) Act and to withhold the issuance of export licenses for sand until the inquiry was completed.

One of the mining companies concerned, acting with the support of the Queensland government, challenged both the constitutional validity of the act and the right of the government to refuse export licenses for environmental reasons. In its *Murphyores* decision, the High Court ruled that the commonwealth was entitled to take into account environmental concerns in determining whether to issue an export license under its overseas trade and commerce powers (§51(1)).[9] This decision opened the way for subsequent environmental laws based, at least in part, on the commonwealth's overseas trade and commerce powers, including the Ozone Protection Act of 1989 and the Wildlife Protection (Regulation of Exports and Imports) Act of 1982.

In the second case,[10] the High Court upheld three other constitutional bases for commonwealth environmental legislation. The case arose in the context of a battle over the construction of a dam in Tasmania, on the Gordon River below its confluence with the Franklin River. In 1982, the dam had the firm backing of the Tasmanian state government (Hutton and Connors 1999, p. 162). The same year, the commonwealth government succeeded in placing the area in which the dam was to be built, the western Tasmanian wilderness, on the list compiled by the World Heritage Convention. The World Heritage Convention calls for its signatories to identify cultural and natural areas deserving of protection given their "outstanding universal value," and establishes an evaluation process for including selected areas on the World Heritage List (Farrier and Tucker 1998, p. 565). Under pressure from environmentalists to protect the area, the commonwealth government announced that it planned to halt the construction of the dam. The government of Tasmania initiated legal proceedings to challenge the commonwealth's decision. In 1983, in order to bolster its plans to block the dam, the commonwealth passed the World Heritage (Properties Conservation) Act, which listed the specific activities that would be prohibited in areas nominated to the World Heritage List, without specific consent of the commonwealth's environmental minister.[11] The Tasmanian government proceeded with its legal challenge regarding the dam and, in addition, challenged the constitutional validity of the new act before the High Court.

The High Court struck down some sections of the act, but generally upheld its constitutional validity and the commonwealth's ability to block construction of the dam.[12] First, the court held that the act was valid under the commonwealth's external affairs power, because it served to comply with Australia's obligations under an international treaty. Second, the court ruled that the commonwealth's corporations power supported the legislation because the act served to prevent a trading corporation from taking an action relating to its trading activities, such as the generation and sale of electricity. Finally, the High Court ruled that the act could be based on the commonwealth's power to make special laws for specific races, insofar as the government's actions sought to protect places of importance to Australia's aborigines.[13] The ruling on the construction of the Franklin Dam secured the constitutional bases for many other pieces of legislation, such as the National Parks and Wildlife Conservation Act 1975, the Ozone Protection Act 1989, and the Protection of the Sea (Prevention of Pollution from Ships) Act of 1983.

Commonwealth intervention in the area of environment has not been limited to regulation and legal tools. As in other policy areas, the commonwealth has used fiscal tools to pressure state governments to pursue commonwealth environmental policy objectives (Murchison 1995,

p. 510). Article 96 of the Australia Constitution empowers the commonwealth to make grants to states. The High Court has ruled that the commonwealth is free to attach conditions to such grants.[14] The Nature Conservation Act of 1974, the Air Quality Monitoring Act of 1976, the Environment Act of 1977, the Soil Conservation Act of 1985, and the Natural Resources Management Act of 1992 all involved making grants to states for environmental purposes. Not surprisingly, states have not challenged the commonwealth's funding schemes.

This overview of the Australian commonwealth's initial foray into environmental policymaking suggests that public attention and subsequent federal intervention concentrated on wilderness and nature conservation issues. And indeed, from the 1960s through the 1980s, environmental groups in Australia focused on wilderness preservation, campaigning against a variety of development projects in pristine areas. Unlike in the United States and western Europe, industrial pollution and urban environmental concerns attracted little national attention (Doyle 2000, p. 65; Hutton and Connors 1999, p. 197). In this context, it is not surprising that the federal role in environmental policy long remained limited to issues of nature conservation. As anticipated by the theory set out in Chapter 1, the Australian commonwealth government intervened only in areas of high political salience.

IMPLEMENTATION AND ENFORCEMENT

With its power to take environmental actions confirmed, the Australian commonwealth took a few coercive actions against state governments during the 1980s. These actions attracted widespread public attention, but they were by no means typical. Aside from these isolated episodes, the commonwealth did very little to ensure that environmental laws were implemented or enforced. It never moved to establish administrative bodies to monitor, implement, or enforce environmental law at the commonwealth level.

One dispute involved the tropical rain forests of northern Queensland. Covering 8,500 square kilometers, the forests are the oldest continuously surviving rain forests on Earth and are exceedingly rich in biodiversity (Toyne 1994, pp. 65–69). Most of the rain forests were owned or controlled by the Queensland government, which under the conservative premier John Bjelke-Petersen, allowed real estate development, mining, burning, and logging in the area throughout the 1970s. The conflict between conservationists and the Queensland government came to a head when the latter supported the construction of a road through the rain forest to the coast (Hutton and Connors 1999, pp. 171–175). Conservationists tried to block the road construction in the Queensland courts, but failed. They then turned to the commonwealth government, asking that it intervene to prevent construction of the road.

In late 1983, conservationists called on the commonwealth Labor government to follow the precedent set in the Franklin Dam episode and nominate the rain forests to the list of the World Heritage Convention so that they could be placed under commonwealth protection. Initially, the commonwealth refused to intervene, preferring to reach a negotiated solution. In 1985 the Commonwealth proposed the National Rainforest Conservation Program, which was to provide funds for the Queensland government to protect the forests by establishing alternative timber supplies, purchasing privately held forests, and creating more parks. But Queensland flatly refused the conditional funding and continued with its logging and development operations. Finally, in June 1987, the commonwealth announced that it would consider nominating the Wet Tropics of North Queensland for World Heritage listing, despite the opposition of the Queensland government. Queensland applied to the High Court for an injunction to prevent the commonwealth from nominating the area, but was rejected. The commonwealth then nominated the area in December 1987.

Conflict between the commonwealth and Queensland escalated in 1988, pending the World Heritage committee's decision on the listing of the rain forests at year's end. Despite the ban on logging in areas pending inclusion on the World Heritage List, logging continued, and it was alleged that the Queensland government tacitly approved of the continued logging. The commonwealth sent in helicopters to monitor compliance with the ban. For its part, Queensland mounted a lobbying campaign to persuade the World Heritage committee to reject the nomination. Shortly before the meeting of that committee in December, the Queensland environment minister stated, "We are totally uncompromising in our determination not to cooperate with the Federal government" (Toyne 1994, p. 81). The committee approved the nomination and the "Wet Tropics of North Queensland" were put on UNESCO's World Heritage List on December 9, 1988. Shortly thereafter, the Queensland environment minister stated that Queensland would not accept commonwealth management plans for the area, and that the commonwealth would have to use the federal police and the army if it wished to enforce them.

After the area was added to the World Heritage List, the Commonwealth placed it under the protection of the World Heritage (Properties Conservation) Act of 1983 and issued regulations prohibiting forestry or road construction in the area without commonwealth approval. Queensland then challenged these commonwealth actions, but the challenge was dismissed by the High court.[15]

While the commonwealth and Queensland were locked in conflict over the Queensland rain forests, a second intergovernmental conflict over forest preservation was brewing in Tasmania. Here the issue concerned logging in the Lemonthyme and Southern eucalyptus forests. As in the previous cases, the state government supported the logging, and conservationists turned to the commonwealth.

Since the 1970s, the production of woodchips for export had become one of the primary commercial uses of the forests. As only the commonwealth had the power to issue or renew export licenses, conservationists saw an opportunity to block, or at least slow, logging in the area. Export licenses for woodchips in Tasmania were set to expire between 1985 and 1988. While the Tasmanian government pressed the commonwealth to extend the licenses, conservationists argued that continued logging would threaten areas of the forest that were listed on the National Estate and that might warrant nomination to the World Heritage List.[16]

The commonwealth demanded that the woodchippers prepare an environmental impact assessment before it would extend the export licenses. After the completion of the assessment, the commonwealth approved the licenses but mandated that the Tasmanian government consult with the commonwealth in preparing its forest management plans for the areas on the National Estate, and promised that the areas would be subject to environmental controls. The commonwealth wanted to maintain a role in the ongoing implementation of forest management in the area.

The Tasmanian government reacted angrily to this intrusion. While it could not deny the commonwealth's power regarding logging intended for woodchip exports, it acted quickly to expand logging and production of lumber for domestic consumption, where the commonwealth had no clear power. Logging continued unabated despite the opposition of the commonwealth. In December 1986, the cabinet called for a year-long moratorium on logging in areas of the National Estate that might be of World Heritage value, pending evaluations. Still Tasmania refused to cooperate.

The commonwealth won temporary protection for the forests by passing legislation[17] that established a formal inquiry commission to consider the area for World Heritage nomination, and by obtaining a court injunction against logging. Eventually, the commonwealth abandoned its more aggressive efforts to have a hand in management of the region and reached a compromise with Tasmania.[18] The Tasmanian government agreed to protect a portion of the forests (approximately 30 percent) in exchange for a $50 million compensation package from the commonwealth, an extension of woodchip export licenses, and a promise that the commonwealth would make no unilateral nominations of areas to the World Heritage List in the future (Toyne 1994, p. 103; Hutton and Connors 1999, p. 183–188).

Another intergovernmental controversy, this time surrounding the environmental assessment of a proposed pulp mill in Tasmania, set the stage for the commonwealth's eventual retreat from implementation activities. In this case, the positions of the commonwealth and Tasmanian government seemed to be in line. Both wanted to see the Wesley Vale Pulp Mill built. The billion-dollar project, backed by an Australian firm (North Broken Hill) and a Canadian partner (Noranda) was to be the largest private investment in Australian history. The approval of both Tasmania and the commonwealth was necessary for the project to go forward and both levels of government claimed that they would demand strict environmental controls. The companies repeatedly threatened to abandon the project if they did not win regulatory approval in a timely fashion. The commonwealth agreed that an environmental impact assessment (EIS) could follow state procedures and that the companies could submit one EIS to both levels of government (Toyne 1994, p. 115). In February 1989, under continuing threats from the companies, the Tasmanian government watered down its proposed environmental controls. When the commonwealth cabinet met a few days later, they approved the project, "conditional upon further environment studies, ongoing monitoring, and the preparation of tougher guidelines by the Commonwealth in the following month." This decision prompted the companies to abandon the project the next day (Toyne 1994, p. 117; Hutton and Connors 1999, p. 206).

The commonwealth and all state governments viewed the entire episode as a failure. Critics argued that the commonwealth failed to provide companies with reliable, consistent guidelines. The failure of the commonwealth to better coordinate its environmental requirements with those of state governments created uncertainty regarding regulatory requirements. Many feared that this regulatory uncertainty would discourage investments in other states as well.

The commonwealth's approach to implementation and enforcement in all these cases was ad hoc. In the matter concerning the Queensland rain forests, the commonwealth coerced Queensland into protecting the rain forests by nominating them to the World Heritage List. In the conflict surrounding the Tasmanian eucalyptus forests, the commonwealth tried to use its power to issue export licenses to coerce Tasmania. In the case of the Wesley Vale Pulp Mill, the commonwealth relied on its authority over environmental impact assessments. Although these episodes revealed the commonwealth's willingness to place pressure on state governments and polluters regarding environmental and conservation issues, they do not add up to a coherent program of implementation and enforcement. The commonwealth's few interventions into policy implementation evoked great hostility on the part of state governments and forced it to turn to a new approach to policymaking.

ESTABLISHING A NEW EQUILIBRIUM

By 1990, state and commonwealth positions regarding environmental protection were beginning to change. Seeing that the High Court approved commonwealth jurisdiction in environmental matters, states had come to accept that the commonwealth would have jurisdiction whether they liked it or not. Perhaps the most striking evidence of this was the fact that while the Tasmanian government opposed the federal intervention in the Wesley Vale Pulp Mill episode, it did not go to the High Court to challenge the commonwealth's authority to intervene. The commonwealth, for its part, increasingly recognized the futility of trying to coerce states into protecting the environment. It could intervene in high profile cases to block a state action, but it lacked the administrative infrastructure necessary to oversee the day-to-day implementation and enforcement of environmental policy.

Prime Minister Hawke called for a "new federalism" that would aim to increase cooperation between states and the commonwealth. He initiated a series of conferences in which he met with the state government premiers and representatives of local government in an effort to improve intergovernmental cooperation. The first such conference was held in Brisbane in October 1990. Environmental policy was a prominent issue on the agenda, and participants announced their intention to draft an Intergovernmental Agreement on the Environment (IGAE).

The text of the agreement was negotiated over the next eighteen months, and the IGAE (Environment Australia 1992) was finally signed on May 1, 1992 by Prime Minister Keating and all six state premiers, along with leaders of the two mainland territories and a representative of the Australian Local Government Association. The agreement included a statement regarding the responsibilities of the various levels of government (commonwealth, state, and local) and set out a procedure for resolving conflicts of interest between the commonwealth and state governments. Signatories committed themselves to eliminating the duplication of functions between the two levels of government wherever possible. The agreement also included "schedules" that detailed the cooperative arrangements to be enacted between state governments and the commonwealth in nine specific policy areas: environmental data, land use decisions and approval processes, environmental impact assessment, environmental protection (standards and goals), climate change, biological diversity, national estate, World Heritage, and nature conservation.

Perhaps most important, the IGAE provided for the establishment of a ministerial council called the National Environmental Protection Council (NEPC).[19] The NEPC, which was established in 1994,[20] consists of one minister from each government that is a party to the agreement. The commonwealth minister serves as the chair and the group makes decisions by a two-thirds majority vote. The council's primary functions are to make national environment policy measures (NEPMs) and to assess their implementation and effectiveness in participating jurisdictions. These NEPMs may contain environmental quality goals, standards, monitoring, and reporting requirements. The council is empowered to issue NEPMs concerning a select number of environmental issues: ambient air and water quality, noise pollution, contaminated sights, hazardous wastes, motor vehicle emissions reuse, and recycling. A NEPM passed by the council automatically becomes law in all participating jurisdictions, unless it is disallowed by either house of the commonwealth's Parliament. NEPMs replace existing laws dealing with the same subject matter, except insofar as existing laws have more stringent requirements. While participating states and territories are required to meet detailed, harmonized reporting requirements and to establish "a uniform hierarchy of offenses and related penalty structures," implementation and enforcement of NEPMs is left in their hands (Environment Australia 1992; Schedule 4).

Prior to the signing of the IGAE, the commonwealth had faced stiff resistance from state governments to its attempts to make and implement environmental policy. The IGAE, and the national council that it envisaged, aimed to win the support of state governments by providing them with a direct voice in national policymaking and by assuring them that implementation would remain in their hands. After a rocky start, including the temporary withdrawal of Western Australia from the agreement, the commonwealth's efforts appear to be succeeding.

The NEPC has produced protection measures on ambient air quality, contaminated sites, interstate shipment of controlled wastes, packaging waste, diesel vehicle emissions, and a national pollutant inventory. The NEPM on air quality, issued in June 1998, illustrates the approach that the council is taking in drafting national standards.[21] The NEPC justifies the need for national standards, stating that the "significant differences" in air-quality requirements among jurisdictions in Australia create uncertainty for business and "[have] the potential to create, or may have already created, market distortions or pollution havens, and may not be in keeping with National Competition Policy" (NEPC 1998, pp. 41–42). The NEPM sets out precise quantitative standards for allowable concentrations of carbon monoxide, nitrogen dioxide, ozone, sulfur dioxide, lead, and particulate matter and establishes a protocol for standardized monitoring and reporting of these pollutants nationwide. At the same time, the measure clearly leaves implementation and enforcement in the hands of state governments: "The NEPC Act deliberately leaves the implementation of the standards to each individual jurisdiction. This allows for local knowledge, conditions and systems to be considered and applied in managing air pollution" (NEPC 1998, p. 5). Even more explicitly, the council explains, "The NEPM imposes a responsibility on jurisdictions to report progress towards meeting the standard but does not require compliance, except for the agreed monitoring and reporting requirements" (NEPC 1998, p. 22).

A recent piece of federal legislation again demonstrates the commonwealth's preference for leaving implementation powers to the state governments. In June 1999, the commonwealth adopted the Environment Protection and Biodiversity Conservation (EPBC) Act, the most significant piece of federal environmental legislation in the past twenty-five years.[22] The act replaces five existing commonwealth statutes—the 1992 Endangered Species Protection Act, the 1974 Impact of Proposals Act, the 1975 National Parks and Wildlife Conservation Act, the 1980 Whale Protection Act, and the 1983 World Heritage Properties Conservation Act—and amends many others. The law clarifies the commonwealth's role in environmental protection by empowering the commonwealth to assess and approve actions that it deems will have a "significant impact" on a set of six specific matters of "national environmental significance."[23] While the 1999 act clarifies the scope of the commonwealth's environmental assessment powers, it does not increase the commonwealth's role in implementation. Quite to the contrary, the act (§§45–48) specifically allows the commonwealth to enter bilateral agreements with state governments in which it delegates the authority to conduct environmental assessments and approvals. Critics suggest that the act paves the way for the commonwealth to retreat even further from its role in implementation and enforcement (*Canberra Times* 1999, p. 8).

The development of the politics of competence in Australian environmental policy fits well with the model of regulatory federalism presented in Chapter 1. Environmental regulation started as a state government function, but as environmental protection became a popular political issue, the federal government entered the policymaking arena. Compared to other federal governments in this study, Australian legislative activities on the national level have been somewhat limited, concentrating primarily on issues of nature conservation. However, this limited scope is consistent with the fact that Australian environmentalists and public environmental awareness have concentrated on issues of nature conservation. The commonwealth initially delved into implementation, but eventually backed away when confronted with the enormous cost that systematic implementation and enforcement would entail. As states demanded a greater say in decisionmaking regarding national standards, the commonwealth acquiesced, recognizing that cooperation with states was necessary to bring about standardization of regulatory requirements at the national level. The commonwealth went further than one might expect based on the model of regulatory federalism, actually establishing a new decision-making body (the NEPC) that provides states with a direct vote on national environmental measures. The establishment of these new decision-making mechanisms, along with the assurance given to states that they will maintain control over implementation, has ameliorated state resistance and made it likely that national standards will be set in a number of new areas as public attention to pollution-related problems increases.

The Politics of Discretion

In step with the politics of competence common to all the federal polities considered in this book, the Australian commonwealth has assumed an increasing role in environmental policymaking, while implementation remains firmly in the hands of the state governments. Given the role of the Australian states in implementing commonwealth policies, we must again address questions of bureaucratic discretion: How much discretion do states have in implementing commonwealth laws? Do those laws include detailed requirements or only vague mandates? Does the commonwealth act to ensure that states apply these laws in practice?

Australia's parliamentary structure of government has resulted in the enactment of legislation that leaves a great deal of discretion to the executive agencies charged with implementing the legislation, whether they be commonwealth or state agencies. The judiciary has largely followed the government's lead, discouraging litigants from challenging the exercise of bureaucratic discretion. Environmental policymaking in Australia has been far less judicialized than that in the United States, and far less even than that in the EU. Neither private parties nor federal authorities have consistently taken action to challenge the actions of state administrations in implementing environmental laws.

Commonwealth environmental statutes are generally vague, often to the point of being unenforceable. Bates summarizes the situation, pointing out that "much of the present law is cast in rather vague terms, leaving the application of the legislation to ministerial discretion that is difficult to challenge in the courts" (Bates 1995, p. 19). Comparing Australian environmental statutes to those in the United States, Murchison notes, "Australia has no environmental statutes that approach the complexity of the federal environmental statutes in the United States" (Murchison 1995, p. 547).

Examples of such vagueness abound. The Impact of Proposals Act of 1974, an early landmark piece of legislation, was designed to allow for ministerial discretion. In announcing the act, the commonwealth minister explained that by introducing environmental assessment, the government wanted to avoid the situation in the United States where litigation was brought frequently to challenge administrative decisions regarding impact assessments (Bates 1995, p. 170). But the circumstances in which an assessment would be required were left vague and unenforceable. As a result, states adopted very different approaches to environmental assessment. Most took a rather flexible approach, which does not allow for judicial review of administrative decisions regarding assessments. Only New South Wales has established a mandatory, legally enforceable process (Bates 1995, pp. 154–170; Lynch and Galligan 1996, p. 221). Most recently, the 1999 Environment Protection and Biodiversity Conservation (EPBC) Act allows the commonwealth to enter bilateral agreements with state governments delegating environmental assessment and approval responsibilities to them. Neither the EPBC Act nor the regulations passed pursuant to it[24] impose detailed substantive or procedural conditions on how states must conduct assessments (Kerr 2000). Once the commonwealth has entered a bilateral agreement with a state government, it has no power under the EPBC Act to override an environmental assessment decision by the state, short of suspending or canceling the entire bilateral agreement.[25] Critics worry that this broad delegation of implementation authority will tempt states to succumb to parochial development interests. Green Party senator Bob Brown argues that "if the degree of state discretion allowed by the [EPBC Act] had been law during some of the most famous environmental stoushes of recent times, the Franklin would have been flooded, Fraser Island would have been mined, and Daintree logged" (*Canberra Times* 1999; Peake 1999).

Other statutes completely lack enforcement mechanisms. For instance, the Agricultural and Veterinary Chemicals Act of 1988 establishes a national council to make decisions regarding the approval of certain toxic chemicals. However, the act does not provide for any enforcement mechanisms in the event that a state simply chooses to ignore a decision of the council or permits the use of a chemical that has not been approved (Bates 1995, p. 450).

The commonwealth very rarely plays a direct role in implementing and enforcing environmental statutes. It does not take enforcement actions directly against polluters to pressure state governments into action, as the U.S. federal government often does. Nor does it follow the approach of the European Commission, which frequently brings states before the European Court of Justice for their failure to implement environmental laws. The commonwealth's implementation activities are limited to primarily those statutes that require the issuance of import or export licenses for such items as dangerous substances or protected species. The federal government can also use its control of export licenses to pursue environmental objectives indirectly, as it did in 1976 when it halted mining on Fraser Island by banning the export of minerals mined there (Hutton and Connors 1999, p. 149). Similarly, where implementation is left exclusively in state hands, as is most often the case, the commonwealth very rarely takes action to ensure that the law is enforced. The instances of commonwealth intervention in matters concerning nature conservation examined earlier, such as the Franklin Dam and the rain forests of northern Queensland, are exceptions to the rule.

Traditionally, judicial review of administrative action in Australia has been limited; those that have occurred ordinarily have been carried out by state and local courts. By the late 1960s, however, there was growing public dissatisfaction with the system of administrative law. As the administration was vested with more and more discretionary powers, it became clear that parliamentary oversight and ministerial responsibility could not adequately protect individual rights (Mullan 1983). In response, between 1975 and 1980 the commonwealth enacted legislation that created a new system for judicial review.[26] Two new institutions were established: the Administrative Appeals Tribunal (AAT), a quasi-judicial body that was empowered to hear appeals to administrative decisions taken under a wide range of statutes, and a federal court that could hear appeals on questions of law from decisions of the AAT. Furthermore, the commonwealth expanded the grounds on which an aggrieved party could seek review of an administrative decision. These innovations have certainly increased the extent to which individuals may challenge decisions of the public administration, and most observers conclude that this oversight has had a salutary effect on public administration in Australia (O'Brien 1991).

The AAT and the federal court established in its wake have jurisdiction to hear appeals concerning a number of environmental statutes, and to this extent have had an impact on environmental regulation. But these bodies and other Australian courts have largely avoided dealing with general challenges to the administration of commonwealth environmental policy by denying access to those who might bring such challenges.[27] Under common law, before a person may commence legal proceedings they must establish standing to sue *(locus standi)*. Private parties may gain standing if their private rights have been violated or if they have suffered a special damage (usually of an economic nature), which distinguishes them from the general population. Australian courts have generally denied standing to individuals and groups seeking to enforce environmental law in the courts, thus discouraging the judicialization of the regulatory process (Lynch and Galligan 1996). Steep litigation costs and a loser-pays rule have also discouraged environmental plaintiffs. The combination of vague federal statutes, infrequent federal intervention, and judicial deference to administrative discretion have left state regulators ample discretion to pursue the informal, cooperative style of regulation they prefer (Murchison 1995, pp. 519, 538).

Environmental Regulation in Canada

The Politics of Competence

The Canadian Constitution (the 1867 British North America Act) made no mention of the environment. Early environmental regulation was pursued at the provincial level. Provinces based their involvement in this regulatory arena on their constitutional authority to regulate municipal affairs, local matters, property rights, and civil rights. Early provincial regulations, such as Ontario's 1884 Public Health Act, provided the legal framework within which provinces could regulate water and air pollution (Morton 1996, p. 38). These provincial public health statutes governed the limited amount of governmental pollution control activities that took place before the second half of the twentieth century (Harrison 2000a, p. 5).

THE EMERGENCE OF FEDERAL POLICYMAKING

Paralleling trends in the United States, Canadian concern about the environment grew during the late 1960s, though it varied across the provinces. Ontario, Alberta, and British Columbia took the lead in environmental regulation, while other provinces, particularly those in Atlantic Canada, lagged behind (Doern and Conway 1994, p. 93; Harrison 1996, p. 71). As in Australia and the other polities we have been considering the Canadian federal government responded to the heightened public concern by entering the realm of environmental regulation.

In 1970 and 1971 the government established a federal department of the environment named Environment Canada and passed the three pieces of legislation that formed the basis for most federal involvement in environmental regulation: the Clean Air Act, the Canada Water Act, and the amendments to the Fisheries Act. As anticipated in the model of regulatory federalism in Chapter 1, these early federal regulations set out broad goals and standards and left implementation and enforcement to the provinces (Skogstad 1996, p. 107; Harrison 1996, pp. 64–71, 103–104). The Clean Air and Canada Water Acts were "enabling" rather than "regulatory" legislation. They enabled the federal government to reach agreements with the provinces and industry on pollution problems. They allowed the federal government to coordinate and fund programs and to provide information, but did not provide for direct federal regulation.

The Clean Air Act authorized the federal government to issue National

Ambient Air Quality Objectives. However, the responsibility for issuing the emission standards necessary to achieve these air-quality objectives was left largely to the provinces. Normally, the federal government could only issue standards for a province if invited to do so by a provincial government. The one instance in which the federal government could issue standards unilaterally was when a particular source presented a significant danger to public health (Harrison 1996, pp. 70–71).

Similarly, the Canada Water Act left implementation to the provinces and allowed for wide administrative discretion. The act called for federal and provincial officials to cooperate in developing joint water-resource and water-quality management plans. In early drafts of the act, while most implementation was left to the provinces, the federal government was granted the power to implement the water-quality plans in "interjurisdictional" waters. However, even this limited degree of federal involvement in implementation was too threatening for provincial governments in Ontario, Alberta, Quebec, and British Columbia. Quebec premier Jean-Jacques Bertrand expressed his concerns in 1970, stating that "Quebec insists on control over its waters and no federal government will ever 'nationalize' them without triggering unyielding opposing from the Quebec government" (Harrison 1996, p. 75). The draft Water Act was amended in 1970 to reemphasize that water-quality standards would not be unilaterally imposed by the federal government and to ensure that implementation of the plans would be delegated to existing provincial agencies.

The Fisheries Act was exceptional in that it provided the federal government with stronger regulatory powers, allowing it to establish national standards for discharges into fish habitats. Even in the area of fisheries, however, the federal government refrained from using its unilateral powers. For example, after issuing pulp and paper effluent regulations under the Fisheries Act, the federal government reached a series of bilateral accords with provinces in which they agreed to implement the objectives set out in the regulations.[28]

Federal legislative activity in Canada abated quickly after 1971. Two additional acts, the Ocean Dumping and Control Act and the Environmental Contaminants Act, were proposed in 1972.[29] Passage was delayed until 1975 and 1976, respectively. Like the three major acts identified above, these two also left implementation and enforcement primarily to the provinces.[30] There were no other major legislative proposals until the Fisheries Act amendments of 1977, which are discussed below.

As in the other polities examined in this study, the Canadian federal government entered environmental policymaking with no explicit constitutional authority. Like the commonwealth in Australia, but unlike the federal government in the United States or the EU, the Canadian government did not possess a wide-ranging interstate commerce power that it could use as the basis for environmental legislation. Canadian courts had not developed a "stream of commerce" doctrine that linked commercial activities within provinces to trade between provinces. With their more restrictive interpretation of interprovincial trade, Canadian courts had limited federal power to regulate commerce to issues clearly involving interprovincial or international commerce. As the federal government could make only limited use of its trade and commerce power ($91(1A)$), federal involvement in environmental regulation in Canada relied on more limited constitutional powers such jurisdiction over seacoast and inland fisheries ($91(12)$), navigation and shipping ($91(10)$), federal lands and waters ($91(1A)$), agriculture (95), Indians and Indian Lands ($91(24)$), criminal law ($91(27)$), and interprovincial public works ($92(10)$). The federal government had to so craft its legislation that it could be justified under one or more of these powers, but in practice this did not limit its ability to issue a wide range of environmental regulations. As in other federal polities, the nation's highest court supported the federal government's claims to an "environmental competence" under constitutional powers not directly related to the environment (Harrison 1996, pp. 36–53, Morton 1996).

IMPLEMENTATION AND ENFORCEMENT

From the 1970s through the mid-1980s, the federal government in Canada avoided conflicts with the provinces regarding implementation of environmental policy. Although the federal government had delegated implementation and enforcement to the provinces through bilateral accords, it did, at least in principle, retain the power to bring enforcement actions should the provinces fail to live up to the conditions of the accords. In practice, however, the federal government rarely intervened, despite widespread nonimplementation and nonenforcement in the provinces (Harrison 1996, pp. 103–107). For example, the Canada Water Act's water-quality provisions were never implemented and only four implementing regulations were issued under the Clean Air Act (Harrison 2000b, p. 58). Similarly, regarding enforcement, until 1988 the federal government had prosecuted only ten cases under the Canada Water Act, the Environmental

Contaminants Act, the Clean Air Act, and the Ocean Dumping Control Act combined. Prosecution under the Fisheries Act, though more common, was still negligible (Doern and Conway 1994, p. 218; Harrison 1996, p. 102).

The federal government did make one notable attempt to expand its implementation capacity during this period. In 1977, Environment Canada proposed a number of revisions to the Fisheries Act, including increases in penalties for noncompliance, a provision authorizing the federal minister to designate federal or provincial officials to promulgate enforceable compliance schedules for individual polluters, and provisions prohibiting the destruction of fish habitats. The provinces adamantly opposed the habitat provisions, fearing that they could allow for increased federal control of development activities. The federal government, which had viewed the amendments as minor changes to facilitate implementation of the Fisheries Act, had not anticipated such intense provincial opposition. This conflict proved to be a turning point. Although the federal government went ahead and enacted the amendments, thereafter it was careful to avoid conflict with the provinces, and the federal government did not use its new powers under the Fisheries Act amendments. It never promulgated enforceable compliance schedules. Doern and Conway (1994, pp. 16–37) quote an Environment Canada official who summarized the department's reaction to the 1977 conflict by saying, "We did not do anything on regulation for almost a decade."

The federal government had two principal reasons to avoid challenging the provinces. First, Environment Canada lacked the resources necessary to take over implementation and enforcement functions from the provinces. Second, the federal government recognized that heavy-handed federal intervention in the provinces could stoke secessionist sentiments in Quebec.

Leaving implementation in provincial hands, however, led to significant discrepancies in enforcement across provinces and to weak enforcement in general (Skogstad 1996, p. 111). In 1987, an advisory council to the federal minister of the environment reported a pattern of almost two decades of systematic nonenforcement of the antipollution provisions of the Fisheries Act in Quebec. This echoed a report produced for the Law Reform Commission of Canada in 1984 that had earlier suggested that provinces throughout Canada were failing to enforce the Fisheries Act (Schrecker 1992, p. 91). By 1987, 70 percent of Canadian pulp and paper mills still failed to meet federal regulations issued in 1971 (Harrison 1996, p. 102).

In the 1980s, a series of toxic waste catastrophes—culminating in the Dow "toxic blob" found in the St. Claire River—led to public demand for federal action on the environment. The failure of the provinces to adequately protect the environment had become widely recognized, and the federal government saw an opportunity to gain popular support by taking a more direct role in the regulatory process. In particular, the federal government wanted to show that it could do something to solve the problem of toxic wastes. Environment Canada began preparing new legislation, the Canadian Environmental Protection Act (CEPA), that called for an increased federal role in the establishment and enforcement of regulations on toxic substances. There was substantial opposition to the CEPA initiative among provincial governments, many of whom questioned the federal government's jurisdiction in the area and opposed the imposition of federal standards.

As Environment Canada was preparing the CEPA, the Canadian Supreme Court handed down a decision that strengthened the federal claim for jurisdiction in the area of toxic wastes. The *Crown Zellerbach* case involved an attempt by the federal government to regulate a logging company's dumping of woodwaste into waters located within British Columbia.[31] Activities in provincial waters were traditionally considered matters of provincial jurisdiction, and the firm contended that the federal Ocean Dumping Control Act did not empower the federal government to regulate its dumping in provincial waters. The governments of British Columbia and Quebec intervened in the case in support of the firm. The federal government maintained that, in the case at hand, the pollution was of "national concern" and that it should be able to act under its constitutional power (§91) "to make laws for the peace, order and good government of Canada." The Supreme Court had long maintained a restrictive interpretation of this federal power (sometimes referred to by the acronym POGG), holding that it applied in only a very limited number of matters of "national concern." The Court's position changed with the *Crown Zellerbach* decision, when it ruled in favor of the federal government and established a new, looser test for "national concern" that drastically expanded the range of environmental issues in regard to which the federal government might intervene.[32]

With federal jurisdiction secured, Environment Canada proceeded with the CEPA. Before the act was signed, however, the provincial governments, led by Quebec, succeeded in adding provisions for "equivalency agreements" between provinces and the federal government. These provisions meant that, if a province and the federal government agree that provincial regulations are equivalent to federal ones, provinces may assume responsibility for regulation. Although the CEPA established stricter conditions for equivalency agreements than those that existed in previous bilateral accords, allowing provinces to opt out of federal regulation was nevertheless a serious concession by the federal government.

ESTABLISHING A NEW EQUILIBRIUM

By the start of the 1990s, environmental politics in Canada reached a new equilibrium. Recognizing that the federal government had the firm backing of the Supreme Court, provincial governments came to accept a federal role in environmental policymaking. Though the Canadian federal government had not adopted as significant a role in setting national environmental standards as other federal polities such as the United States, the EU, and Germany, its policymaking competence was well established. For its part, the Canadian government recognized that efforts to impose federal standards on the provinces unilaterally sparked substantial resistance, and that it needed the cooperation of provincial governments in order to effectively implement environmental policy. Finally, the federal government recognized that the provinces would only cooperate in the implementation of federal environmental policies if they were given a greater voice in the crafting of national standards (Harrison 1996, p. 143; Van Nijnatten 2000, p. 27). Recognizing that they would have to work together, federal and provincial authorities established new intergovernmental forums in which to set harmonized national environmental standards to coordinate environmental protection activities. As in the case of the Australian NEPC, the intergovernmental forums established in Canada stand outside the existing federal legislative institutions (namely, the federal Parliament).

Since 1961 there had been one such intergovernmental forum that brought together leaders from the federal and provincial governments to discuss resource and environment issues.[33] In 1988, this institution was reorganized, provided with a significant increase in staff, and renamed the Canadian Council of Ministers of the Environment (the CCME). The CCME drafted a "Statement on Interjurisdictional Cooperation (STOIC)," which was signed by the federal government and all provincial and territorial governments in 1990. The statement called on the CCME to play a central role in harmonization of provincial and federal environmental legislation and environmental assessment procedures.

In the course of the 1990s, the CCME has emerged as a major forum for the establishment of national environmental standards. In January 1998, after contentious negotiations and one significant false start,[34] the federal government and the provincial governments, with the exception of Quebec, signed the Canada-Wide Accord on Environmental Harmonization (hereafter the Canada-Wide Accord) and three subAgreements (the Canada-Wide Environmental Standards Sub-Agreement, the Sub-Agreement on Environmental Assessment, and the Canada-Wide Environmental Inspections Sub-Agreement).[35] The Canada-Wide Accord establishes a set of fundamental principles that are to guide intergovernmental relations on environmental matters. The subagreement on standards provides for the establishment of "Canada-wide" environmental standards. These standards are a substitute for true federal standards, but are not produced by the federal government.[36] Rather, they are agreed on by the provincial ministers and the federal minister who are members of the CCME. The standards subAgreement does not set forth a fixed decisionmaking procedure for the establishment of Canada-wide standards. Rather, it provides that "Ministers will agree on the process for the development of standards on a case by case basis."[37] Pursuant to the subAgreement, members of the CCME have produced a number of Canada-wide standards for particulate matter, ozone, mercury emissions, benzene, petroleum hydrocarbons, dioxins, and furans, and are in the process of developing others.

The CCME serves the federal government's interests in that provincial governments are more willing to accept nationally harmonized standards if they have a role in crafting them. The CCME serves provincial interests in that it promises to substitute intergovernmental decisionmaking for unilateral decisionmaking by the federal government. Indeed, provinces such as Alberta and Quebec, which vigorously oppose federal intervention, strongly supported the CCME and the Statement on Interjurisdictional Cooperation (Harrison 1996, p. 143). How successful the CCME will be in harmonizing environmental standards remains to be seen. What is certain is that the federal government's willingness to delegate what are essentially lawmaking tasks to an intergovernmental body not envisaged in the Canadian Constitution represents a startling admission that the federal government is unable, on its own, to harmonize regulatory standards in Canada. For EU scholars, the fact that the Canadian government has delegated standard setting to an intergovernmental body akin to the EU's Council of Ministers is particularly striking.

The Politics of Discretion

As in other politics explored in this book, the Canadian federal government took on a policymaking role in environmental regulation, while provinces maintained control over implementation. This division of competence raises questions concerning provincial discretion: Do federal laws include detailed requirements or only vague mandates? Do courts play an active role in constraining executive discretion? Does the federal government act to ensure that provinces apply these laws in practice? Ultimately, how much discretion do provinces have in implementing federal laws?

Federal legislative and executive power in Canada's parliamentary system are concentrated in the cabinet. Rather than binding their hands with detailed standards, procedural requirements, and invitations for judicial oversight, Canadian governments have opted for legislation that leaves them a great deal of discretion (Green 1999, pp. 180–182). As discussed above, nearly all environmental legislation in Canada takes the form of "enabling" statutes. Such statutes confer on the executive discretionary powers to regulate in pursuit of a general policy goal, but they do not contain detailed provisions that mandate specific executive actions. The drafting of such vague statutes has clearly served to promote executive discretion and discourage judicial review in environmental matters (Schrecker 1992, pp. 88–89; Knopff and Glenn 1996, p. 192).

However, outside the environmental policy arena, unprecedented legal changes were encouraging courts to take a more active role in judicial review. The role of the courts in Canada was profoundly changed with the introduction of the Charter of Rights and Freedoms in 1982, which represents the most significant legal development in Canada in the twentieth century (Cotler 1996). The charter was part of the Constitutional Act of 1982, which also provided for the final severance of formal constitutional ties with the United Kingdom. The charter guaranteed Canadians a number of individual freedoms and rights—including political rights, mobility rights, legal rights, equal opportunity rights, and minority language rights—and it explicitly authorized judicial review to enforce these rights. While judicial activism has increased since 1982, it has been limited by the institutional features of parliamentary government.

Before the introduction of the charter, Canadian courts generally deferred to the decisions of the legislature and executive.[38] They refused to overturn statutes or administrative decisions unless they found that a government (provincial or federal) had overstepped its jurisdiction. The charter called on the courts to protect a wide range of constitutionally guaranteed rights and to thus increase the scope of their judicial review. Canadian courts took up this call enthusiastically. In the twenty years prior to the introduction of the charter, the Supreme Court had only once invalidated a federal statute on the grounds that it violated individual rights. By contrast, in the first seven years after the charter, the Supreme Court overturned eight federal statutes for violations of individuals' rights. In addition to overturning statutes, the court became much more active in overruling administrative decisions (Baar 1991; Knopff and Glenn 1996; Cotler 1996).

The charter, which makes no mention of environmental rights, has had only and indirect impact on the role of the courts in environmental regulation. Litigants have attempted to use the charter's guarantees regarding "security of the person" in environmental cases, but the courts have thus far rejected these attempts (Morton 1996, p. 50). However, while the charter has had little direct impact on environmental policy, the general increase in judicial activism resulting from it has spilled over into the environmental policy arena and has emboldened courts to overturn executive decisions in matters of environmental policy.

In *Finlay v. Canada*, [1986] 2 S.C.R. 607, the Supreme Court eased the requirements for standing in public-interest-related litigation. In ruling that a Manitoba welfare recipient had standing to challenge a cabinet decision concerning a welfare program, the Court held that "discretionary standing" to challenge administrative decisions may be granted to persons or groups who failed to meet the traditional requirement for standing—that of suffering some specific harm. This decision opened the courtroom doors to interest groups dissatisfied with administrative decisions, including environmental groups.

Environmental groups seized on the relaxation of standing requirements in order to challenge executive actions in the courts. Two landmark cases—in which environmental groups challenged executive discretion in conducting environmental impact assessments under the federal Environmental Assessment Review Process (EARP)—illustrate both the increase in judicial activism regarding environmental issues and its limits. In the *Rafferty-Alameda Dams* case, the Canadian Wildlife Federation challenged decisions regarding the construction of two dams in Saskatchewan.[39] In the *Oldman Dam* case, a local NGO, Friends of the Oldman River, challenged the construction of a dam in southern Alberta.[40] In each instance, the federal government preferred to let the projects proceed and sought to delegate its environmental assessment responsibilities to the provinces.

The EARP had not been established by binding legislation, but by an administrative "Guidelines Order" (SOR/84–467) that the federal government and most observers considered to be totally discretionary. However, the Federal Court and the Supreme Court interpreted the guidelines order to impose binding duties on the federal government (Knopff and Glenn 1996, p. 189; Harrison 1996, pp. 48–51). The courts also held that the federal government could delegate assessment responsibilities to the provinces only if provincial assessment processes were identical to those in the federal guideline. The courts' interpretation of the guidelines forced the federal government to perform environmental assessments on major projects in cases where it preferred not to, and in doing so prompted significant judicial activism. Moreover, the decisions spurred environmental groups across Canada to initiate litigation seeking to force the federal government to perform environmental assessments on a range of projects (Harrison 1996, p. 134).

While the *Rafferty-Alameda Dams* and *Oldman Dam* decisions illustrate the increased willingness of Canadian courts to constrain executive discretion, the political reaction to the cases serves as a reminder of the underlying institutional constraints on judicial activism in the Canadian polity. The federal government reacted to the decisions by pushing new environmental assessment legislation through Parliament that restored the executive discretion that the federal courts had attempted to limit. The new legislation, the Canadian Environmental Assessment Review Act of 1992 (CEAA) replaced the existing EARP and thus trumped the Supreme Court's restrictive interpretation of it. The new act made it clear that the federal environment minister would have wide discretion in deciding when to delegate environmental assessment to the provinces and when public hearings were warranted.

The ability of the executive to overrule judicial decisions that it finds troublesome explains the persistence of judicial deference in cases concerning environmental regulation. Courts have been more active in challenging the executive over issues covered in the Charter of Rights and Freedoms, because these issues are entrenched in the Canadian Constitution. Environmental regulations have no such constitutional anchor, and judicial interpretations of them are therefore more susceptible to legislative overrides. This explains why courts continue to defer and why litigation has not become an important part of regulatory politics (Howlett 1994; Swanson and Hughes 1990, p. 103; Knopff and Glenn 1996).

Conclusion

The similar federal structures in Australia and Canada have channeled intergovernmental relationships concerning environmental regulation along similar paths. In both cases, the high courts have supported the expansion of federal policymaking competence, upholding federal jurisdiction under a variety of constitutional powers not directly related to the environment. Meanwhile, federal courts have refrained from placing restrictions on ministerial discretion. As a result, regulatory politics have not become heavily judicialized in either case, and state governments continue to enjoy great room for maneuver in implementing federal laws.

Finally, federal and state governments have established intergovernmental policymaking forums outside of regular parliamentary institutions. The parallels between the Canadian Council of Ministers of the Environment (CCME) and the Australian National Environmental Protection Council (NEPC) are unmistakable. Both institutions serve to bring state governments into the policymaking process at the national level. Federal governments have backed these institutions because they recognize that the cooperation of state governments is necessary for the implementation of harmonized regulatory standards, and that states will only acquiesce to such harmonization if they have a hand in shaping the standards. These arrangements have developed further in Australia, where measures enacted by a two-thirds majority of the NEPC become law in all participating jurisdictions, unless they are disallowed by either chamber of the commonwealth Parliament. When such measures are adopted it can well be said that environmental regulatory policymaking in Australia relies more on intergovernmental bargaining and allows less of a role for Parliament than it does in the European Union. These findings highlight the irony of the Australian and Canadian comparison. Australia and Canada are moving to intergovernmental policymaking just as the EU is moving away from it. States and provinces in Australia and Canada are coming to play a role in federal policymaking similar to that of EU member states, and they are actually granted far more discretion in implementing federal law than their EU counterparts.

6 | Food and Drug Safety Regulation in the EU

The comparisons in the preceding chapters demonstrate that the theory of regulatory federalism set forth in Chapter 1 explains variations in patterns of environmental regulation across federal systems. This chapter expands the empirical analysis to two other areas of social regulation in the European Union (EU): food and drug safety. Regulation in both areas provide useful tests of whether the theory of regulatory federalism may be generalized, and each focuses attention on different aspects of the argument. The findings of these two case studies generally support the theory, although they do reveal important differences when compared to the developments in environmental policy. When analyzed alongside environmental policy, they highlight an aspect of EU regulatory federalism that is not particularly salient when the area of environmental regulation is viewed in isolation—namely, the growing role of EU-level regulatory agencies. Therefore, after analyzing food and drug policies in some detail, I turn to a more general analysis of the role of regulatory agencies in the EU.

Food safety regulation provides a useful comparison with environmental regulation because they share important similarities, but food safety has emerged as a salient policy concern only very recently. Whereas the boost in public attention that kicked-off the expansion of EU environmental regulation occurred at the beginning of the 1970s, the jump-start of the politics surrounding EU food safety regulation occurred only in the early 1990s. In the twenty intervening years, the EU underwent significant institutional developments, most notably an increase in the European Parliament's power. Analyzing the politics of EU food safety regulation makes it possible to assess whether, and if so how, recent changes in the EU's institutional structure may influence developments in newly emergent policy areas.

Drug safety regulation provides a useful test of the theory of regulatory federalism for a different reason. The theory suggests that a federal government enters new areas of social regulation in order to realize two basic preferences: an increase in public support and an expansion of competences. In the case of drug safety regulation, however, it appears that the first of these incentives did not play a role. Whereas the EU's involvement in both environmental and food safety regulation developed largely in response to dramatic increases in public concern regarding those issues, no such jump in public concern occurred in the area of drug safety. Nevertheless, the EU's involvement in drug safety regulation has increased dramatically. The expected outcome occurred, but due to a different set of causes than those postulated by the theory. Analysis of the politics of drug safety regulation thus suggests that demands from industry for centralization may substitute for significant public concern as a stimulus for federal regulation.

In food and drug safety regulation, as in environmental regulation, efforts to centralize regulatory power at the EU level sparked proposals for the creation of "independent" EU regulatory agencies. These proposals were linked to a wider debate concerning such agencies. To understand why they were created and how they were structured we must analyze the politics of agency design in the EU. Political struggles between the Commission, the member states in the Council, and later the European Parliament (EP) influenced the designs of these EU agencies. In particular, I explain how principal-agent concerns and political compromise between the main EU institutions shaped the design of EU agencies. Finally, I argue that the EU agencies are likely to have a significant impact on regulation in the EU by encouraging member state administrations to harmonize their regulatory processes and by increasing the transparency of EU regulatory processes.

The first section of this chapter turns the lens of regulatory federalism on the development of food safety regulation in the EU. In particular, the analysis focuses on how the growing power of the European Parliament has influenced the dynamics of regulatory politics in the EU. The second section examines the politics of drug safety regulation, highlighting how a highly centralized system of regulation has emerged even in the absence of strong public demands. The third section analyzes the politics of bureaucratic, or Eurocratic, structure in the EU, showing how the EU's institutional structure has influenced the design of EU-level regulatory agencies and assessing what impact these agencies are likely to have on regulatory policy.

Food Safety Regulation

The Politics of Competence

Eating in Europe is a transboundary activity. European diners regularly consume food products made in a number of member states. Food safety regulations in exporting states has an impact on the health of the consumers in importing states. Under such conditions, food-borne disease outbreaks—which are bound to occur from time to time—take on an EU dimension. When such outbreaks occur, consumers are likely to demand that their government protect them from imported foodstuffs that they distrust. Measures taken by importing states to ensure food safety may then generate trade tensions. In particular, exporting states may suspect that safety controls or other import restrictions enacted in the name of public health have more to do with protecting domestic producers from foreign competition than with protecting public health.

THE EMERGENCE OF EU FOOD SAFETY POLICY

Since its founding, the European Community has sought to establish a common market in foodstuffs (Vogel 1995, pp. 24–43). Initially, EU food regulation focused on the most obvious impediments to trade in foodstuffs—labeling and composition requirements. The EU paid much less attention to issues of food safety. Its first food safety legislation dealt with, quite literally, meat and potatoes issues. In 1964 the Community enacted a directive concerning trade in live cattle and pigs and another concerning fresh meat, and in 1969 it adopted two directives concerning potato diseases.[1] Legislation on the part of the Community expanded slowly, as it adopted a total of twenty-three directives concerning a variety of products prior to 1990 (Commission 1997a, pp. 34–35). As with all Community directives, implementation of those relating to food safety was left to member states. The Commission conducted limited oversight, though in the mid-1980s the EU did establish a rapid-alert system to deal with food safety emergencies and a small veterinary inspection service within the directorate general for agriculture. Under the rapid-alert system, when a food emergency arose, the Commission would notify member state authorities and would coordinate a set of national or Community-wide restrictions to contain the problem. Member state authorities conducted actual inspection and enforcement of food safety requirements, with Commission veterinary inspectors accompanying them on occasion.

The politics of food safety changed profoundly with the outbreak of mad cow disease in the United Kingdom. Mad cow disease—or bovine spongiform encephalopathy (BSE)—is a fatal degenerative brain disorder that afflicts cattle. BSE had been detected in cattle in the UK as early as 1982. In 1986, the UK informed other member states of the problem through the Standing Veterinary Committee. Tension surrounding BSE escalated between 1988 and 1990. A 1988 study found evidence that BSE could be transmitted to mice, and in the same year the British government took a number of precautionary measures to halt the spread of the disease. In July 1989, the Community banned exports of British cattle born before 1988, thus demonstrating its mounting concern regarding BSE and lending a vote of confidence to the safety measures enacted by the British in 1988. However, in the winter of 1989–1990, a massive outbreak of the disease occurred in the UK. Other member states responded quickly. First, in January 1990 Germany, which is known for its strict food purity laws, banned imports of British beef.[2] France and Italy soon enacted their own bans. In April 1990, the Commission banned the use of meat from BSE cattle for human consumption. Trade tensions mounted as the British accused other member states of using BSE as an excuse to erect unjustified barriers to British beef. Finally, in June 1990, tensions subsided as the EU Agricultural Council brokered a settlement in which the British agreed to enact new controls, the other member states agreed to lift their embargoes, and the Community as a whole erected limited restrictions on British beef exports. While trade tensions subsided temporarily, the BSE problem did not disappear. The number of cases continued to climb through 1992, and the European Parliament began expressing grave concern over the crisis.

Meanwhile, the Commission used the concerns regarding BSE as an impetus to expand its regulatory capacity in the area of food safety regulation. In December 1991, the Commission established the Office of Veterinary and Phytosanitary Inspection and Control (OVPIC) within Directorate General VI (Agriculture). OVPIC's approximately thirty inspectors were empowered to conduct inspections of food production and processing facilities in a range of areas covered by EU food safety legislation, including live animals, fresh meat (beef, pork, poultry, and fishery products), hormone use, animal welfare, and plant health.[3] Also during this period, the EU enacted legislation calling on the Commission to evaluate member states' general systems of food safety control, in both food production and retail. Visits by Commission officials to national food authorities began in February 1995 (Commission 1998b).

Though OVPIC gained considerable inspection powers, its staff and re-source limitations greatly restricted the scope of its activities. OVPIC could not cover all of the areas that fell within its mandate and chose to conduct on-site inspections only in the area of meat safety. As part of the Commission hierarchy, OVPIC had to compete for staff lines with other directorates general (Chambers 1999). The Commission found it difficult to attract sufficient funding and staffing for OVPIC, and by 1995 con-cluded that the best way to sustain and eventually expand OVPIC would be to transform it into an independent European agency with its own source of funding.[4] The Commission then prepared a proposal for trans-forming OVPIC into an independent agency, to be named the Euro-pean Agency for Veterinary and Phytosanitary Inspection (Commission 1996e).

On March 20, 1996, the British government announced that it could not rule out a link between BSE and Creutzfeld-Jacob disease (CJD), a fa-tal human disease that had been afflicting farmers and children in the UK. The announcement was front-page news across Europe. Most member states immediately took unilateral emergency measures to address public concerns. A week later, the Commission announced a ban on the export of British beef and beef products.[5]

The British government was furious about the ban, viewing it as an at-tempt by other member states to wipe out the British beef industry. On May 21, after the Standing Veterinary Committee refused to lift the ban,[6] the British government instigated the "Mad Cow Crisis," the most direct challenge to the EU's operating procedures since De Gaulle's Empty Chair Crisis (Westlake 1997). The UK government announced that it would adopt a policy of noncooperation in all EU affairs. It declared that it would withhold its vote on all matters that required the unanimous ap-proval of the Council of Ministers. This stalemate lasted for a month, end-ing only when the other member states agreed to phase out the ban gradu-ally in exchange for the UK slaughtering more herds of cattle.

IMPLEMENTATION AND ENFORCEMENT

The EU's reaction to the Mad Cow Crisis demonstrates how the increased political standing of the European Parliament has influenced the dynamics of regulatory policy. The EP seized on the Mad Cow Crisis as a vehicle to exercise new powers and new political stature it had won in the Maastricht Treaty. In July 1996, it convened a committee of inquiry to investigate the

Commission's handling of the matter.[7] The Parliament was eager to exercise its new might on BSE, as the issue provided it a high-profile opportunity to act as a defender of public health. On February 7, 1997, the committee produced a report critical of the Commission's handling of BSE (European Parliament 1997b). On February 18, the EP issued a conditional censure of the Commission, calling on it to implement the recommendations in the committee of inquiry's report by October 1997.

Under pressure from the parliamentary inquiry, the Commission debated various proposals for reform (Southey 1996; *Agence Europe* 1997c). Finally, on February 7, 1997, the very day the parliamentary committee reported its findings, the Commission announced a major reform of the way it dealt with food health issues (Commission 1997a). The reform involved a substantial upgrading of the size and responsibilities of the Consumer Policy Directorate General (DGXXIV), which was renamed the Consumer Policy and Health Protection Directorate. The reform also separated the services responsible for drawing up legislation on food safety from those responsible for monitoring implementation. The Commission arranged this separation by transferring OVPIC to the strengthened Consumer Policy and Health Directorate (DGXXIV), while leaving policy-making in the hands of the Agriculture Directorate (DGVI). Along with the move, the Commission renamed OVPIC the Food and Veterinary Office (FVO) and announced plans to expand the number of FVO inspectors from thirty to approximately two hundred. In addition, pursuant to an earlier agreement in the Council of Ministers, the FVO would be relocated from Brussels to a new headquarters in Ireland. The Commission's internal reorganization did not, however, settle the question of whether the FVO should be transformed into an independent agency (Commission 1997a, p. 28). The Commission's 1996 proposal (Commission 1996e) remained on the table and debate inside the Commission and other EU institutions continued.

The EP was happy to see the Commission take decisive action to address mad cow disease, but it was sceptical of the Commission's proposal to transfer control of food safety inspections to an independent agency, outside of Commission control.[8] The Commission's 1996 proposal had called for placing control of the new agency charged with food safety inspection in the hands of a management board composed of representatives of member state governments. Many members of the European Parliament (MEPs) feared that by transferring control from the Commission to a member-state dominated board, the new structure might lead to a "renationalisation of Community policy" (Interviews, European Commission, November 28, 1996, June 19 and June 25, 1997; European Parliament 1997b).

The Commission, too, had reasons to hesitate before transferring the FVO out of its control. The Commission's original proposal to transform the FVO into a separate European agency had been developed before the revelations surrounding the impact of BSE on humans. At that time, the Commission could not secure the resources it needed for a major expansion of its food safety inspectorate, largely because some member states opposed increasing the Commission's power in this area. The Commission proposed transferring food safety inspections to an autonomous European agency, which would be controlled by a management board dominated by member state appointees, as a way to win the support of reluctant member states for an increase in the EU's capacity in the field of food safety inspection.

After the Mad Cow Crisis had garnered public concern, the Commission saw that it might be able to drastically enlarge its inspection service, while at the same time maintaining direct control. Given this potential and given the EP's opposition to the agency proposal, the Commission decided in January 1998 to reverse its position on transforming the FVO into an independent agency (Commission 1998a; *Agence Europe* 1998). It withdrew its earlier proposal for the creation of an agency and explained that it planned to keep the FVO within the Commission. Justifying its *volte face*, the Commission explained that the independence of any food safety inspection service would be better ensured within the Commission than in an independent European agency (Commission 1998a). In other words, in the Commission's view, an office within the Commission hierarchy would be more independent than a supposedly "independent" European agency, controlled by a member-state dominated management board.

The corruption scandals of 1998–1999, which involved allegations of fraud, mismanagement, and nepotism in the Commission, and the ensuing resignation of the entire Commission, put further reform of the EU's food safety services on the back burner. However, shortly after taking office, the new Commission president Romano Prodi announced that food safety would be among his central policy concerns. In November 2000, the Commission (2000a) proposed a regulation establishing a European Food Authority (later renamed the European Food Safety Authority (EFSA).[9] The legal basis of the regulation called for the use of the reformed co-decision procedure, ensuring that the EP would have a strong influence over the EFSA's design.

In January 2002, after months of negotiation, the European Parliament and Council finally agreed on a regulation establishing the European Food Safety Authority.[10] Both the Commission's original proposal and the final regulation that emerged from the legislative process reflect the increased power of the EP. In contrast to the management boards of earlier agencies that were dominated by hand-picked member state appointees, members of the EFSA's management board are appointed by the Council in consultation with the EP. Under EFSA's founding regulation, member states are not guaranteed a representative on the management board, and four of the fourteen members appointed by the Council and Parliament have backgrounds in consumer organizations and other interest groups involved in the food sector (art. 25(1)). The candidate selected by the management board to serve as executive director of the EFSA is required to face a hearing before the European Parliament (art. 26(1)). Finally, the regulation establishes a number of transparency provisions, including requirements to hold meetings in public and to specify and publish its internal procedures (art. 38).

The Parliament was able to leverage its legislative power under the co-decision procedure in order to entrench institutional structures in the EFSA that allow the Parliament and its interest group allies to play a powerful role in ongoing oversight. Throughout the negotiations over the design of the EFSA, the EP insisted on management structures and operating procedures that would provide it with opportunities for oversight and control (Telephone Interviews, European Commission Secretariat General, December 7, 2001; European Parliament, December 7, 2001). The Parliament has secured a powerful role in the appointment of the EFSA's management board. Transparency provisions and the inclusion of board members with backgrounds as interest group representatives facilitates interest group access to the decisionmaking process and thus allows the Parliament to engage in indirect, "fire-alarm" monitoring (McCubbins and Schwartz 1984; McCubbins, Noll, and Weingast 1987).

The limited scope of the EFSA's powers also reflects the increase in the European Parliament's power and the changed political circumstances following the Mad Cow Crisis. As mentioned above, in 1996 the Commission had proposed relinquishing control over its food safety inspectorate (OVPIC/FVO) to an independent European agency, which it saw as a way to overcome opposition to expanding the EU role in inspections.

EFSA, by contrast is limited to "risk assessment" activities, such as information gathering, analysis, and the provision of scientific advice, while inspections and other such risk management activities remain responsibilities of the Commission's inspectorate, the FVO. Empowered by backing from the EP, the Commission succeeded in expanding the EU's information gathering and analysis capacity through the EFSA, while at the same time expanding and maintaining control over its own inspection and enforcement force (the FVO).

The Politics of Discretion

While the degree to which EU institutions will limit the discretion of member states in the area of food safety regulation remains uncertain, recent developments suggest that a strict system of controls is emerging. In the area of BSE alone, dozens of measures have been enacted dealing with issues ranging from the design of heat treatment systems, to worker safety requirements, to the removal of bovine vertebral columns, to notification requirements (Commission 2002).

The EU has made significant strides in developing its monitoring and enforcement capacity. The FVO's inspection capacity was increased significantly in 1997, after the Parliament provided funding for thirty-five new inspectors.[11] As of 2000, the FVO employed ninety-two inspectors (Commission 2000f). FVO inspectors conduct hundreds of inspections annually. These include general audits of the member state authorities responsible for food safety and on-the-spot inspections of individual food processing plants to assess the level of control by national authorities and to ensure that operational records presented to the FVO reflect the actual situation. The results of these inspections in turn have provided the foundations for Commission infringement actions against laggard member states. For instance, in the summer of 1997, inspections conducted by the FVO in cooperation with the Commission's anti-fraud unit discovered deficiencies in the UK's system for inspecting beef for export (Commission 1998d, p. 4). Based on this finding and on other detections of food safety violations across the EU, the Commission initiated a number of infringement proceedings in 1997 (*Agence Europe* 1997e). The Commission continues to monitor the UK closely, demanding bimonthly reports on its progress to eradicate the disease and conducting frequent inspections through the FVO. The EFSA, with an estimated staff of over three hundred, will further enhance the EU's monitoring capacity and create increased pressure for the harmonization of food safety regulation among the member states.

Meanwhile, parliamentary oversight of the Commission and member states continues. The Parliament's BSE follow-up committee highlighted deficiencies in member states' implementation of the Commission's decision regarding heat treatment systems (European Parliament 1997b). Also, the Parliament harshly criticized member states for their failure to provide detailed reports to the Commission regarding their inspection staffs. The EP's position in the debate on the creation of the EFSA demonstrates that it continues to demand increased transparency and accountability in the implementation of EU food safety regulations.

Finally, as in environmental policy, the EU has started to promote decentralized implementation of food safety regulation. In the wake of the Mad Cow Crisis, the Commission proposed, and the Parliament actively supported, a revision of the EU's product liability directive to extend the principle of strict liability to primary agricultural products.[12] The Council quickly adopted the Commission's amendment.[13] This amendment clearly was intended to ease the burden of proof for victims seeking compensation from agricultural producers. However, given the difficulties inherent in establishing a causal link between the consumption of a particular producers' food and the development of a disease years later, product liability litigation is unlikely to provide consumers with redress in this area. Therefore, victims rights groups, particularly in the UK, have demanded the establishment of a no-fault compensation scheme. The Commission and Parliament have stated that they would support payments to victims made by member states with a contribution from the Community budget. The Commission specifically suggests providing such funding through payments to such nonprofit associations as the Creutzfeld-Jacob Disease Families Association (Commission 1997c).

The development of EU food safety regulation reflects a pattern similar in many ways to that observed in environmental policy. The EU gradually entered the policy area during a period when enforcement was left primarily to member states. As implementation failures became evident, the Commission created new enforcement bodies and generally increased its vigilance in monitoring and enforcement, thus decreasing member state discretion. Despite these similarities, two clear differences between food safety and environmental regulation stand out. First, the Commission's formal powers in food safety long exceeded those in environmental protection, as EU inspectors had the power to conduct direct inspections in food production facilities. When the Mad Cow Crisis became a matter of considerable public concern, the Commission was able to dramatically increase its use of this formal power. Second, the Parliament took a stronger stand vis-à-vis the Commission regarding food safety than it had in any policy area. The EP's extensive inquiry and its conditional censure of the Commission regarding BSE went beyond previous oversight activities. Parliamentary influence over the design of the EFSA, and its insistence on a variety of transparency measures and other strict controls over the EFSA, demonstrates the Parliament's ability to shape the design of the EU's regulatory bureaucracy. Together these developments suggest that the growing power of the EP will further decrease the discretion of member states in implementing EU law.

Drug Safety Regulation

The Politics of Competence

Although the Treaty of Rome made no specific mention of drugs, the pharmaceutical sector clearly fell within the scope of the common market envisioned by the Community's founders. The EU began its effort to harmonize drug regulation in the early 1960s with the aim of promoting trade in pharmaceuticals (Vogel 1998). Regulation of drug safety by national governments was already extensive at that time—entailing safety testing and authorization, supervision of manufacturing processes, and monitoring for potential adverse affects of drugs that had been approved for sale (pharmaco-vigilance). Most important from a trade perspective, each member state government in the EU required separate safety testing and authorization processes before they would allow a product on to their consumer market. These drug safety standards and approval times varied among member states, creating a serious barrier to trade in pharmaceuticals in the EU. Large pharmaceutical companies, which treated each member state as a separate market, sometimes found the separate regulations so onerous they simply did not seek approval for a product in some states (Vogel 1998).

The theory of regulatory federalism suggests that a federal government like the EU would enter a new area of social regulation in order to satisfy two basic preferences: increasing public support and increasing its own regulatory competences. While entering the field of drug safety regulation certainly promised to increase interstate commerce and to give the EU a new area of competence, it offered little promise of attracting broad popular support. Although European consumers have long been concerned with the safety of drugs, the issue has not gained political prominence in the EU in recent decades. There has been no marked jump in public concern regarding drug safety in the EU similar to those that precipitated the EU's involvement in environmental regulation or its increased role in food safety regulation.

One can easily envision a public health crisis involving a pharmaceutical product that might have sparked increased EU involvement in drug safety regulation. Just such a crisis regarding thalidomide led to increases in federal involvement in the United States.[14] However, no such crisis has played a similar role in EU drug safety regulation. Nevertheless, the EU's involvement in regulating pharmaceuticals has increased dramatically. These developments suggest that an upsurge in public concern regarding an issue is not necessary for centralization of regulation to occur. The EU's desire to promote the growth of the pharmaceutical sector by eliminating barriers to trade and its desire to extend the reach of EU competences, coupled with the consistent support of the pharmaceuticals sector, have provided sufficient stimulus for the centralization of regulation. The absence of a strong public concern, however, did have an impact on the institutional structures that were established to run the new centralized drug regulation system.

THE EMERGENCE OF EU DRUG SAFETY POLICY

The EU adopted its first directive dealing with drug safety in 1965.[15] This directive established baseline safety criteria that must be met by newly developed drugs before they are approved for marketing. As in other areas of the common market, progress on harmonization was slow in the ensuing years. It was not until 1975 that the EU issued its next important initiatives to reduce regulatory barriers to trade in pharmaceuticals.[16] That year the EU established a multistate procedure for drug approval. The process provided that a drug company that had received approval for its product from one member state could then submit "concurrent applications" to at least five other member states. The national authorities in these states then had four months to authorize the product. If they refused to do so, they were required to offer a "reasoned objection" to a special EU advisory committee—the Committee for Proprietary Medicinal Products (CPMP).

This committee then had two months to offer its opinion on the objection.[17] The EU also issued a directive calling on member states to establish national pharmaco-vigilance systems to track possible adverse effects of drugs.[18] The multistate procedure proved ineffective, as the CPMP's opinions were nonbinding and many member states chose to ignore them. Member states mostly refused to accept each other's assessments of drugs and continued to conduct their own tests. The deadlines stipulated in the multistate procedure were violated frequently and little progress was made in speeding up drug approval in Europe.

When the drive to complete the EU's internal market was revitalized in the mid-1980s, the European Commission identified the pharmaceutical sector as an important target. The Cecchini Report on the completion of the single market blamed lengthy drug authorization procedures for impeding the development of the pharmaceutical industry (Cecchini 1988, p. 67). New regulations covering manufactured medicines—including vaccines, blood derivatives, radiopharmaceuticals, and homeopathic medicines—were all adopted before the 1992 deadline for completion of the single market.[19] Changes to product approval procedures were also made. In 1987, in order to address the weaknesses of the multistate procedure, the EU adopted a new centralized procedure that would apply to high-tech medicinal products, in particular those derived from biotechnology.[20] The new procedure allowed the producer of a high-technology medicinal product to apply directly to the CPMP for product approval, without first going to one of the member state authorities. However, the CPMP could only issue a nonbinding evaluation of the product. Member states still had the final say on granting marketing authorization. Finally, in 1990 the Commission proposed the creation of a new European agency to deal with medicinal products and the establishment of a more centralized system of product approval.[21]

IMPLEMENTATION AND ENFORCEMENT

In 1993, the EU made a major move to centralize drug safety regulation by establishing the European Agency for the Evaluation of Medicinal Products (EMEA) and by making EU-level drug approvals binding on member states.[22] The EU established two new approval procedures for medicinal products and gave the EMEA a central role in each (Kingham, Bogaert, and Eddy 1994). In the *centralized procedure*, applications for a European Marketing Authorization for a product are submitted directly to the EMEA in London, which then has 210 days in which to evaluate the product and offer its opinion to the European Commission. The Commission then has ninety days to decide whether to issue the authorization allowing the product to be marketed across the entire EU. Use of this centralized procedure is mandatory for biotechnology products and is available as an option for other pharmaceutical products. In the *decentralized procedure*, after an applicant gains approval of the product in one member state, it may request the extension of the approval to other member states. If other member states do not recognize the original approval, the matter is submitted to the EMEA's scientific committee for binding arbitration. That committee then reaches a position on the matter and makes a recommendation to the European Commission, which takes responsibility for the final decision.

In addition to its role in drug assessment, the EMEA was given responsibilities in other areas, including overseeing efforts to monitor manufacturing of medicinal products, educating the public about medicinal products, and advising companies on how to conduct necessary safety tests.

As noted above, the EMEA and the new procedures were not created in reaction to any jump in public concern over drug safety. The EU's desire to promote growth in the pharmaceuticals industry across Europe and its desire to expand EU competences provided powerful motivations for the creation of the new system (Vogel 1998). Moreover, there was strong industry support for the centralization of drug approval. Whereas industry is often divided on the question of increasing federal powers in the area of environmental protection, in the drug sector manufacturers generally supported the centralization of product approval processes. Centralized approval promised to save firms millions of ECUs on testing and filing fees. More important, by speeding up drug authorization, centralization promised to enable firms to realize profits on new drugs more quickly.

Despite pressure from industry and the European Commission, some national governments, in particular Germany and Denmark, resisted ceding control of drug approval to the EU (Kingham, Bogaert, and Eddy 1994, p. 303). Debate over the Commission's proposal for the creation of a centralized procedure directed by a European agency went on for over two years. The structure of the European drug authorization system that was established in 1993 was the product of political compromise that preserved a central role for national regulatory authorities.

The EMEA is part of the Community's legal framework, but it is not part of the EU's primary executive organ—the European Commission.

The EMEA's operations are overseen by a management board that consists of two representatives from each member state, two representatives appointed by the Commission, and two appointed by the European Parliament. Decisions of the management board require a two-thirds majority vote.[23] Although the Community marketing authorizations that the EMEA recommends constitute a powerful form of centralized regulation, the EMEA's actual drug assessment process relies on networking with existing national drug assessment agencies. The EMEA acts as the hub of a network of national drug testing authorities. When the EMEA in London receives an application for a Community marketing authorization for a new medicinal product, it delegates the assessment of the product to two national testing authorities—a rapporteur and a co-rapporteur.[24] The laboratories of these national authorities do the actual testing of the product and report their findings back to the agency in London.[25]

In essence, the EMEA orchestrates a system whereby national authorities take turns assessing drugs, subject to EMEA requirements. In one instance, a drug produced by a German company might be tested by French and Spanish regulators. In another case, a drug produced by a Belgian firm might be tested by British and Italian regulators. Regardless of which labs do the testing, they must satisfy EMEA testing requirements. If the new drug in question satisfies the national labs and their overseers at the EMEA, it gets the EMEA's stamp of approval and, barring unusual developments, eventually receives a Community marketing authorization from the Commission.

The EMEA also relies on national authorities in the area of inspections. The EMEA does not have its own inspectors. When considering a marketing authorization application, the agency's scientific committee may request an inspection of the product's manufacturing process. If the product is manufactured in one of the EU member states, then the competent national authority of that member state will conduct the inspection on behalf of the agency. If the product is manufactured outside the EU, a European team, composed of representatives of the "supervisory" member state and of the national rapporteurs, conducts the inspections. The EMEA coordinates these inspections and reviews inspectors' reports, but does not participate directly (Interview, EMEA Official, February 11, 1997).

The Politics of Discretion

With the founding of the EMEA at the start of 1995, the EU's new drug approval system came into operation. On October 20, 1995, following a recommendation from the EMEA, the Commission granted the first Community marketing authorization for a new drug, Gonal-F, an infertility drug produced by an Italian-Swiss company. This authorization permitted the sale of Gonal-F in all EU member states (EMEA 1996, p. 19). By the end of 2001, 182 such authorizations had been granted (EMEA 2001b). To the extent that pharmaceutical manufacturers rely on this centralized procedure for product approval, member states have almost no discretion, for they cannot block the marketing of a product in their country that has been approved through the centralized procedure.[26] Member states have more discretion when it comes to supervising the production of drugs and monitoring their effects (pharmaco-vigilance); however, the creation of the EMEA has increased the degree of central control over these functions as well.

The new centralized procedure for drug approval has proven popular with pharmaceutical companies.[27] Nevertheless, the vast majority of applications for conventional medicinal products come to the agency through the decentralized or "mutual recognition" procedure. Use of the procedure has increased rapidly, from thirty new product submissions under the decentralized procedure in 1995 (EMEA 1996, p. 23) to 587 submissions in 2002 (EMEA 2002, p. 23). The power of the EMEA in this procedure stems from its authority to arbitrate disputes between member states when they arise and to issue binding decisions pursuant to such arbitration. Although very few arbitrations concerning new products have taken place under the decentralized procedure, this does not reflect any weakness in the procedure. Rather, when compared with the failure of mutual recognition before 1995, the dramatic increase in the number of successfully completed decentralized procedures since then suggests that the mere threat of binding arbitration has been sufficient to induce member states to accept one another's authorization.

Along with increases in its role in drug authorization, the EMEA has increased its activities in monitoring of drug manufacturing facilities and of the effects of drugs (pharmaco-vigilance). EMEA officials do not conduct actual inspections of manufacturing practices at applicant firms. Rather, national inspection authorities conduct inspections at the request of the agency.[28]

In the area of pharmaco-vigilance, member states agreed to send a listing of all reported serious adverse drug reactions occurring in their territory every two weeks by email. In 2001, the EMEA implemented a new EU-wide electronic database, the Eudravigilance system, for gathering data on cases where drugs have adverse effects. Thousands of such cases have been reported since the EMEA began operations and the number is increasing rapidly (EMEA 2001a, p. 18). The EMEA's system for monitoring the health impact of drugs after they are authorized compares favorably with similar systems in other political systems. For instance, the U.S. Food and Drug Administration's program for monitoring adverse drug reactions operates on a voluntary basis and without the benefit of a computerized reporting system (Kalb 1998).

The system of drug safety regulation in the EU is still relatively new, but its prospects for growth are good. The agency's budget and staff have grown steadily. Its 1995 budget was 14.41 million ECUs, financed by a contribution from the EU and from fees collected from applicants for drug approvals. The budget for 2003 was estimated at 78 million euros (EMEA 2002, p. 44). Moreover, the EMEA has become increasingly self-financing as the percentage of its budget supported by application fees has increased while its Community subsidy has decreased.[29] During its first year of operation, the EMEA's staff grew to sixty-seven. By 2002, the staff had grown to nearly 250 (EMEA 2002, p. 37).

Since the start of 1998, all new medicines in the EU have had to be approved through either the centralized or decentralized procedure, unless they are to be marketed in only one member state. Both the number of centralized marketing authorizations granted and the number of binding arbitrations are increasing. Industry seems likely to continue supporting the agency and the new procedures. Producers who have used either procedure have reported a high level of satisfaction (EMEA 1997a, p. 16). Many major pharmaceutical companies have set up liaison offices next to the EMEA headquarters in London. Bayer, the German pharmaceutical giant, has relocated its European headquarters there (Vogel 1998). Industry now views the EMEA in London as the nexus of regulatory power in the EU.

Litigation by private parties has not played a role in the enforcement of EU drug safety policy. Consumers groups have no legal standing to challenge centralized EU marketing authorization decisions. Individuals injured by defective medicinal products may pursue product liability claims under the EU's product liability directive, which harmonized, and in most cases greatly strengthened, the position of consumers in product liability law.[30] To date, however, there are few reported cases in national courts based on the directive and no statistics are available on claims made or compensation paid in product liability cases (Commission 2000g). Clearly, though, there has not been a flood of product liability litigation related to defective medicinal products. A number of disincentives discourage such litigation across the EU—including the tendency of European judges to make low damage awards, the absence of punitive damages, and the absence of contingency fee arrangements and class actions in most countries. Finally, the comprehensive medical, sick pay, and disability coverage provided by many member states reduces the incentive to seek compensation from manufacturers.

While decentralized litigation has not played an important role, EU regulators recognize that public interest groups may seek to challenge their administrative practices in the future. The EMEA has made efforts to gain the support of consumer and patient groups, inviting organizations such as the European Association of Consumers' Unions (BEUC) to meetings in London where it briefs them on the findings of its scientific committees in relation to product applications. The EMEA is developing its rules on transparency and access to documents for concerned parties. These efforts have thus far won the support of consumers' groups such as BEUC, which find that the creation and operation of the EMEA has dramatically increased the transparency of the drug approval process in the EU (Interview, BEUC, January 16, 1997).

Agencies in the EU

During the 1990s, proposals for the creation of European-level regulatory agencies have been central in debates concerning environmental protection, food safety, and drug safety.[31] This is no coincidence. While these policy areas are distinct, they have been linked as part of the wider development of the role of regulatory agencies in the EU. The establishment of EU regulatory agencies is one of the most significant recent developments in EU regulatory policy, and these agencies are sure to play an important role in the future dynamics of EU regulatory federalism. Between May 1990 and November 1994 the EU established six new European agencies dealing with regulatory matters. Subsequently, the EU established five more—the Monitoring Centre on Racism and Xenophobia, the European Agency for Reconstruction, the European Food Safety Authority, European Maritime Safety Agency, and the European Aviation Safety Agency—and discussion of the creation of agencies in other policy areas has continued (Majone 2000; Yataganas 2001; see Table 2). At the Laeken Summit in December 2001, member state negotiators clashed over the siting of a dozen planned agencies (Macpherson 2001).

Table 2 New European agencies

Agency	Location	Primary functions
The European Environment Agency (EEA)[a]	Copenhagen, Denmark	Information gathering and publication. Networking of national administrators.
The European Monitoring Centre for Drugs and Drug Addiction (EMCDDA)[b]	Lisbon, Portugal	Information gathering and publication.
The European Agency for the Evaluation of Medicinal Products (EMEA)[c]	London, UK	Evaluating applications for Community-wide marketing approvals.
Office for Harmonization in the Internal Market (OHIM-Trademarks and Designs)[d]	Alicante, Spain	Registration of Community trademarks. Licensing and publication.
European Agency for Safety and Health at Work[e]	Bilbao, Spain	Research and publication. Promotion of dialogue between social partners.
Community Plant Variety Office (CPVO)[f]	Angers, France	Granting of property rights for new plant varieties.
European Monitoring Centre on Racism and Xenophobia (EUMC)[g]	Vienna, Austria	Information gathering and publication.
European Food Safety Authority (EFSA)[h]	Brussels, Belgium[i]	Risk assessment (information gathering, analysis, and advice).
European Maritime Safety Agency (EMSA)[j]	Brussels, Belgium[i]	Implementing Community legislation. Information gathering and publication.
European Aviation Safety Agency (EASA)[k]	Brussels, Belgium[i]	Implementing Community legislation. Inspections and product certification.

a. Reg. 1210/90 on the establishment of the European Environment Agency and the European environment information and observation network ([1990] OJ L120, May 11, 1990).

b. Reg. 302/93 establishing a European Monitoring Centre for Drugs and Drug Addiction ([1993] OJ L36, Feb. 12, 1993).

c. Reg. 2309/93 establishing a European Agency for the Evaluation of Medicinal Products ([1993] OJ L214, Aug. 24, 1993).

d. Reg. 40/94 establishing an Office for Harmonisation in the Internal Market ([1994] OJ L11, Jan. 14, 1994).

e. Reg. 2062/94 establishing a European Agency for Safety and Health at Work ([1994] OJ L216, Aug. 20, 1994).

f. Reg. 2100/94 establishing a Community Plant Variety Office ([1994] OJ L227, Sept. 1, 1994).

g. Reg. 1035/97 establishing a European Monitoring Centre on Racism and Xenophobia ([1997] OJ L151, June 15, 1997).

h. Reg. 178/2002 laying down the general principles and requirements of food law, establishing the European Food Safety Authority, and laying down procedures in matters of food safety ([2002] OJ L31/1, Feb. 1, 2002).

i. Temporary location.

j. Reg. 1406/2002 establishing a European Maritime Safety Agency ([2002] OJ L208/1, Aug. 5, 2002).

k. Reg. 1592/2002 on common rules in the field of civil aviation and establishing a European Aviation Safety Agency ([2002] OJ L240, Sept. 7, 2002).

At one level, the establishment of European agencies seems unsurprising. Legislators in many polities choose to delegate discretionary rule-making and adjudicative powers to bureaucratic agencies, which can provide necessary technical expertise (Shapiro 1988; Rose-Ackermann 1995; Majone 1996, p. 16; Thatcher 2002). In addition to the functional justifications for agencies, they are often justified as a means to separate administration from politics. Legislators often grant agencies some degree of independence in order to enhance the credibility of their policy commitments (Majone 2000). With these considerations in mind, the establishment of EU agencies may appear a natural response to the expansion of the EU's regulatory role in the late 1980s.

However, functionalist accounts do not provide an adequate explanation of the creation of EU agencies. While much of the rhetoric surrounding the new agencies emphasizes the need to delegate to "independent" authorities, the Commission itself can be thought of as a generalist independent agency established by member states to promote the completion of the internal market (Shapiro 1997, p. 281; Harlow 1999, pp. 267, 273; Yataganas 2001, p. 41). Why then, instead of delegating more authority to the Commission, were new European agencies created? What exactly were these agencies intended to be independent of? The literature on American politics concerning delegation and the design of bureaucratic agencies offers a number of theoretical insights that we can apply to the EU. To understand why the agencies were created and, in particular, why they were structured as they were, we must analyze the politics of bureaucratic, or Eurocratic, structure in the EU.

The establishment of European agencies requires the approval of the Council of Ministers, the European Commission, and in some cases, the European Parliament. Like political principals in other polities, these institutions struggle with each other over the design of bureaucratic agents. One major concern facing lawmakers in designing a bureaucratic agency is "bureaucratic drift," the possibility that the agency will not perform its mandated tasks effectively and will develop and pursue its own policy agenda. A series of studies of agency design in the American context has identified a number of *ex ante* and ongoing control mechanisms that politicians use to limit bureaucratic drift. Such mechanisms include appropriations powers (Calvert, Moran, and Weingast 1987; Kiewiet and McCubbins 1991), appointment powers (Calvert, McCubbins, and Weingast 1989), limits on agency jurisdiction and authority (Calvert, McCubbins, and Weingast 1989; Epstein and O'Halloran 1994, 1999), administrative procedures (McCubbins, Noll, and Weingast 1987, 1989, 1999), and judicial review (McCubbins, Noll, and Weingast 1987; Mashaw 1990; Shipan 2000).

A second major concern facing lawmakers is "political drift," the possibility that their political opponents who might come to power in the future will dismember their agency and reverse their preferred policies (Moe 1989, 1991; Horn 1995; Shepsle 1992; McCubbins, Noll, and Weingast 1999; Epstein and O'Halloran 1994). Therefore, the agency creators will favor bureaucratic structures, administrative procedures, and statutory mandates aimed at insulating the agency against future political interference.

Finally, in polities such as the United States or the EU that fragment political power between a number of veto players, the need for political compromise between proponents and opponents of regulation is likely to influence agency design (Moe 1989, 1990, pp. 125–127; Epstein and O'Halloran 1999, pp. 11, 129–133). Opponents of regulation will oppose plans to create a strong, well-insulated agency, preferring instead that the agency, if it is to be established at all, have a weak fragmented structure and a vague, nonenforceable mandate.

To explain the creation of EU agencies, we must understand how strategic interactions between the Commission, the Parliament, and the member states in the Council have affected the design of the agencies. Furthermore, we must consider the role of the European Court of Justice (ECJ), as expectations concerning the role of the judiciary may have influenced the strategies of the political actors engaged in agency design.

Principal-agent concerns and political compromise between the major EU institutions have had a significant influence on agency design in the EU. In short, as the single-market initiative expanded the EU's regulatory tasks, the Commission saw a need and an opportunity to expand the EU's regulatory capacity. Recognizing that additional transfer of power and resources to the European Commission would be unacceptable to the Council of Ministers, the Commission proposed the establishment of specialized, European agencies (Shapiro 1996b, 1997; Kelemen 1997). The member states in the Council agreed to the establishment of agencies, but limited the scope of their authority and demanded that they be subject to intergovernmental control.

Since the mid-1990s, the increasing power of the European Parliament has led to significant changes in the politics of EU agency design. The EP, which gained increased powers under the Maastricht and Amsterdam

Treaties (Tsebelis and Garrett 2001), has voiced increasing concern about the democratic accountability of European agencies and has asserted a greater role in agency design. Whereas the Council has a well-established preference for ongoing intergovernmental oversight structures, the Parliament has demanded the establishment of monitoring and control structures that emphasize transparency and opportunities for participation by concerned interests.[32]

The First Wave of European Agencies

The creation of the first six new EU-level regulatory agencies was coordinated by the Commission's secretariat general.[33] The outcome of the first wave of agency creation can best be understood as the result of a political compromise between the Commission, which was focused on expanding the EU's regulatory capacity, and the member states in the Council, a number of which were determined to maintain intergovernmental control. The Parliament had little direct influence, as legislative procedures restricted it to a mere consultative role. Because member states opposed to the creation of powerful independent agencies had a significant role in the agency design process, agencies were granted limited powers and were structured with management boards and operating procedures designed to provide opportunities for member state oversight and control.

The initial impetus for the creation of agencies came from the Commission. The single-market initiative provided the Commission with an exceptional opportunity to expand its regulatory activity. However, with its small staff, the Commission was ill equipped to handle the flood of new information gathering, rule making, and product licensing tasks (Dehousse 1997). Given the Commission's well-known tendency for self-aggrandizement, one might have expected the Commission to respond by demanding an increase in its staff and resources. However, the Parliament and Council placed strict limits on increases of the Commission's personnel budget, and Commission president Jacques Delors and later President Jacques Santer must have recognized that attempting to expand the size of the Commission would invite attacks from Euro-sceptics critical of what they viewed as a burgeoning "Eurocracy" in Brussels.

Given the limits on its enlargement, the Commission turned to the idea of establishing independent agencies.[34] The idea of creating independent agencies to administer statutory regulation was gaining popularity in many member states (Majone 1996; Kreher 1996; Thatcher 2002). This idea appealed to the Commission both because it promised an avenue by which the Commission could expand the EU's regulatory capacity, and because it allowed the Commission to "off-load" some highly technical, laborious, and resource-sapping activities.[35] Some lower-level *fonctionnaires* saw agencies as a threat to their turf; however, Delors and other high-ranking officials foresaw that delegating technical work to independent agencies would expand the EU's regulatory capacity while allowing the Commission to concentrate on its core competences—namely, policymaking and long-term strategic planning (Interviews, European Commission, November 29, 1996; EEA Taskforce, May 1994).

The Commission set in motion the wave of agency creation in January 1989. With environmental issues high on the Community's policymaking agenda, Commission president Delors proposed establishing the European Environment Agency (EEA), suggesting the agency would improve the Community's monitoring and implementation capacity (Ladeur 1996; Everson et al. 1999, pp. 86–87). Establishing the EEA required the unanimous approval of the member states in the Council, but only required consultation with the European Parliament.[36] The EP, with its consistently pro-integration and pro-environment stance, readily lent its support to the Commission proposal. In the Council, there was disagreement among member states concerning what powers the environment agency should be granted. Proponents of strict implementation, such as Germany and the Netherlands, supported granting the EEA substantial rulemaking, monitoring, and enforcement powers, while other member states, such as Britain and Spain, opposed granting a Community agency such far-reaching powers (*Financial Times* 1994; Interview with William K. Reilly, former EPA administrator, May 1994). After nearly ten months of negotiation, the Council adopted a regulation establishing the EEA. Member states opposed to the creation of a powerful, independent regulatory agency at the EU level were successful in limiting the EEA's powers to the coordination of information-gathering activities, and did not grant it any authority to engage in rulemaking, inspections, or enforcement.[37] These member states also insisted on the establishment of management structures that would allow for ongoing member state oversight. Thus, the EEA was subject to the control of a management board dominated by member state appointees.

The creation of the EEA caught the attention of Commission officials in other policy areas, and calls for establishing additional agencies came from a number of directorates general. The Commission's secretariat general then stepped in to oversee and coordinate the process of agency design (Interview, European Commission, November 29, 1996). To satisfy Council demands for intergovernmental control of the agencies, the Commission followed the EEA example and designed management structures dominated by member state appointees. Control over each agency was vested in a management board, which was empowered to select an agency director and a scientific committee.[38] The management boards were composed of representatives of the member states and the Commission, and in some cases also included representatives of the European Parliament, industry, and labor. However, in all cases member state representatives greatly outnumbered representatives of the Commission and the EP. Thus, to the extent that regulatory responsibilities were transferred from the Commission to one of the new agencies, they would be placed more firmly under intergovernmental control.

The Parliament played little direct role in the design of the agencies. The regulations establishing each of the agencies in this first wave were subject to the consultation procedure, which limited the EP to a consultative role.[39] Some members of the European Parliament (MEPs) expressed concerns regarding the agencies' accountability, in particular on financial matters (Interviews, European Commission, November 28–29, 1996; Brinkhorst 1996). Nevertheless, the Parliament generally supported the agencies, and accepted the Commission's view that they provided a promising means by which to expand the EU's regulatory capacity.

In terms of the scope of their authority, the early agencies can be divided into two groups: information-gathering agencies and regulatory agencies. The mandates of agencies in the first group—the EEA, the European Monitoring Centre for Drugs and Drug Addiction, and the European Agency for Safety and Health at Work—were limited to the gathering and dissemination of information and the development of networks of national administrators and technical experts. The second group of agencies—the European Agency for the Evaluation of Medicinal Products, the Office for Harmonization in the Internal Market, and the Community Plant Variety Office—were given more extensive regulatory powers. Most prominently, the EMEA was given authority to evaluate applications for Community-wide marketing authorizations.

The operating procedures of all the European agencies were designed to subject the agencies to intergovernmental control and to minimize any threat they posed to existing national administrations. Member state governments were sensitive to the threat that European agencies posed to their national administrations. Therefore, the Commission proposed that the agencies operate as the hubs of networks of national administrative agencies, research centers, testing laboratories, and other expert bodies. In this way the European agencies would rely on, rather than directly compete with, national agencies. The EMEA's procedures, discussed above, for testing and authorizing new drugs and monitoring drug manufacturing facilities exemplify this approach.

Agency Design after Maastricht

As the European Parliament gained new legislative powers, in the Maastricht and Amsterdam treaties, it began to demand more say in the design and oversight of European agencies. The reason for this shift is straightforward: the delegation of extensive implementation powers to agencies controlled by member state appointees threatened to undermine the EP's influence at the implementation stage. In order to ensure that the new legislative powers it had gained translated into influence over policy outcomes, the Parliament needed to extend its influence over the EU's executive organs.

From 1995, the EP showed increasing concern regarding the accountability of the new European agencies. First, it used its budgetary powers to place some agency budgets on reserve, discharging funds on an ongoing basis subject to its approval of the agency's financial management. Next, the Parliament began to press for agency designs that would provide it with increased opportunities for direct and indirect oversight. In the wake of the Mad Cow Crisis, the EP made it clear that it was skeptical of European agencies. MEPs criticized the fact that the European agencies were controlled by member-state dominated management boards, and expressed concern regarding the transparency and democratic accountability of the agencies. The Parliament pressed for increased representation on agency management boards. Recognizing that it had limited resources to conduct ongoing, direct oversight, the Parliament also demanded the establishment of formalized, open, transparent administrative procedures that would create opportunities for its interest-group allies to engage in indirect oversight and control.

As the Parliament weighed in on debates over agency design, the Commission altered its strategy vis-à-vis the Council. In the early 1990s, when the Commission had believed the establishment of agencies to be the best politically acceptable means by which to expand the EU's regulatory capacity, it had favored delegating extensive competences to the agencies, including the power to issue implementing regulations. By the late 1990s, however, after the Parliament had come out against the creation of powerful regulatory agencies, the Commission realized that where it had the support of the Parliament, it might expand the EU's regulatory capacity without delegating extensive powers to agencies controlled by the member states. These post-Maastricht politics of agency design are well illustrated by the politics surrounding the creation of a European food safety authority described above.[40]

The Limits on European Agencies

While future European agencies may be created and the authority of European agencies in the regulatory process may increase, such expansions face a number of obstacles. The EU's institutional structure ensures that delegation to European agencies requires the agreement of a number of veto players. The Council, the Commission, and the European Parliament all have opportunities to block the delegation of authority to existing or new European agencies. Opposition of powerful member states in the Council has derailed proposals for European agencies, as for instance in the area of telecoms (Johnstone 1997; Pelkmans and Young 1995; Thatcher 2001). More generally, member states are reluctant to delegate powers to European agencies that would threaten the existence of national bureaucracies. Where member states do agree to the establishment of agencies, they are likely to continue to demand that the agencies be controlled by member-state dominated management boards and serve as hubs of regulatory networks that rely on national administrative agencies.

The EP is likely to play a powerful role in the creation and oversight of future agencies and in the oversight of existing ones. As noted above, the Parliament has already used its budgetary powers to exert control over existing agencies. In policy areas subject to the reformed co-decision procedure, the Commission is likely to bring any proposals for new agencies under co-decision, thus providing the Parliament with substantial influence over agency design. Where the EP does agree to delegate decisionmaking authority to agencies, it will demand the creation of structures that enable it to maintain direct or indirect oversight, as in the case of the EFSA. The Parliament is also likely to demand increased transparency, codification, and judicial review of agency administrative procedures. Although the agencies functioned in a more open and transparent manner than had comitology committees, their operating procedures were not subject to any sort of uniform, judicially enforceable administrative guidelines. Already, the Parliament has supported inquiries by the European Ombudsman into the administrative procedures of the European agencies and has pressed them to adopt and publicize administrative codes of conduct, detailing procedures they will follow in dealing with citizens (European Ombudsman 1999).

The Commission also may block delegation to agencies, most likely in policy areas where it already has far-reaching competences. For instance, in the area of competition policy, where its powers are extensive, the Commission has consistently opposed the German proposal for the creation of an independent European cartel office and has refused to submit a proposal for the creation of such an agency (Van Miert 1996).[41] Similarly, in the area of food safety discussed above, the Commission only proposed delegating inspection powers to a European agency when it appeared that there was no other way to expand its existing internal inspectorate. After the Mad Cow Crisis, when the Commission gained the political backing it needed to expand its inspectorate, it chose not to delegate its inspection powers to the proposed European Food Safety Authority. The Commission is likely to resist the creation of agencies that strip it of authority in areas where it has well-established powers, and given its role in policy initiation, it is well positioned to do so.

Finally, while the ECJ plays no direct role in the design of agencies, concern over potential legal challenges has influenced the design of EU agencies. (Vos 1997). The ECJ's longstanding *Meroni* doctrine limits the Commission's ability to delegate broad, discretionary executive powers to bodies not foreseen in the treaties.[42] In keeping with the *Meroni* doctrine, where European agencies have been granted discretionary executive powers, such as the EMEA's authority to grant marketing authorizations for pharmaceuticals, the Commission reviews and maintains ultimate legal responsibility for the decisions. However, regardless of *Meroni*, it seems unlikely that the ECJ would block the establishment of or substantially limit the authority of an agency that had won the approval of the European Parliament, Council, and Commission.

EU agencies will not approach the size of their American counterparts. Nevertheless, despite the obstacles to agency expansion in the EU, new EU regulatory agencies are likely to have a significant impact on regulation. By gathering comparable information across the EU, the agencies will improve the EU's monitoring capacity. By creating and coordinating networks of national administrators, they will encourage the spread of common administrative practices across the member states (Majone 1996, 1997, 2000; Kreher 1997). Under pressure from the EP and the ECJ, these administrative practices are likely to emphasize transparency and detailed codification (Shapiro 1997, 2001; Harlow 1999; Dehousse 1998). Through the European agencies and their network structure that coordinates activities of existing national authorities, the EU is managing to federalize regulatory policy and limit member state discretion without eclipsing national regulatory authorities.

Conclusion

The patterns of development of food and drug safety regulation in the EU generally support the theory of regulatory federalism. The politics of competence in food safety are developing in a way that by now should be familiar. Claiming that it was prompted by increasing public concern, the EU entered the area to deal with impediments to trade caused by differences in national regulation. Initially, the EU left implementation and enforcement largely in the hands of the member states. When the Mad Cow Crisis sparked public cries for enforcement of food safety rules, the Commission increased its role in enforcement dramatically. The politics of competence in drug safety differs somewhat in that the EU developed a large role in the area, despite the absence of a jump in public concern. In both areas, the EU's separation-of-powers structure encouraged the drafting of detailed regulations. In the area of food safety, litigation has already emerged as an important tool and proposals to encourage litigation by private interests are on the table. In the area of drug safety, however, litigation has yet to play a significant role, as regulation has focused primarily on product assessment. Finally, a comparison of environmental, drug safety, and food safety regulation sheds light on the politics of agency creation in the EU and on the role that "independent" regulatory agencies are likely to play in EU regulation.

7 | Institutional Structure and Regulatory Style

The formal structures of a political system provide opportunities and constraints that empower certain actors and favor certain strategies, while weakening other actors and rendering other strategies ineffective. In democratic polities, where the rule of law forces political actors to follow the rules of the game, basic constitutional structures channel the development of politics. This book focuses primarily on how the institutional structures of the European Union (EU) influence the development of environmental regulation and other forms of social regulation in the EU. Most scholars view the EU either as a particularly well-developed international regime controlled by sovereign states, or as a unique, multilevel supranational polity that surrounds and enmeshes its member states. I have advanced an alternative perspective on regulation in the EU, arguing that the EU's regulatory regime functions as a federal system.

By comparing the development of regulation in the EU with that in other federal polities, this study contributes to our understanding of both the EU and federal institutions more generally. It focuses exclusively on regulation and does not claim that the EU is a "federal state" in some larger sense. While regulation constitutes only one piece of the EU puzzle, it is a large and vital piece. The EU has focused much more on regulation than on other public policy functions such as redistribution, defense, and, until recently, macro-economic stabilization. Understanding the dynamics of regulation in the EU reveals a great deal about how the EU actually functions.

European leaders have exhibited great concern with the questions of institutional design and regulation explored in this book. In the context of recent EU intergovernmental conferences and the Convention on the Future of Europe, European leaders have debated such basic constitutional questions as the roles of the Commission, the European Parliament (EP), the Council of Ministers, and the European Court of Justice (ECJ). German foreign minister Joschka Fischer's May 2000 speech at Humboldt University reinvigorated debate about the relevance of federalism to the EU's future development (Joerges, Mény, and Weiler 2000; *Le Monde* 2000; *Economist* 2000). Politicians and journalists regularly compare the Convention on the Future of Europe and the Philadelphia Convention of 1787.

EU scholars and leaders have also shown great interest in the politics of regulatory competence and discretion. The ongoing debate over "subsidiarity," a central issue at the Convention on the Future of Europe, centers on the question of how regulatory *competences* should be divided between member states and EU institutions. Recent proposals by national governments and the Commission to simplify EU directives and improve enforcement of EU law reveal a concern with the politics of *discretion*. These debates reflect a number of fundamental questions that are of great concern to European leaders and citizens alike: Are common standards necessary to prevent a "race to the bottom" in environmental and social regulation? Is power being increasingly centralized in the hands of Brussels-based Eurocrats? Will the "Europeanization" of regulation strip away national differences and lead to excessive homogeneity across Europe?

I have examined these questions through the lens of comparative federalism. The theory of regulatory federalism explains how strategic interactions between the various branches of the federal government, state governments, and courts—all acting within a given institutional context—influence the division of regulatory competences and the degree of state discretion. The theory, and the case studies that support it, show how various federal institutional arrangements encourage the development of distinct patterns of regulation.

The remainder of this chapter is divided into two sections. The first summarizes the findings of the case studies. The second considers the implications of those findings for the EU, examining how social regulation is likely to develop in the future and what impact such developments are likely to have on the EU more generally.

Findings

The theory of regulatory federalism I introduced in Chapter 1 contains two hypotheses. First, the division of power between federal and state governments common to all federal systems leads to a similar division of regulatory *competences*. In all federal systems, strategic interaction between state and federal governments leads to a similar outcome: federal governments take on a large role in policymaking and state governments retain control over most implementation. Second, differences in the concentration of power within the federal government explain differences in the *discretion* granted to states in their role as the implementers of federal policies. The greater the concentration of power within the federal government, the greater the degree of discretion granted to states. The case studies presented in Chapters 2–5 generally lend strong support to these hypotheses, although they did suggest a few anomalies. I discuss each hypothesis and the relevant findings in turn.

The Politics of Competence

Observers who are skeptical of the EU's power point out that member states retain control over implementation and enforcement of EU law, which those skeptics take as a sign of the EU's weakness. I suggest a different perspective on policy enforcement in the EU. Member state control of implementation and enforcement need not be viewed as a sign of weakness. Delegation of implementation and enforcement to member states does not distinguish the EU from other federal-type polities. Well-established federal governments—such as those in the United States, Germany, Australia, and Canada—also delegate most implementation and enforcement of regulatory policy to state governments.

The comparative case studies of environmental regulation in Chapters 2–5 show that the politics of competence in the United States, Canada, Australia, and the EU developed along similar lines, following the pattern hypothesized in Chapter 1. In each instance, states originally had jurisdiction over environmental issues, which had been of little public concern for decades. But concerns about the environment gained widespread public attention in each case during the late 1960s and early 1970s. Initially, some state governments adopted environmental controls, though standards varied among states depending on the influence of proponents and opponents of regulation in their jurisdictions. Subsequently, federal governments assumed lead roles in environmental policymaking. They took these initiatives for three reasons: to gain public support for addressing a popular issue, to prevent impediments to interstate commerce, and to expand federal authority.

Federal courts supported federal regulation, as it served to expand the scope of federal law. When federal competence in environmental matters was challenged, federal courts approved it. The legal bases that the federal governments relied on to justify their role in regulation varied, but in every case they were able to find legal bases acceptable to the federal courts.

Unfunded mandates proved universally popular. In each case, inconsistent implementation by states led to calls for an increased federal role in implementation and enforcement. While the federal polities did increase their activities in these areas, they never moved to strip the state governments of their primary responsibility for implementation and enforcement. The scope of federal enforcement efforts varied, with the U.S. federal government taking on the most powerful direct role in implementation and enforcement of any case in the study. Nevertheless, in all the case studies the federal governments continued to rely on states for most implementation and enforcement, passing off a good deal of the costs to them in the process.

In Canada, Australia, and the United States, where the political systems did not provide state governments with a direct role in federal policymaking, the states demanded the establishment of institutions that would give them a voice at the federal level. The development of such institutions has been greatest in Australia, where an intergovernmental body, the National Environmental Protection Council, adopts legislative proposals by a qualified majority vote that become law in all participating jurisdictions, unless they are vetoed by either chamber of the commonwealth Parliament. In the EU and Germany, such institutions are unnecessary, as member state governments already are ensured a powerful role in federal policymaking through their position in the Council of Ministers and the *Bundesrat* respectively.

The politics of competence in Germany proved somewhat anomalous. The case study findings were similar to those in the other polities considered, insofar as the federal government was responsible for making policy and the states for handling implementation and enforcement. The major difference in the German case was that this division of competences was established explicitly in the German Constitution (the Basic Law). In the other federal systems, the federal governments considered or actually attempted to take on at least some of the implementation and/or enforcement responsibilities. In the German case, this possibility was never raised, as no one challenged the constitutional provision that states are responsible for the implementation of federal law. Finally, Germany's membership in the European Union had an impact on the politics of competence. The increase in environmental policymaking at the EU level contributed to the shift in legislative power from the states to the federal government within Germany.

The Politics of Discretion

While there are certainly deficiencies in policy enforcement in the EU, it compares favorably with some federal systems. Community directives and regulations place more detailed requirements on member states than do Canadian or Australian laws. The European Commission and the ECJ do more to enforce EU environmental law than do the central authorities of Australia or Canada or Germany. Only in the United States does the federal government clearly take a more direct and extensive role in policy implementation and enforcement through its direct prosecution of polluters. In terms of enforcing state compliance with federal laws, however, the EU arguably takes the most coercive stance. Viewing the EU in comparative perspective, the impact of the EU's institutional structure on the development of regulatory policy becomes evident. It is no coincidence that the level of regulatory detail and the role of courts in the regulatory process in the EU resemble those in the United States. In both cases, the fragmentation of power in the basic institutional structure of the polity has encouraged these developments.

This finding may seem counterintuitive and does contradict much accepted wisdom. James Madison and the other framers of the U.S. Constitution, some of the most celebrated analysts of political institutions, saw federalism and the separation of powers as complementary means for limiting the federal government's ability to exercise power in a coercive manner (Madison 1987, no. 51).[1] They thought both together would serve to prevent tyranny by fragmenting power: federalism would provide for a vertical division between federal and state governments, while the separation of powers between the executive and legislature would provide for a horizontal division at the federal level. By contrast, the theory and findings presented in this study suggest that the interaction between these two institutions may actually encourage the federal government to act coercively. This insight has important implications for the EU.

The theory of regulatory federalism presented in Chapter 1 posits that the greater the fragmentation of power within the federal government, the lower the degree of discretion granted to states. In other words, where federal power is divided, as in separation-of-powers federal systems, the federal government takes a more coercive approach to controlling states. The causal logic I hypothesized to underlie this theory emerged in detail during the case studies. In brief, where federal power is fragmented, the federal government produces detailed laws and the federal judiciary plays a powerful role in regulation. Court involvement, in turn, encourages an adversarial, litigious approach to enforcement. Federal agencies and/or private parties bring legal actions that pressure states to implement the detailed requirements of federal regulations. By contrast, where federal power is highly concentrated, as in parliamentary federal systems, the federal government produces vague laws and federal courts play little role in the regulatory process. Few enforcement actions are brought and state governments enjoy wide discretion in implementing federal laws.

Table 3 summarizes the findings of the comparative case studies of environmental regulation in the United States, the EU, Germany, Canada, and Australia. The politics of discretion in the United States follow the pattern presented in the fragmented power model in Chapter 1. Power is highly fragmented in the U.S. federal government. Control of the executive is separated from control of the legislature, and the latter is divided into two powerful chambers. The fragmentation of power between these veto players makes it difficult to assemble the coalitions necessary to pass new legislation. Once laws are enacted, however, it is difficult to overturn them with new legislation. Therefore, when advocates of environmental regulation control a legislative majority, they seek to seal their victories by creating statutory rights and by placing detailed mandates on the administration. Advocates of regulation use detail in an attempt to control the discretion of state and federal administrators, anticipating that they will be able to enforce these requirements before the courts should administrators fail to implement them.

Table 3 Summary of cross-polity comparisons

	Fragmentation of power in federal government	Detail of regulations	Judicialization	State discretion
EU	High	High	Medium–high	Medium
United States	High	High	High	Low
Germany	Medium	Medium	Medium	Medium
Canada	Low	Low	Low	High
Australia	Low	Low	Low	High

Courts in the United States are often willing to make rulings that force the hand of reluctant administrators, because they recognize that administrators would have difficulty summoning the support in Congress necessary to pass new legislation to override such decisions. When the federal government first entered the field of environmental policy, courts took on an active role in the regulatory arena. Although the U.S. Supreme Court and lower federal courts have reduced judicial interference in the implementation process and have acted to exclude some potential litigants, the regulatory process in the United States remains highly litigious.

The institutional structure of the EU, like that of the United States, fragments power at the federal level. The Council of Ministers, the Commission, and increasingly the European Parliament act as veto players in legislative processes. Moreover, divisions between member states in the Council increase the fragmentation of power. The Commission and Parliament's distrust of the member state administrations, coupled with the member states' distrust of each other, has encouraged the drafting of detailed directives and regulations. The success of efforts to simplify legislation has been limited. The enforcement process has become highly judicialized. As Harlow (1998, pp. 12–13) aptly put it in an analysis of trends in EU administrative law, "Litigation is itself a form of juridification to which the EC system has already capitulated." The Commission actively prosecutes member states for their failure to implement detailed requirements of EU law. Recently, the Commission began to use the threat of fines to pressure states into compliance. However, the Commission's resource limitations continue to limit the effectiveness of its enforcement efforts. Decentralized litigation by private parties has played a limited role in EU environmental policy, but recent developments concerning the opportunities and incentives for such litigation discussed in Chapter 2 point toward an increase.

The recent developments in EU food and drug safety regulation discussed in Chapter 6 reveal patterns similar to those observed in EU environmental policy. The EU has adopted detailed requirements in these policy areas. In food safety regulation, the Commission has recently commenced a number of cases against member states for nonimplementation. In drug safety regulation, Community institutions already play a direct role in approving new drugs. Also, the Community has started monitoring drug manufacturing practices.

The institutional structure of German government provides for a concentration of power that falls between that in the highly concentrated parliamentary federalism model and the highly fragmented separation-of-powers model. As a result, the politics of discretion in Germany falls somewhere between the patterns depicted in the two models. In Germany, control of the federal government is fused with control over the lower house; however, the upper house remains a significant independent player. Also, the Basic Law safeguards the independent role of courts in the protection of individual rights. The courts have played an active role in environmental regulation, but only in a narrow range of cases. Courts have refrained from challenging the government on general matters of policy and have focused almost exclusively on licensing decisions concerning specific projects where the rights of neighbors are at stake.

The nature and role of detail in German environmental law is linked to this pattern of judicial review. German federal and state administrators use detailed regulatory requirements as a means for minimizing judicial interference in the regulatory process. The federal legislature does not use detail to control the administration; federal environmental statutes are actually quite vague. Nevertheless, when implementing any given statute, the federal bureaucracy, with the consent of state governments, issues highly detailed regulations and administrative guidelines that specify precisely how state and local officials are to implement any given environmental statute. Federal and state administrators bind themselves with these detailed requirements in order to shield themselves from administrative courts. Regulators recognize that if they were to adopt vague regulations, court rulings regarding individual cases could set precedents that would bind other administrators in future cases. Regulators choose to tie their own hands to prevent courts from doing the tying for them.

The politics of discretion in both Canada and Australia resembles that depicted in the model of a concentrated power federal system presented in Chapter 1. In both cases, institutional structures encourage the concentration of power within the federal government. In Canada, federal power is concentrated in the hands of a federal government, formed by the majority in the lower house. The government has enacted vague environmental statutes, which place very few specific requirements on provincial governments. Courts have played little role in the regulatory process. They sometimes grant environmental advocates standing to sue, but nearly always defer to the administration. In other areas of law, there has been some increase in the role of courts since the 1982 Charter of Rights was enacted, but this has not yet extended to environmental policy. The federal government generally does not intervene in matters of implementation and enforcement of federal environment laws, leaving that up to the provinces.

The pattern in Australia is similar. Most federal power is concentrated in the hands of the government, which is formed by the majority in the lower house. The Australian Senate is more powerful than the Canadian and can in some cases act as a veto player. Despite the power of the Senate, governments are still able to push through vague enabling statutes that give the administration and states ample discretion. Though Australian courts have heard a few high-profile environmental cases, the regulatory process has not become heavily judicialized because courts routinely deny standing to environmental plaintiffs. The commonwealth has intervened to enforce environmental requirements in a few instances, but generally leaves such matters to the states.

Implications: A European Rights Revolution?

The experience of federal polities suggests that the creation of rights for individuals under federal law enhances the power of the federal government over state governments (Katz and Tarr 1996; Baar 1991). Where federal law creates a right that every citizen is entitled to enjoy, the federal government has the authority to enforce that right against state governments that might seek to infringe on it. Moreover, citizens themselves may seek to secure their rights under federal law by bringing court actions. The relationship between the creation of rights and the expansion of federal power in the United States is instructive. The dramatic expansion of federal power that occurred in the years following the 1960s has been linked to the equally dramatic increase in the number of federally guaranteed rights. The "rights revolution" was initiated by the civil rights movement, which sought to ensure an equal standard of civil rights protection for citizens in every state in the Union. To this end, civil rights advocates enacted federal statutes to protect civil rights and pressured the federal government to enforce these rights against recalcitrant states. In addition, civil rights advocacy groups brought litigation of their own to enforce federal laws. Advocates of social regulations—such as environmental regulation, workplace health and safety regulation, and consumer protection regulation—soon followed suit and invoked a similar "rights" rhetoric (Sunstein 1990; Kincaid 1994a; Epp 1998; Vogel 1981).

New agencies were established to help enforce these new rights, including the Environmental Protection Agency, the Occupational Safety and

Health Administration, the Consumer Product Safety Commission, the Equal Employment Opportunity Commission, and the National Highway Traffic Safety Administration. All told, between 1970 and 1979 the budgets of major federal regulatory agencies increased by 537 percent and employment grew by 216 percent (Sunstein 1990, pp. 27–28). However, in most areas of social regulation federal agencies constituted only the tip of the iceberg. Because state governments were responsible for most implementation, they had to establish state agencies to implement and enforce federal requirements.

The rights revolution in the United States led not only to an increase in federal control over state governments, but also to an associated boom in litigation. A number of comparative studies of regulation in advanced industrial democracies indicate that U.S. regulatory processes are more detailed, complex, costly and, litigious than are regulatory processes in other nations (Kagan 1996, 2001; Kagan and Axelrad 1997). The adversarial nature of the regulatory process and the volume of litigation increased dramatically with the rights revolution. (The emergence of environmental litigation in the United States was detailed in Chapter 3.) Similarly, between 1960 and 1980 the number of civil rights cases brought against the government in federal courts increased nearly a hundredfold, while cases concerning unfair labor practices nearly quadrupled (Kagan 1997, pp. 170–171). Such litigation allowed private parties to often serve as the watchdogs of the federal government, ensuring that federal, state, and local agencies, as well as other private parties, adhered to the requirements of federal law. Rights litigation also produced many rulings in which federal courts interpreted statutes expansively, thereby pressuring the federal government to extend its control over state regulatory practices (Melnick 1996).[2]

The European Union has created a number of legally enforceable rights for European citizens. This study has focused on rights created by Community directives and regulations in the areas of environmental protection and food and drug safety regulation. Many rights have been created in other areas of social regulation including worker health and safety, consumer protection, and equal treatment of the sexes. The decision by member state governments at the Nice Summit not to fully incorporate the Charter of Fundamental Rights into the treaties blocked one potentially powerful basis for rights-based litigation. The catalogue of rights mentioned in the treaties remains limited, and some of the existing rights are unlikely to have direct effect (de Búrca 1995; Shaw 1997). For instance, Flynn (1999, p. 1132) notes that the list of implied rights contained in Article 13 of the Treaty of Amsterdam (rights concerning discrimination based on sex, race/ethnicity, religion/belief, disability, age, and sexual orientation) was drafted explicitly to not create direct effect. Nevertheless, in many areas of social regulation, Community law already provides bases for rights-based litigation. In light of the American experience, the creation of these rights all the EU level raises an important question: Is the establishment of rights by EU institutions encouraging a dramatic increase in the power of EU institutions over the member states in regulatory affairs? Is the increase in Community law encouraging the development of an American-style, litigious approach to regulation?

The findings of this study suggest that the answer to both of these questions is yes. While some aspects of political and legal culture in Europe and some domestic legal institutions may discourage the development of this litigious approach to regulation, the basic institutional structure of the EU encourages it.[3] While institutions do not determine political outcomes, they create opportunities for and place constraints on political actors that influence both strategies and outcomes (Thelen and Steinmo 1992; Weaver and Rockman 1993). The EU and the United States have similarly fragmented political structures. In the United States, this fragmentation of power in the federal government has encouraged both the proliferation of rights under federal law and the spread of an adversarial, litigious approach to policy enforcement. The EU's political structures have contributed to similar developments.

Political power in Brussels is fragmented among the member states in the Council of Ministers, the Commission, and the European Parliament. The increasing power of the EP in recent years has exacerbated this fragmentation. The Commission and Parliament's distrust of the member state administrations, coupled with the member states' distrust of each other, has encouraged proponents of social regulation to create rights and enact detailed requirements that later can be enforced in court. The fragmentation of power in Brussels has emboldened the ECJ to enforce these laws against recalcitrant member states. The ECJ has also created rights that place further pressure on member states to implement EU laws faithfully, most notably through the principles of direct effect and state liability.

The creation of new rights under Community law has been coupled with the establishment of new, EU-level regulatory bodies, including agencies outside the Commission hierarchy such as the European Environment Agency and the European Agency for the Evaluation of Medicinal Products. These European regulatory bodies promise both to improve the EU's capacity to monitor policy implementation and to encourage harmonization of regulatory practices in the member states. Given the power of entrenched national bureaucracies, these European bodies are unlikely to grow into expansive "Eurocracies" on par with U.S. federal agencies. Rather, they will most likely continue to pursue an approach based on networking with national bureaucracies.

Arguments, such as Siedentop's (2001), that the EU is sliding toward a massive centralization of power and bureaucratic despotism emanating from Brussels are misguided. The greatest increase in monitoring and enforcement of EU law is not likely to come from EU institutions, but rather from European citizens and interest groups that seek to enforce their rights under European law before national courts. The U.S. experience with the enforcement of social regulations suggests that private parties, such as concerned citizens and interest groups, can play a vital role in the enforcement of federal law. The same potential for private parties to act as watchdogs for Brussels exists in the EU. In the EU, private parties may bring challenges before national courts if a member state violates their rights under Community law. National courts may rule on such cases themselves, or may refer them to the ECJ. Litigation brought by private parties to enforce Community law has played a vital role in some areas of Community law. To date, it has had a limited impact on the areas of social regulation examined in this study, but there are many indications that such litigation will increase.

Every year, EU directives and the ECJ's interpretations of them create new rights in various areas of social regulation, which all Europeans are entitled to enjoy. Although the opportunities for private litigants to gain standing to sue vary among the member states, a number of Community laws have begun to generate litigation across the EU. In a number of areas of regulation the Commission has called for increased enforcement by private parties bringing cases before national courts. The ECJ has encouraged an increase in private enforcement by establishing that states may be held liable for damages caused as a result of nonimplementation.

The Commission recognizes that, given its resource limitations, it is incapable of ensuring adequate implementation of Community law by the member states. Recent increases in the Commission's enforcement powers coupled with the establishment of European-level regulatory agencies and networks will have a great impact on regulation in the member states.

However, the EU will not have to construct a powerful bureaucracy in order for this impact to take place. Rather as Kagan (1997, p. 178) recently observed, "When federal governments cannot deploy bureaucrats, they can respond to political demands by allowing citizens to deploy lawyers and lawsuits." It is by encouraging such litigation that the EU will ultimately place the greatest constraints on national governments and have the greatest impact on regulation in Europe.

Notes

References

Cases Cited

Index

Notes

1. Regulatory Federalism and the EU

1. The distinction between economic and social regulation (sometimes referred to as "the new social regulation" or "protective regulation") is common in the literature on regulatory policy (Vogel 1981; Moe 1989; Kagan 1993; Dehousse 1992; Rose-Ackerman 1992; Majone 1993). Most authors include only safety, health, environmental, and consumer regulations in the category of social regulation, while others include regulations aimed to provide rights for members of particular groups (e.g., women, minorities, the disabled).
2. I follow a common practice in literature on Community law and use the word "competence" to refer to powers or responsibilities held by a jurisdiction (Haagsma 1989).
3. As discussed in Chapter 5, power is more fragmented in Australia than in Canada, given the greater power of the upper house in Australia.
4. A handful of other studies, though not focusing specifically on regulation, do apply a comparative federalism framework to the EU. See, for instance, Friedrich 1968; Forsyth 1981; McKay 1999, 2001; Goldstein 2001; Burgess 2000.
5. The intergovernmentalist approach draws heavily on theories of international regimes. See Krasner 1983 and Keohane 1984.
6. Moravcsik (1995) seeks to explain this anomaly by arguing that the ECJ was granted more autonomy than the Commission because the scope of ECJ action, and therefore the potential cost of the ECJ pursuing its own agenda, is narrower than that of the Commission. This, he argues, results from the fact that the ECJ has to deal with specific cases and does not make general policy. This auxiliary hypothesis can be rejected on two grounds. First, given the wide-ranging impact of the precedents established in some ECJ decisions, the assertion that the scope of ECJ action is narrow is dubious at best. Second, and more important, this auxiliary hypothesis does not fit well within the intergovernmentalist paradigm.

175

7. For an earlier elaboration of this model, see Kelemen 2000.

8. Many such tactics have been used against the U.S. Supreme Court (Gely and Spiller 1992; Rosenberg 1992; McCloskey 1960) and the ECJ (Garrett, Kelemen, and Schulz 1998).

9. It is, of course, possible that a founding constitution could delegate competence for social regulation to the federal government. However, the assumption that state governments have jurisdiction holds true for all federal polities I have examined.

10. Health and safety concerns may become more salient as a result of a combination of factors: mounting pollution; industrial accidents; increased activism by environmental, consumer, and public health organizations; and international diffusion effects. The increased salience of such problems can be considered endogenous to the extent that the problems result from the lack of regulation.

11. It may be difficult to distinguish legitimate social regulations and those imposed as a tool of trade protectionism, because legitimate advocates of social regulation sometimes find support among local producers who see the regulations as a means to protect their commercial interests. Vogel (1995) refers to these unlikely partnerships as "Baptist-bootlegger" coalitions, referring to the fact that bootleggers—for obvious economic reasons—supported Prohibition.

12. The question of whether these competitive economic pressures lead strict states to reduce the stringency of their regulations is the subject of extensive debate. See, for example, Stewart 1977, 1993b; Revesz 1992, 1997, 2001; Vogel 1995; Engel 1997; Scharpf 1996b; Engel and Rose-Ackerman 2001; Esty and Geradin 2001; Faure 2001; Oates 1997.

13. McCubbins, Noll, and Weingast (1999) use the term "political drift." In earlier work, Moe (1989) refers to the same concept with the term "political uncertainty," while Shepsle (1992) uses the term "coalitional drift."

2. Environmental Regulation in the EU

1. In this respect, the EU's structure most closely resembles that of Germany, where states *(Länder)* are directly represented in the upper house *(Bundesrat)*. By contrast, in the United States, since 1913 senators have been directly elected representatives of the people of their state, rather than representatives of their state government. Even before 1913, when senators were elected by state legislatures, their voting in the Senate was not directly controlled by their state government. For more in depth discussions of the Council, see Westlake 1995; Ludlow 1991; Nugent 1994, pp. 123–152.

2. Direct elections to the European Parliament were first introduced in 1979. Before that, Members of the European Parliament (MEPs) were nominated by national parliaments from amongst their members. The number of MEPs has increased over time as the Community has enlarged to include new member states.

3. The Commission's closest analogue is the Swiss collegial executive, the Federal Council. See Lijphart 1999, pp. 34–35.

4. The five largest member states appoint two commissioners each, the other ten states appoint one each.

5. While Article 214 of the Maastricht Treaty subjects the Commission as a whole to a vote of approval by the EP, it only gave the EP the right of consultation regarding the nominee for Commission president. In 1994, however, the EP interpreted its right to consultation as a right to vote, and did so. The Amsterdam Treaty incorporated this interpretation into EU law. See Hix 1999, p. 46. On new procedures called for in the Treaty of Nice, see Yataganas 2001.

6. According to the treaty, harmonization measures adopted under Article 100 were to be subject to qualified majority voting; however, following the 1965 "Luxembourg compromise" nearly all measures were adopted by unanimity. The member states agreed to the Luxembourg compromise after France demanded that states be allowed to veto proposals in the Council of Ministers whenever "vital" national interests were at stake. This agreement had no legal basis, but nevertheless governed decisionmaking in the Community until the ratification of the Single European Act.

7. Exceptions where the consultation procedure (with unanimity voting) still applies are fiscal measures, land use planning and water management measures, and measures affecting choice of energy supply (art. 175 (former art. 130(s))).

8. Directive 67/548, [1967] OJ Spec. Ed. 234.

9. Directive 70/157, [1970] OJ Spec. Ed. 111; and Directive 70/220, [1970] OJ L76/1.

10. Commission SEC(71) 2616, final, July 7, 1971.

11. Declaration of the First Summit Conference of the Enlarged Community, reprinted in E.C. Bull. no. 10, at 14, 20 (1972).

12. The program was formally adopted in November 1973 ([1973] OJ C112/1, December 20, 1973). Environmental action programs are political declarations of principles and goals, rather than legally binding measures. Subsequently, the EU adopted five more multi-annual environmental action programs.

13. Directive 75/716, [1975] OJ L307/22.

14. Directive 85/210, [1985] OJ L96/25.

15. Directive 78/1015, [1978] OJ L349/121.

16. The first restrictions concerned PCBs polychlorinated biphenyls (PCBs) and polychlorinated terphenyls (PCTs) (Directive 76/769, [1976] OJ L262/201). Subsequent amendments of this directive extended the list of restricted substances.

17. Directive 75/440, [1975] OJ L194/26.

18. Directive 76/160, [1976] OJ L31/1.

19. Directive 79/409, [1979] OJ L103/1.

20. Directive 84/360, [1984] OJ L188/20.

21. Directive 75/442, [1975] OJ L194/23.

22. Directive 78/319, [1978] OJ L84/43.

23. Directive 85/337, [1985] OJ L175/40.

24. C-91/79, *Commission v. Italian Republic,* [1980] ECR 1099; and C-92/79, *Commission v. Italian Republic,* [1980] ECR 1115.

25. C-240/83, *Procureur du Roi v. Association de défense des bruleurs d'huiles usagées,* [1985] ECR 531.

26. See Kelemen 1995 for a further elaboration of this argument. For contrasting views, which describe the inclusion of an environmental article in the treaty as an outright victory for proponents of Community-level regulation, see Hildebrand 1993; Sbragia 1993a; and Wurzel 1993.

27. Since 1980 the Commission had advocated a "new approach" to eliminating barriers to trade in the internal market, relying largely on the principle of mutual recognition. The Commission derived this principle from the ECJ's controversial ruling in the landmark *Cassis de Dijon* case (C-120/78, *Rewe-Zentral A.G. v. Bundesmonopolverwaltung (Cassis de Dijon),* [1979] ECR 649). See Alter and Meunier-Aitsahalia 1994, p. 551; Commission 1985; Sun and Pelkmans 1995.

28. A qualified majority required fifty-four of the seventy-six votes that were distributed among the member states, roughly according to their populations. The four largest member states—Germany, France, Italy, and the UK—had ten votes each, Spain had eight votes, Belgium, Greece, the Netherlands, and Portugal each had five votes, Denmark and Ireland had three votes, and finally the smallest member state, Luxembourg, had just two votes.

9. States with strict standards had fears about qualified majority voting as well, namely, that they might be outvoted and forced to lower their national standards. These states, led by Denmark, demanded that Article 100a include an "opt-up" clause, permitting them to maintain higher standards even where the Community agreed to harmonize. This provision is contained in Article 100a(4), which also requires that member states notify the Commission of any national measures it takes that surpass harmonized standards. The Commission must verify that such measures do not serve as disguised restrictions on trade.

30. In the Commission's original proposal for Article 130s, it called for qualified majority voting (Krämer 1990, p. 88; Wurzel 1993, p. 183). However, the Council revised this article so that environmental provisions would require unanimity voting.

31. C-300/89, *Commission v. Council,* [1991] ECR I-2867 (regarding Directive 89/428, [1989] OJ L201/56).

32. Conflicts over which decisionmaking procedures should apply to environmental measures did not end with the *Titanium Dioxide* ruling. Subsequent cases (such as C-155/91, *Commission v. Council,* [1993] ECR I-939) revisited the issue, and ECJ rulings placed some constraints on the use of Article 100a in the environmental arena. See Jupille 1997.

33. Golub (1994, pp. 18–22) presents evidence that the British invoked sub-

sidiarity in opposing the directives on species and habitat protection and on chromium in water. However, it seems that the use of subsidiarity was very infrequent. Ludwig Krämer (1995, p. 60), former head of the legal service in the Commission's environmental directorate, stated that he knew of "not one single environmental measure where the Council has decided or even discussed whether a measure could be better adopted at Community level than at the level of Member States."

34. In 1983, with the budgetary support of the European Parliament, the Commission proposed establishing an "environmental fund" to provide Community financing for actions undertaken at the national level to promote clean technologies and habitat protection (Proposal for a Council Regulation on Action by the Community Relating to the Environment (ACE), [1983] OJ C30/8; Haagmsa 1989, p. 344; Krämer 1995, p. 25. The Council did not accept this proposal, as some member states anticipated that such funding could lead to excessive Community meddling in implementation. Instead, the Council agreed to a much more restricted "mini-fund" that, along with support from the member states, would co-finance a limited number of demonstration projects (Regulation 1872/84, [1984] OJ L176/1). This fund provided only 13 million ECUs over three years. It was extended in 1987 to provide 24 million ECUs over four years (Regulation 2247/87, [1987] OJ L207/8).

35. Fourth Environmental Action Programme, [1987] OJ C328/1.

36. The practice of including temporary derogations in environmental legislation was not new. Many pieces of legislation passed prior to Maastricht had included such clauses (Krämer 1995, p. 74.) While this treaty provision did not introduce a new policy, it did serve to reassure poorer states that this practice would continue.

37. Article 3b(2) of the Maastricht Treaty reads, "In areas which do not fall within its exclusive competence, the Community shall take action, in accordance with the principle of subsidiarity, only if and in so far as the objectives of the proposed action cannot be sufficiently achieved by the Member States and can therefore, by reason of the scale or effects of the proposed action, be better achieved by the Community."

38. Under Article 130s, the Maastricht Treaty called for the use of the cooperation procedure. See Kelemen 1995, pp. 320–321.

39. One important reason that EEA supporters abandoned efforts to expand its mandate was budgetary constraints. Ken Collins, former chairman of the EP's committee on the environment, suggested that adding inspection functions to the environment agency would require an untenable several fold increase in the agency's budget. Also, advocates of an expanded role for the EEA and EEA officials themselves became convinced that adding enforcement functions to the agency's mandate would interfere with its information gathering functions (Interviews, EEA Officials, April 1997; European Parliament Environment Committee, May 1997; European Commission, November 1996).

40. Common Position (EC) no. 24/2000, OJ C137, pp. 1–10.

41. The EP's distrust of member state administrations also helps explain its reluctance to rely on voluntary agreements between government and industry as an instrument for implementation.

42. The UK is exceptional in this regard. While the British government has not typically advocated strict Community standards, it does, for the most part, apply them conscientiously. The UK advocated a more active Commission role in enforcement in order to ensure that other member states will have to implement Community regulations as well as it does.

43. C-387/97, *Commission v. Greece,* [2000] ECR I-5047.

44. Of course, the state may choose to ignore the ECJ ruling. This possibility, and recent actions taken to remedy it, are discussed later in this chapter.

45. Directive 79/409, [1979] OJ L271/44.

46. C-355/90, *Commission v. Spain,* [1993] ECR I-4221.

47. The court has also ruled against member states in similar cases involving directives on waters for fresh water fish and shellfish. See C-322/86, *Commission v. Italy,* [1988] ECR 3955.

48. C-3/96, *Commission v. Netherlands,* [1998] ECR I-3031; Commission 1999c, §2.12.5.

49. Council Directive 76/160/EEC.

50. The UK had added the beaches to its list of bathing waters, but only belatedly. It claimed that the time limits for achieving water-quality levels should run from the time it added the beaches to its list, rather than from the time the directive came into force.

51. Case 56/90, *Commission v. United Kingdom* [1993] ECR I-4109.

52. C-427/00, *Commission v. United Kingdom,* [2001] ECR I-8535.

53. C-361/88, *Commission v. Germany,* [1991] ECR I-2567.

54. Ibid., 2602–2603. The Court has made a number of similar rulings. See C-131/88, *Commission v. Germany,* [1991] ECR I-825; C-58/89, *Commission v. Germany,* [1991] ECR I-4893 (concerning the surface waters directive); C-59/89, *Commission v. Germany,* [1991] ECR I-2607.

55. Three of the cases were brought against Germany and two were brought against Italy. The penalties proposed in the cases ranged from 26,400 to 264,000 ECUs per day (*Agence Europe* 1997b).

56. Directive 75/442/EEC on waste and Directive 78/319/EEC on toxic and dangerous waste.

57. C-45/91, *Commission v. Greece,* [1992] ECR I-2509.

58. C-387/97, *Commission v. Greece,* [2000] ECR I-5047.

59. Nontransposition involves the failure of a member state to notify the Commission of measures taken to transpose a directive into national law before the deadline for transposition.

60. This relates to the failure of a member state to correctly or completely transpose the directive into national law.

61. The Commission occasionally visits the site of an alleged infringement. However, no actual investigation is carried out. Thus, the former director of

DGXI's legal service explains that these are better viewed as fact finding missions than as inspections (Krämer 1995, p. 143).

62. See C-325/94, *An Taisce—The National Trust for Ireland and World Wide Fund for Nature (WWF) v. Commission*, [1996] ECR I-3727; C-321/95 P, *Stichting Greenpeace Council (Greenpeace International) v. Commission*, [1998] ECR I-1651.

63. C-26/62, *Van Gend en Loos v. Nederlandse Administratie der Belastingen*, [1963] ECR 1.

64. See Hartley 1994, pp. 199–206, for a discussion of these conditions. The ECJ first established that directives may have direct effect in C-41/74, *Van Duyn v. Home Office*, [1974] ECR 1337. Later it clarified that directives only have direct effect after their national deadline for implementation has passed (C-148/78, *Pubblico Ministero v. Tullio Ratti*, [1979] ECR 1629).

65. The ECJ established the doctrine of the supremacy of Community law over national law in C-6/64, *Costa v. Ente Nazionale per L'Energia Elettrica (ENEL)*, [1964] ECR 585. See Stein 1981 and Weiler 1991 for general discussions of the development of the doctrines of supremacy and direct effect.

66. C-148/78, *Pubblico Ministero v. Tullio Ratti*, [1979] ECR 1629.

67. C-131/88, *Commission v. Germany*, [1991] ECR I-825, concerning Directive 80/68 on dangerous substances in ground water ([1980] OJ L20); C-361/88, *Commission v. Germany*, [1991] ECR I-2567, concerning Directive 80/779 on sulphur dioxide and suspended particles in air ([1980] OJ L229); C-58/89, *Commission v. Germany* ECR [1991] ECR I-4983, concerning Directives 75/440 and 79/869 on drinking water and measurements methods for drinking water ([1975] OJ L194/26 and [1979] OJ L271/44); C-59/89, *Commission v. Germany*, [1991] ECR I2607, concerning Directive 82/884 on limit values for lead in the air ([1982] OJ L378/15).

68. See, for instance, C-131/88, *Commission v. Germany*, [1991] ECR I-825, para. 8, where the court ruled that the procedural rules of a Community ground-water pollution directive created rights for individuals. Also see C-72/95, *Kraaijeveld BV v. Gedepudteerde Staten van Zuid-Holland*, [1996] ECR I-5403, concerning procedural requirements of the directive governing environmental impact assessments.

69. Categorizing environment cases differently, Krämer (1996, p. 4) reports a figure of only twenty-one cases during the same period.

70. C-33/76, *Rewe v. Landwirtschaftskammer*, [1976] ECR 1989, para. 5.

71. The UN's Economic Commission of Europe (ECE) Convention on access to information, public participation in decisionmaking, and access to justice in environmental matters. Signed June 23–25, 1998, Aarhus, Denmark. Available at *www.unece.org/env*. Also see IMPEL (2000). To date, the EU has not ratified the Aarhus Convention and only two member states, Denmark and Italy, have done so.

72. EC Treaty Article 230 (former Article 173) provides that private parties can bring cases before the ECJ that challenge the legality of an act by a Commu-

nity institution, if they are directly and individually concerned with the act (art. 230(4)). As mentioned above, since the establishment of the Court of First Instance, cases brought by private parties (nonprivileged plaintiffs) are heard first by the CFI and must then be appealed to the ECJ.

73. C-321/95, [1998] ECR I-1651.

74. Articles 6(2) and 8 of Directive 85/337 provide for public participation in the environmental impact assessment process.

75. Joined cases C-6/90 and C-9/90, *Francovich and Others v. Italy,* [1991] ECR I-5357.

76. Joined cases C-46/93 and C-48/93, *Brasserie du Pêcheur and Factortame,* [1996] ECR I-1029; C-392/93, *R v. HM Treasury ex parte British Telecommunications,* [1996] ECR I-1631; C-5/94, *Hedley Lomas,* [1996] ECR I-2553; Joined cases C-178, 179, and 188–190/94, *Dillenkofer and Others,* [1996] ECR I-4845.

77. For an up-to-date review of ECJ and national case law concerning the doctrine of state liability see the European Environmental Law Homepage's Dossier on State Liability for Breaches of Community law—"Francovich Follow-Up," *www.eel.nl.*

78. Directive 85/337, [1985] OJ L175/40.

79. See, for instance, C-396/92, *Bund Naturschutz in Bayern e.V. and Richard Stahnsdorf and Others v. Freistaat Bayern, Stadt Vilsbiburg and Landkreis Landshut,* [1994] ECR I-3717; C-435/97, *World Wildlife Fund (WWF) and Others v. Autonome Provinz Bozen and Others,* [1999] ECR I-5613.

80. Directive 90/313, [1990] OJ L158/56.

81. Member states are permitted to refuse access under certain conditions, but any refusal must be accompanied by a specific statement of reasons for denying access (Krämer 1995, p. 24). Similarly, at the EU level, the Commission must provide adequate reasons for denying access to Commission documents, including documents concerning environmental policy decisions. See C-T-105/95, *WWF UK (World Wide Fund for Nature) v. Commission,* [1997] ECR II-0313.

82. The EU is not unique in this regard. Although the U.S. federal government actively prosecutes polluters, the German federal government does not, instead delegating such enforcement to *Länder* authorities. See Chapters 3 and 4.

3. Environmental Regulation in the United States

1. See Percival 1995, pp. 1152–53, for a discussion of other similar cases.

2. Examples of the few state laws enacted in this period include the Minnesota Law 395, §11 (1945) on water pollution; California Statute 632, §1 (1947) on air pollution; and New Jersey Laws 212, §1 (1954) on air pollution. See Humphrey and Paddock 1990, p. 11.

3. The federal government's involvement in conservation stemmed from its ownership of vast tracts of public lands, particularly in the western states. The fed-

eral government owns nearly one-half of the land in the eleven western states (Arizona, California, Colorado, Idaho, Montana, New Mexico, Nevada, Oregon, Utah, Washington, and Wyoming) (Nelson 1997, p. 23). The conservation movement of the late nineteenth century succeeded in convincing Congress to set aside some public lands as national parks, forests, recreation areas, wildlife refuges, and grazing lands. Conservationists were an important element in Teddy Roosevelt's Progressive coalition, and during his presidency (1901–1909) Roosevelt set aside millions of acres of public lands as national parks, forests, and wildlife reserves. (Caulfield 1989; Vig 1994, p. 73; Percival 1995, pp. 1147–48).

4. Federal involvement began with the Water Pollution Control Act of 1948. The federal government had required permits for dumping waste into navigable waters as early as 1899, but that law (the Refuse Act of 1899) went unenforced (Davies and Davies 1975).

5. For instance, the Water Pollution Control Act of 1948 authorized funding both for research and for grants to state water pollution control programs (Davies and Davies 1975). In 1955 Congress adopted legislation providing funding for both research on air pollution problems and for aid to state and local government air pollution control agencies (Jones 1975, pp. 29–38).

6. The 1955 Air Pollution Control Act authorized the Department of Health, Education and Welfare (HEW) and the Public Health Service to fund research and to coordinate information collection to assist state and local authorities (Air Pollution Control Act ch. 360, §1, 69 Stat. 322, 322 (1955); see Jones 1975, pp. 29–38.

7. Clean Air Act, Pub. L. No. 88–206, §5(c), 77 Stat. 392, 396 (1963); Motor Vehicle Air Pollution Control Act, Pub. L. No. 89–272, §202(a), 79 Stat. 992, 992–993 (1965); Air Quality Act of 1967, Pub. L. No. 90–148, §2, 81 Stat. 485–501.

8. 84 Stat. 1676, 42 U.S.C. §1857b.

9. 86 Stat. 816, 33 U.S.C. §1401.

10. 88 Stat. 1661, 42 U.S.C. §300f.

11. 86 Stat. 965, 7 U.S.C. §135.

12. 90 Stat. 2005, 15 U.S.C. §2601.

13. 90 Stat. 45, 42 U.S.C. §6901.

14. See Reorganization Plan no. 3 of 1970, 3 C.F.R. 1072 (1970).

15. The EPA is frequently referred to as an independent agency. This is misleading. "Independence" in this context is normally associated with the various independent regulatory commissions, headed by multimember panels whose members are appointed by different administrations. By contrast, the EPA is headed by a single administrator appointed by the president. Structurally, the EPA resembles a cabinet level department, such as the Department of Interior or Health and Human Services. It differs only in name and reputation.

16. Unlike the EU's legislative bodies, the U.S. Congress is under no obligation to cite a constitutional basis for the legislation that it enacts.

17. In a series of judgments, the Court had developed a "stream of commerce"

doctrine that allowed for federal regulation of local commercial matters, so long as it could be argued that they had some effect on interstate commerce. See, for example, *Wickard v. Filburn,* 317 U.S. 111 (1942).

18. In *Hodel v. Surface Mining and Reclamation Ass'n Inc.,* 452 U.S. 264 (1981), the Supreme Court indicated that Congress had plenary authority concerning environmental regulation under its interstate commerce power (Pfander 1996, p. 81). See Soper (1974, p. 24) who discusses case law concerning the constitutional bases for federal environmental regulation.

19. The 1967 Air Quality Act had provided the federal government with a very limited enforcement competence. The federal government could only act when there was an "imminent and substantial" public health threat and when state and local authorities had failed to address it (Humphrey and Paddock 1990, pp. 7, 15).

20. However, only $2.8 billion of this went toward the EPA's administrative activities. The remainder went to construction grants for waste treatment facilities ($2.1 billion) and to the Superfund Trust for the cleanup of hazardous waste sites ($1.6 billion).

21. The Clean Air Act provides for complete federal preemption in setting motor vehicle emission standards, except that it permits California to adopt stricter standards (the "California waiver"). The act then gives states the choice between adopting federal standards or California standards (42 U.S.C. §7543).

22. For instance the Federal Insecticide, Fungicide and Rodenticide Act (7 U.S.C. §136v(b)) makes federal labeling and packaging requirements for toxic substances exclusive, barring any state requirements. See Pfander 1996, p. 121.

23. States are typically asked to submit a state implementation plan (SIP) for federal approval (Kincaid 1996, pp. 79–102; Lester 1994, pp. 52, 58). As discussed below, the Supreme Court has recently reaffirmed that states cannot be forced to implement federal laws on behalf of the federal government. They must be given the choice of leaving responsibility for implementation to the federal government. However, as I explain below, this choice is often highly constrained.

24. 42 U.S.C. §7410(a)(1).

25. 42 U.S.C. §7410(c)(1).

26. The Clean Air Act Amendments of 1970 provided that the EPA could take direct enforcement action only if a violation continued thirty days after the EPA notified both the polluter and the state of the violation. 42 U.S.C. §§7413(a)(1), 7410(a)(3).

27. 33 U.S.C. §1319(a)(1).

28. 42 U.S.C. §6928.

29. Executive Order No. 12,291, 3 C.F.R. 127 (1981).

30. RCRA was strengthened by the Hazardous and Solid Waste Amendments of 1984 (Pub. L. No. 98–616, 98 Stat. 3221). In 1986, Superfund (the Comprehensive Environmental Response, Compensation and Liability Act—or CERCLA) was reauthorized with the Superfund Amendments and Reau-

thorization Act (SARA) (Pub. L. No. 99–339, 100 Stat. 1613 (1986). Also in 1986, the Safe Drinking Water Act was reauthorized and strengthened (Pub. L. No. 99–339, 100 Stat. 642).

31. Pub. L. No. 104–4, 109 Stat. 48.

32. The steering committee was established to implement the reforms called for in a report the EPA had commissioned (Report of the Task Force to Enhance State Capacity: Strengthening Environmental Management in the U.S., pp. 4–7 (July 1993)). The report called for a radical transformation in how EPA and states work together. See Emison 1996, p. 236.

33. For instance, the National Conference of Commissioners on Uniform State Laws, formed in 1892, has preempted unwanted federal regulation in some areas by issuing model legislation (such as the Uniform Commercial Code) that states enact voluntarily. See Kincaid (1994b, p. 44).

34. In the United States, as in Canada and Australia, federal institutions provide no representation for state governments as actors in their own right. By contrast, in Germany and the EU, state governments send representatives to the upper federal chamber, providing them with a direct say in federal policy-making processes.

35. Section 304, 42 U.S.C §7604(A)(2) (amended 1990).

36. Clean Air Act §707, 42 U.S.C.§7604 (1988) and Supp. II (1990); Resource Conservation and Recovery Act §7002, 42 U.S.C. §6972 (1988); Federal Water Pollution Control Act §505, 33 U.S.C. §1365 (1988); Comprehensive Environmental Response, Compensation and Liability Act §113, 42 U.S.C.§9659 (1988); Toxic Substances Control Act §20, 15 U.S.C. §2619; Oil Pollution Act §1017, 33 U.S.C. §2717 (Supp. II) 1990. See Kibel and Klinski 1994, p. 67; Sunstein 1990, p. 165; Garrett 1991, p. 68; Craig 2001, p. 93. Rose-Ackerman (1995, p. 152) emphasizes that all environmental statutes contain such provisions except the Federal Insecticide, Fungicide, and Rodenticide Act, 7 U.S.C. §§136–136y (1988).

37. Senate Rep. No. 1196, 91st Cong., 2nd Sess., 37 (1970).

38. The EPA had to hire two hundred employees and write fifty-five new regulations within the first two years after the passage of the 1990 Amendments in order to implement new requirements (Rosenbaum 1994, p. 126).

39. According to former EPA administrator William K. Reilly, EPA has met less than 20 percent of congressionally imposed deadlines (Lazarus 1991, p. 323).

40. See Shapiro 1988, pp. 36–77. This judicial activism contrasted with the deferential posture courts had taken toward regulatory agencies since being badly beaten in their conflict with the New Dealers (Sunstein 1990, p. 23; Rosenberg 1992; McCloskey 1960, pp. 174–179). Before 1970, courts had maintained a number of barriers to discourage plaintiffs from challenging administrative decisions, including denying them standing to sue, claiming a lack of jurisdiction, holding that plaintiffs had not exhausted all available administrative remedies, and finding that they had failed to meet substantive evidence test.

41. Federal Administrative Procedures Act (APA), 5 U.S.C. §§551–706 (1988). Sections 551–559 and 701–706 establishes standing requirements. In particular, §702 grants standing to any "person suffering legal wrong because of agency action within the meaning of a relevant statute, is entitled to judicial review thereof."

42. In *Sierra Club v. Morton*, 405 U.S. 727 (1971), the Court held that environmental groups can sue under the APA so long as members can claim standing under APA §702. Also in this case, the Court held that plaintiffs could claim standing for having suffered noneconomic, "environmental" injuries. Standing reached its zenith in 1973 with *United States v. Students Challenging Regulatory Agency Procedure (SCRAP)*, 412 U.S. 669 (1973), when the Supreme Court ruled that the magnitude of the plaintiff's injury did not matter in determining standing. The decision granted standing to a group of students who alleged that they might suffer loss of enjoyment of an area where they hiked if railroad rates on recycled materials were higher than those on virgin materials. Later, in *Duke Power Co. v. Carolina Environmental Study Group, Inc.*, 438 U.S. 59 (1978), the Court held that for standing to be granted, a plaintiff's injury need only be "fairly traceable" to the challenged government action and that there need only be a "substantial likelihood" that judicial action would diminish or prevent the alleged injury.

43. *Kennecott Copper Corp. v. EPA*, 462 F.2d 846 (D.C. Cir. 1972); *Portland Cement Assoc. v. Ruckelshaus*, 486 F.2d 375 (D.C. Cir. 1973). See Melnick 1983, pp. 239–244, 263–269; Bryner 1987, pp. 94–98.

44. See, for instance, *Monroe v. Pape*, 365 U.S. 167 (1961), which authorizes individuals to bring cases directly to federal courts, without exhausting their opportunities in the state court system, if their constitutional or federal statutory rights have been violated by someone acting "under the color of state law."

45. See, for instance, *Vermont Yankee Nuclear Power Corp. v. Natural Resources Defense Council, Inc.*, 435 U.S. 519 (1978); *Heckler v. Chaney*, 470 U.S. 821 (1985); *Chevron, U.S.A., Inc. v. NRDC, Inc.*, 467 U.S. 837 (1984).

46. In an empirical study of the impact of *Chevron* on federal court decisions, Schuck and Elliott (1990) found that while federal courts generally increased their discretion to agencies, the powerful D.C. Circuit actually remanded a higher percentage of cases to agencies after *Chevron* than before.

47. *New York v. United States*, 505 U.S. 144 (1992); *Printz v. United States*, 521 U.S. 898 (1997).

48. 42 U.S.C. §§2021b *et seq.* (Supp. IV 1980).

49. This "anti-commandeering" principle was by no means new. The principle originated during the debates over the ratification of the U.S. Constitution, and the Supreme Court applied it as early as 1861 in *Kentucky v. Dennison*, 65 U.S. 66, 107–108 (1861). However, federal courts generally gave the principle a narrow interpretation allowing disputed federal mandates to remain in place. See, for instance, *Federal Energy Regulatory Commission v. Mississippi*, 456 U.S. 742 (1982), where the Supreme Court upheld the legality of a Pub-

lic Utility Regulatory Practices Act (PURPA) requirement that state utility regulators enact energy conservation programs (Tolley and Wallin 1995, pp. 78–83).

50. I thank Robert Kagan for suggesting the notion of levers.

51. 42 U.S.C. §4321.

52. For instance, the Federal Water Pollution Control Act, 33 U.S.C. §1365(d), and the Clean Air Act, 42 U.S.C. §7604(d).

53. Court-ordered payments cover the costs associated with litigating the case, but do not cover many related costs such as those incurred while conducting background studies and identifying violations (Interview, Natural Resources Defense Council, San Francisco, June 25, 1998). The tax code also provides an incentive to litigate, in that organizations can be tax exempt if they litigate on behalf of the causes they support, but not if they lobby on behalf of them (Rose-Ackerman 1995, p. 151).

54. Fines are paid to the EPA or relevant state environmental agency and not to the group that brought the "citizen suit." However, if a violator chooses to settle out of court with the group prosecuting the case, it may agree to pay the group a portion of the sum that might have been paid to the government had the litigation continued.

55. Environmental groups had first used the courts in the mid-1960s when mounting challenges to the authorization of DDT (Rose-Ackerman 1995, p. 151).

56. By the end of the 1970s, the Supreme Court had overturned many lower court rulings against the government for violations of NEPA. Thereafter, federal courts began treating NEPA's EIS requirement as a "paper exercise," ruling in favor of the government, so long as it prepared an EIS. See Wenner 1994, p. 152.

57. Enforcement suits under the Clean Air Act were particularly difficult because proving violations required expertise in control technologies and dispersion modeling that most groups lacked at this time (Melnick 1983).

58. 16 U.S.C. §1536 (1988).

59. This was a return to its earlier position. Prior to the 1970s, the Court had long held that Article III of the Constitution restricted standing to plaintiffs with a concrete individual interest in particular "cases and controversies" (Melnick 1983, p. 9).

60. Justice Scalia explained that "although a suitor may drive great comfort and joy from the fact that the United States Treasury is not cheated, that a wrongdoer gets his just deserts, or that the Nation's laws are faithfully enforced, that psychic satisfaction is not an acceptable Article III remedy because it does not redress a cognizable Article III injury" (*Steel Co.*, 523 S. Ct. at 107).

61. See, for instance, *Friends of the Earth, Inc. v. Crown Central Petroleum Corp.*, 95 F.3d 358 (5th Cr. 1996), where the Fifth Circuit denied Friends of the Earth standing under the Clean Water Act, citing the criteria for standing developed in *Lujan II*.

62. See, for instance, *Long Island Soundkeeper Fund v. New York Athletic Club,* U.S. Dist. LEXIS 3383 (S.D.N.Y. 1996), where a district court in New York rejected a defendant's claim that plaintiff lacked standing to sue under the Resource Conservation and Recovery Act. For a recent list of such cases, see EPA 1997a.

4. Environmental Regulation in Germany

1. Germany does have a federal president, but the president is not elected in a popular vote and plays a primarily ceremonial role. See Currie 1994, p. 137.
2. See ibid., p. 140. One qualifier to this reversal of control is that the smaller party in the coalition government may threaten to exit the coalition.
3. On environmental legislation, see Jarass and DiMento 1993, p. 52; Boehmer-Christiansen and Skea 1991, p. 104.
4. The number of states increased from eleven to sixteen with reunification. The number of representatives each state has in the *Bundesrat* is related to population size, varying from three to six. There are currently sixty-eight members. Much like the EU's Council of Ministers, the *Bundesrat's* actual composition varies according to the matter at issue; for instance, when the *Bundesrat* considers environmental issues environmental ministers participate. A state's representatives to the *Bundesrat* do not vote as individuals, but instead cast their state's votes as a block.
5. Greve (1989, pp. 237–239) traces the roots of this emphasis on individual rights back to a nineteenth-century debate among German legal theorists. Prussian legal theorists argued that administrative courts should be part of the administration, entrusted with the task of ensuring that rules were followed precisely. Theorists in southern states argued that administrative courts should be independent and that their aim should be to protect individual rights. When the Nazis rose to power they supported the former view, which thereafter was understood to be guilty by association. With the establishment of the Federal Republic after the war, the model of independent courts focused on protecting individual rights was seen as fundamental to the establishment of a liberal democracy.
6. The Constitutional Court has held this to mean that reviewing courts must examine facts *de novo* and not rely on findings recorded by administrators. See Currie 1994, p. 163.
7. This remedy was established by statute after the founding of the Federal Republic and was enshrined in the Constitution by an amendment made in 1969 (art. 93, I N.4a). See Currie 1994, p. 164.
8. Half of the Constitutional Court's members are chosen by the *Bundestag* and half by the *Bundesrat.* For a more general discussion of the guarantees of judicial independence in Germany, see Currie 1994, pp. 153–162.
9. The other four federal supreme courts focus on civil and criminal law *(Bundesgerichtshof)*, tax law *(Bundesfinanzhof)*, administrative law *(Bundesverwaltungsgericht)*, labor law *(Bundesarbeitsgericht)*, and social law *(Bundes-*

sozialgericht). Lower, state-level courts are divided along the same lines. See Von Oertzen 1983, p. 266.

10. Criminal and civil courts play a role. They hear environmental cases where plaintiffs seek compensation for infringements of their property rights and cases involving criminal violations by polluters. See Schlemminger and Wissel 1996, pp. 195–237. If environmental cases involve questions of constitutional law, they may be brought before the Federal Constitutional Court.

11. Lehmbruch (1989) discusses the earlier history of this division of competences. Although the postwar Constitution provides the relevant frame of reference for this study, the practice of delegating implementation of federal laws to the states goes back to the nineteenth century.

12. By 1980 there were over 1,100 such citizens groups active throughout Germany, though not all had joined the BBU (Boehmer-Christiansen and Skea 1991, p. 85).

13. Within the coalition government, much of the impetus for pushing an ambitious environmental program came from the FDP Interior Minister Genscher. See Kloepfer 1994, p. 99.

14. Previous air pollution control regulations had been adopted under the federal competence regarding economic affairs (Basic Law, art. 74(11)).

15. The act is sometimes translated into English as the Federal Emission Control Act.

16. For a more detailed overview (in German) of the development of federal legislation in this period, see Kloepfer 1994, pp. 96–104.

17. The original Water Resources Act went into effect in 1960 and established a federal framework for a permitting system to control effluents. Under its general guidelines, states set actual water quality standards. The Waste Water Charges Act requires polluters who hold effluent permits to pay fees that vary depending on the noxiousness of their discharges (Rose-Ackerman 1995, pp. 29, 166; Jarass and Dimento 1993, pp. 61–62).

18. *Strafgesetzbuch* §§324–330; *Burgerliches Gesetzbuch* §§862, 906–907. See Greve 1989, p. 223.

19. Chemicals are regulated under the Chemicals Act (*Chemikaliengesetz* (ChemG)). Subsequently, the federal government has taken on some additional implementation duties under the Plant Protection Act (*Pflanzenschutzgesetz* (PflSchG)) and the Gene Technology Act (*Gentechnikgesetz* (GenTG)).

20. The Greens's vote share dropped to 3.9 percent in 1990 as public attention focused on reunification. The Greens resurged in the 1994 election, forming a coalition with an East German Group, *Bündnis 90,* and capturing 7.3 percent of the vote. In the 1998 election, the Greens/*Bündnis 90* won 6.7 percent of the vote and subsequently entered a federal government for the first time, as part of a coalition with the Social Democrats. The Greens increased their vote share to 8.6 percent in the 2002 election and remained part of the coalition government.

21. On the general effect that the EU had on the centralization of policymaking

within Germany, see Benz 1991, pp. 591–592; Hrbek 1999; and Schneider (1999).

22. However, in some areas, such as urban waste-water treatment, EU directives are transposed into German law by state-level regulations (Interview, European Commission Directorate General XI, March 1998).

23. Directive 85/337, [1985] OJ L175/40.

24. Directive 90/313, [1990] OJ L158/56.

25. Act on Environmental Impact Assessment (*Gesetz über die Umweltverträglichkeitsprüfung* (UVPG)) (1990).

26. Environmental Information Act (*Umweltinformationsgesetz* (UIG)) (1994).

27. Administrative Court Procedure Act *(Verwaltungsgerichtsordnung)* §42(2). See Rose-Ackerman 1995, p. 193.

28. Basic Law, arts. 84(2), 85(2); Rehbinder 1989, p. 9.

29. *TA Luft* was originally formulated in 1964, before the Federal Emission Protection Act was even adopted, and has been modified on several occasions subsequently to update technical requirements and to increase the stringency of controls (Rose-Ackerman 1995, pp. 58–59, 79; Boehmer-Christiansen and Skea 1991, pp. 171–173; Schlemminger and Wissel 1996, pp. 37–39).

30. Administrative Procedures Act *(Verwaltungsverfahrengesetz)* §§28, 66–71.

31. The Federal Air Pollution Control Act (BImSchG) §51, the Waste Avoidance and Waste Management Act (AbfG) §16, and the Chemicals Act (ChemG) §§17(1),(7) all include such requirements. However, the Water Management Act (WHG) §7a does not. See Greve 1989, p. 205, and Rose-Ackerman 1995, p. 67.

32. In addition, private parties affected by the implementation of a state regulation may challenge its constitutionality before the courts. However, such cases have played an insignificant role. See Schlemminger and Wissel 1996, p. 211; Rose-Ackerman 1995, pp. 72–81.

33. Basic Law, art. 19(4). By contrast, neither the constitutions nor any supreme court decisions in the other polities in this study guarantee judicial review of administrative action as a general matter. Regarding the United States, see Currie 1994, p. 163.

34. 8 BVerfGE 274, 326 (1958); 11 BVerfGE 168, 192 (1960). See Currie 1994, p. 163.

35. The German Constitution can be amended with the support of two-thirds of the members of the lower house and with two-thirds of the votes in the upper house (Basic Law, art. 79(2)).

36. Law for the Relief of Courts in the Administrative and Financial Judiciary *(Gesetz zur Entlastung des Gerichts in der Verwaltungs- und Finanzgerichtsbarkeit)* §2(9).

37. See *Baugeseztbuch* §§214–215.

38. 65 BVerwGE 313, 320 (1982) and 29 BVerGE 37, 42 (1984); BIMschG §5(1)(ii); 61 BVerwGE 256 (1981); AtG §7(2)(iii).

39. On the limited role of federal ministries more generally, see Mayntz and Scharpf 1975, pp. 45–46.

40. There is an exception in the area of water pollution control, where federal officials can by threaten to withhold federal subsidies to *Länder* for water treatment plants (Rehbinder 1989, p. 9).

41. See Administrative Court Procedure Act *(Verwaltungsgerichtsordnung)* §42(2). Nature protection is an exception. In implementing the Federal Nature Protection Act *(Bundesnaturschutzgesetz)*, several states have adopted provisions permitting selected nature conservation organizations to bring challenges in the administrative courts in the general interests of nature (Rose-Ackerman 1995, p. 90).

42. Along with challenging the specific administrative decision in question, private parties may challenge the constitutionality of the relevant state regulation or guideline, but such claims have had a very limited impact (Greve 1989, p. 213; Schlemminger and Wissel 1996, p. 211).

43. BnatSchG §§29(1)–(2). The approval process has a corporatist flavor. In order to be officially licensed to participate in administrative proceedings, a group must demonstrate that it promotes environmental protection on a permanent basis, that it is organized regionally or nationally, and that it can guarantee an adequate performance of its tasks. See Greve 1989, p. 215.

44. The Administrative Procedures Act §42(2) and the Federal Nature Protection Act §29(1) permit states to adopt more extensive judicial review procedures than those permitted under federal law (Schwarze and Schmidt-Assmann 1992, p. 27; Von Oertzen 1983, p. 271; Greve 1989, p. 215).

45. C-361/88, *Commission v. Germany*, [1991] ECR 2567.

46. See, for instance, C-131/88, *Commission v. Germany*, [1991] ECR I-825; C-58/89, *Commission v. Germany*, [1991] ECR 4893; C-59/89, *Commission v. Germany*, [1991] ECR 2607; C-262/95, *Commission v. Germany*, [1996] ECR 5729.

47. See C-431/92, *Commission v. Germany*, [1995] ECR 2189; C-301/95, *Commission v. Germany*, [1998] ECR 6135.

48. Directive 80/778, [1980] OJ L229.

49. C-237/90, *Commission v. Germany*, [1992] ECR 5973. See Hessel and Mortelmans 1993, pp. 918, 935.

50. Directive 91/271, [1991] OJ L135.

51. C-297/95, *Commission v. Germany*, [1996] ECR 6739.

52. C-422/92, *Commission v. Germany*, [1995] ECR 1097.

5. Environmental Regulation in Australia and Canada

1. The Australian government departs from the Westminster model somewhat, in that the Senate is a powerful independent actor. The impact of the Senate is analyzed below.

2. The Senate may also propose or amend legislation. In practice, however, only senators from the party that holds a majority in the lower house of Parliament can introduce bills in the Senate. (Nongovernment senators have only succeeded in passing a handful of bills during the ninety-six years of the Senate's

existence.) The Senate committees that review legislation are chaired by members of the governing party, regardless of whether that party controls a majority in the Senate. See *Odger's Australian Senate Practice*, 10th ed., available at *www.aph.gov.au/senate/pubs/html/httoc.htm*.

3. Only the small parties, such as the Greens, might advocate such legislation. As partners in Senate majority coalitions, these parties have been in the position to demand amendments, but they have lacked the power to demand a total reorientation in the style of environmental legislation.

4. While the Constitution granted the commonwealth government no powers specifically relating to the environment, it did give the commonwealth power over fisheries beyond territorial waters and quarantine, which had some relevance to the environment.

5. This explains the curious fact that "national" parks in Australia are actually controlled by state governments. See Murchison 1995, p. 515.

6. One exception was the bird protection groups that, in 1909–1910, pressed the federal government to use its customs power to prohibit the export of endangered bird species. See Hutton and Connors 1999, pp. 17–26.

7. The environment had gained status in the cabinet a year earlier with the creation of the portfolio for Environment, Aborigines and Arts (Gilpin 1980).

8. Commonwealth involvement in environmental regulation was justified by its powers to regulate external affairs, corporations, and races, but for the most part not by its power to regulate interstate commerce. The power to regulate interstate commerce, which proved so potent in the United States, has had less of an impact in Australia, where the High Court has not developed a "stream of commerce" doctrine linking intrastate commerce to interstate commerce. See Gilpin 1980, p. 146; Murchison 1995, pp. 510–517.

9. *Murphyores Inc. Pty. Ltd. v. Commonwealth*, 136 C.L.R. 1 (1976). See Toyne 1994, p. 23; Bates 1995, p. 78; Saunders 1996, p. 60; and Hutton and Connors 1999, pp. 146–149.

10. *Commonwealth v. Tasmania*, 46 A.L.R. 625 (1983).

11. World Heritage Properties Conservation Act 1983 (Cth).

12. The court struck out sections of the act that made "blanket" prohibitions on classes of activities, holding that the prohibition of such activities might not always be necessary in order to protect an area under the World Heritage Convention and that, therefore, such prohibitions would have to be made on a case-by-case basis.

13. In the case of the Franklin Dam, the races power was held to apply because the construction of the dam threatened to submerge some caves of historical significance to the aborigines.

14. *Victoria v. Commonwealth*, 99 C.L.R. 575 (Austl. 1957).

15. Queensland argued that the rain forests did not satisfy the criteria to warrant protection under the 1983 act, despite the fact the area had been accepted onto the World Heritage List. The High Court refused the application on the grounds that Queensland did not make a sufficient case for why the area did not warrant listing. *Queensland v. Commonwealth*, 62 *ALJR* 143 (1988).

16. The National Estate had been established in 1975 with the Australian Heritage Commission Act, which created a commission to hear nominations and make decisions regarding the listing of sites on the National Estate. Once an area is listed on the National Estate, the commonwealth government is obliged to minimize the negative impacts on the area of any actions it takes.

17. The Lemonthyme and Southern Forests (Commission of Inquiry) Act 1987.

18. The inquiry commission presented its conclusions in May 1988. The majority recommended that only a small portion of the area be nominated for World Heritage listing. The commonwealth ignored these findings and instead negotiated an agreement with Tasmania.

19. Originally the body was to be called the National Environmental Protection Authority, but the name was subsequently changed to the National Environmental Protection Council.

20. National Environmental Council Act 1994 (Cth)., available at *www.austlii .edu.au/au/legis/cth/consol_act/nepca1994432/index.html#longtitle*. In 2001, the NEPC was incorporated within the Environment Protection and Heritage Council (EPHC).

21. National Environment Protection Council (Ambient Air Quality) Measure, available at *www.ephc.gov.au*.

22. For the text of the act, see *http://scaleplus.law.gov.au/html/comact/10/6006/ top.htm*.

23. These matters are World Heritage properties, Ramsar wetlands of international significance, listed threatened species and ecological communities, listed migratory birds, commonwealth marine areas, and nuclear actions (including uranium mining).

24. The Environment Protection and Biodiversity Conservation Regulations 2000, available at *www.erin.gov.au/epbc/about/index.html*.

25. EPBC Act §§57–64, available at *http://scaleplus.law.gov.au/html/comact/10/ 6006/top.htm*.

26. Administrative Appeals Tribunal Act of 1975; the Federal Court Act of 1976; and the Administrative Decisions (Judicial Review) Act of 1977.

27. The requirements for standing before tribunals are more lax than those for actual courts. Section 27 of the AAT provides that "an organisation or association of persons, whether incorporated or not, shall be taken to have interests that are affected by a decision if the decision relates to a matter included in the objects or purposes of the organisation or association" (Bates 1992, p. 355).

28. The federal government reached accords with only seven provinces, as Quebec, Newfoundland, and British Columbia refused to sign (Skogstad 1996, p. 108).

29. The Ocean Dumping Control Act was passed to implement an international agreement to which Canada was a party, the 1972 London Convention on ocean dumping.

30. The Environmental Contaminants Act did provide that the federal government could issue federal regulations for hazardous substances, but only if it concluded, after mandatory consultation with provincial governments, that

provincial laws would not adequately address the hazard (Doern and Conway 1994, p. 217).

31. *R. v. Crown Zellerbach Ltd. et al.*, [1988] 1 S.C.R. 401.

32. The crucial element of the new "national concern" test was the "provincial inability" test: could provincial failure to deal effectively with the intraprovincial aspects of the matter have an adverse affect on interprovincial interests? If so, the matter might be one of national concern (Hughes, Lucas, and Tilleman 1993, p. 49). But see Lucas and Sharvit 2000, p. 140, where the authors maintain that the Supreme Court's POGG test will still limit the federal government from setting minimum standards for ambient levels of pollution.

33. In its first incarnation, this institution was called the Canadian Council of Resource Ministers. In 1970, environmental ministers joined the group and it was renamed the Canadian Council of Resource and Environment Ministers (Harrison 1996, p. 72).

34. See Harrison 2000a, pp. 8–10, regarding the failed 1995 Environmental Management Framework Agreement (EMFA).

35. Soon after signing the Canada-Wide Environmental Inspections Sub-Agreement, parties to the agreement decided that the agreement should be subsumed into a broader subagreement on inspections and enforcement, which would link these two activities.

36. The term "national standards" was avoided in deference to Quebec's sensitivity regarding the terms "nation" and "national," but Quebec nevertheless chose not to sign the agreement.

37. Canada-Wide Environmental Standards Sub-Agreement art. 5.2.1, available at *www.mbnet.mb.ca/ccme/3e_priorities/3ea_harmonization/3ea2_cws/3ea2a .html.*

38. See Swanson and Hughes 1990, pp. 110–111, for a discussion of judicial deference in environmental matters.

39. *Canadian Wildlife Federation Inc. v. Canada (Minister of the Environment)*, [1989] 3 F.C. 309 (T.D.).

40. *Friends of the Oldman River Society v. Canada (Minister of Transport)*, [1992] 1 S.C.R. 3.

6. Food and Drug Safety Regulation in the EU

1. Directives 64/432/EEC; 644/433/EEC; 69/464/EEC; 69/465/EEC.

2. The German beef ban followed a ban they had enacted on imports of British meat-and-bone meal (a suspected disease vector for BSE) in May 1989.

3. When OVPIC inspectors conducted direct inspections, they always did so accompanied by and in cooperation with national inspectors (Interviews European Commission, November 28, 1996, June 19, 1997 and June 25, 1997).

4. OVPIC's staffing problem stemmed in part from the Council's 1993 decision to relocate the OVPIC to Ireland, where many inspectors refused to relocate (Interview, European Commission, November 28, 1996).

5. Commission Decision 96/239/EC, [1996] OJ L 078, pp. 47–48.

6. The Standing Veterinary Committee (SVC) is a type IIIa regulatory committee (a "contre-filet" committee). Under the comitology procedures that apply to this type of committee, Commission proposals go into effect if they win a qualified majority vote in the committee. If not, the proposal goes on to the Council, which may adopt it by qualified majority, reject it by simple majority, or do neither, in which case the Commission can adopt the proposal on its own responsibility.

7. Article 138c of the Maastricht Treaty gave the Parliament the power to establish such committees. The BSE committee was only the second one established. See Smith and Kelemen 1997).

8. The Parliament opposed the relocation because it feared that the location would isolate inspectors from activities in Brussels (European Parliament 1997c; *Agence Europe* 1997d).

9. The Commission had first suggested the creation of a European Food Authority in a January 2000 white paper. See Commission 1999a.

10. Regulation 178/2002 laying down the general principles and requirements of food law, establishing the European Food Safety Authority, and laying down procedures in matters of food safety ([2002] OJ L31/1, February 1, 2002).

11. The Commission's staffing goal follows on the recommendation of a report by the inspector general's service. See Commission 1998a, p. 4.

12. The directive had previously left member states the option of exempting primary agricultural products. Council Directive on the Approximation of the Laws, Regulations and Administrative Provisions of the Member States Concerning Liability for Defective Products, Council Directive 85/374, OJ L210/29.

13. Directive 1999/34/EEC, OJ L141, p. 20.

14. Thalidomide is a sedative that was once prescribed to pregnant women and only later was found to cause serious birth defects. The scandal surrounding thalidomide led to the expansion of federal drug safety regulation in the United States (Quirk 1980).

15. Directive 65/65/EEC, OJ 22, February 9, 1975, p. 369/65. This directive has been amended many times since its passage in 1965 and still forms an important basis of the EU's involvement in drug safety regulation.

16. Directive 75/318/EEC, OJ L147, June 9, 1975, p. 1, on the approximation of the laws of the member states relating to analytical pharmaco-toxicological and clinical standards and protocols for testing medicinal products. Directive 75/319/EEC, OJ L147, June 9, 1976, p. 13, on approximation of provisions laid down by law, regulation, and administrative action relating to proprietary medicinal products. See Vogel 1998, pp. 5–7.

17. In 1981, the EU established similar provisions for veterinary medicinal products, including a parallel advisory committee—the Committee for Veterinary Medicinal Products (CVMP). See Directive 81/851/EEC, OJ L317, November 6, 1981, p. 1; Directive 81/852/EEC, OJ L317, November 7, 1981, p. 16.

18. Directive 75/319/EEC, OJ L147, June 9, 1976.

19. See, for example, Directive 89/342 EEC, laying down provisions for immunological medicinal products consisting of vaccines, toxins, or serums and allergens (OJ L142, May 25, 1989, p. 14); Directive 89/343/EEC, laying down additional provisions for radiopharmaceuticals (OJ L142, May 25, 1989, p. 16); Directive 89/381/EEC, on proprietary medicinal products and laying down special provisions for medicinal products derived from human blood or plasma (OJ L181, June 28, 1989, p. 44); Directive 91/356/EEC, laying down the principles and guidelines of good manufacturing practice for medicinal products for human use (OJ L193, July 17, 1991, p. 30).

20. Directive 87/22/EEC, OJ L15, January 17, 1987, p. 38.

21. See OJ C330, December 31, 1990, p. 1; OJ C310, November 30, 1991, p. 7.

22. Council Regulation 2309/93, OJ L214, August 24, 1993. The advisory committees for human and veterinary medicinal products that had played a role in previous Community-level drug evaluation, the CPMP and the CVMP, were incorporated into the new agency.

23. The management board appoints an executive director for the agency, on a proposal by the Commission. The executive director serves a five-year term during which he or she manages the operations of the agency.

24. The details of the procedure are somewhat more intricate. An agency scientific committee (the CPMP or the CVMP, depending on the product in question) is charged with the assessment of a product. The committee designates one of its members to serve as rapporteur and another to serve as co-rapporteur. The rapporteur then enlists his or her national laboratories to conduct the actual testing.

25. This procedure was established with the founding of the agency and its details were formalized in a partnership agreement signed in 1997 (EMEA 1997b).

26. A member state may revoke authorization for a centrally approved product on an emergency basis if it detects a risk to human or animal health or the environment. However, such decisions are subject to review by the Commission. Council Regulation 2309/93, art. 18, OJ L214, Augustt 24, 1993.

27. I focus here on medicinal products for human use. Similar patterns have developed for veterinary medicinal products, though less products have been submitted via the centralized procedure. See EMEA 2000.

28. The EMEA supervised over two hundred such inspections in its first five years of operation. See EMEA 2001a, p. 41, for recent figures.

29. In 1995, a subsidy from the regular EU budget financed approximately 70 percent of the EMEA's budget, while application fees made up most of the remaining 30 percent. By 2000, the EU subsidy dropped to approximately 25 percent and fees provided over 70 percent (EMEA 1996, 2000).

30. Council Directive on the Approximation of the Laws, Regulations and Administrative Provisions of the Member States Concerning Liability for Defective Products, Council Directive 85/374, OJ L(210/29). See Kelemen and Sibbitt (2003).

31. This section draws on Kelemen (2002).

32. For instance, Pollack (1997) discusses the member states' use of comitology committees as "police patrol" oversight mechanisms. On differences between the member states' and EP's preferences regarding oversight mechanisms, see Franchino 2000. More generally, see McCubbins and Schwarz 1984.

33. The agencies were allowed to commence operations only after the European Council announced a package deal agreeing on locations for the agencies and other decentralized EU bodies, such as the European Central Bank and Europol (Official Bulletin, EC, October 29, 1993, pp. 12–13). In addition to the agencies listed in Table 2, the Council also agreed on sites for the European Central Bank (Frankfurt), Europol (the Hague), the European Training Foundation (Turin), and the Translation Centre (Luxembourg). It also agreed on a relocation of the European Centre for the Development of Vocational Training (from Berlin to Thessaloniki) and of the Commission's Office of Veterinary and Plant Inspection and Control from Brussels to Ireland (to a site to be specified by the Irish government). The site of the Community Plant Variety Office was not mentioned in this package deal and was not finally settled until the 1996 intergovernmental conference.

34. The idea of establishing independent bodies within the Community framework was not new. In the 1960s and 1970s, the Commission made a number of proposals for the establishment of independent agencies. However, member states opposed most of these proposals and only two weak agencies, the European Centre for the Development of Vocational Training and the European Foundation for the Improvement of Living and Working Conditions, were established during that period (Shapiro 1996b; Kelemen 1997).

35. Even a self-aggrandizing bureaucracy may support the delegation of regulatory functions to agencies outside its control where the loss of bureaucratic turf allows the agency to focus on its core competences. See Wilson 1989, pp. 182–183; Yataganas 2001, p. 42.

36. The proposal was based on Article 130(s) of the Single European Act and was subject to the consultation procedure.

37. In a compromise with advocates for a stronger agency, such as Germany, the Netherlands, and the EP's environment committee, the agency's founding regulation included a clause calling for a review of its functions after two years—with the possibility that monitoring and inspection activities would be expanded (Interview, EEA Taskforce Official, May 1994).

38. Most agency directors are appointed by the management board following a proposal from the Commission, usually for a renewable five-year term. There are some exceptions to this pattern. For instance, the president and vice-president of the Office of Harmonization are appointed by the Council from a list of candidates prepared by the administrative board. Members of the agencies' scientific committees, too, are appointed by the management boards.

39. Kreher (1996, p. 11) notes that the Council acted to limit the Parliament's influence through its choice of legal bases. Where the Commission tried to base proposals for agencies on treaty articles subject to the cooperation procedure,

the Council changed the legal basis back to the Treaty of Rome's Article 235, which was subject to the consultation procedure.

40. The legal bases for the proposals for the Monitoring Centre on Racism and Xenophobia and the European Agency for Reconstruction did not call for the co-decision procedure. Therefore, the EP was not in the position to exert significant influence over their designs.

41. Advocates of a European cartel office hoped to establish the agency via the intergovernmental route at the 1996 Intergovernmental Conference (IGC), but failed to win the support of enough member states.

42. C-9/56, *Meroni v. High Authority,* [1957–1958] ECR 133. See also the parallel judgment of June 13, 1958 in C-10/56, *Meroni v. High Authority,* [1957–1958] ECR 157. Also see Lenaerts 1993, p. 41; Everson 1995, pp. 196–198.

7. Institutional Structure and Regulatory Style

1. For a recent elaboration of this argument, see Bednar, Eskridge, and Ferejohn 2001.

2. Eskridge and Ferejohn (1994, p. 1545) suggest that the structure of American political institutions encourages Congress and the courts engage in a "virtual logroll" in which "the court asserts a rights creating power for those issues it cares most about, while deferring to the most intense rights-creating preferences of Congress."

3. On the impact of variations in domestic legal aid structures and access to justice provisions, see Conant 2001; Harlow 1999; Caporaso and Jupille 2001; Alter and Vargas 2000.

References

ACIR (Advisory Commission on Intergovernmental Relations). 1984. *Regulatory Federalism: Policy, Impact, Process and Reform.* Washington, D.C.: GPO.

———. 1993. *Federal Regulation of State and Local Governments: The Mixed Record of the 1980s.* Washington, D.C.: U.S. Advisory Commission on Intergovernmental Relations.

Adelberger, Karen. 1999. "Federalism and Its Discontents: Fiscal and Legislative Powersharing in Germany, 1948–1999." Working Paper no. 99–16. University of California at Berkeley, Institute of Governmental Studies.

Afifalo, Ari. 1999. "Towards a 'Common Law' of Europe: Effective Judicial Protection, National Procedural Autonomy and Standing to Litigate Diffuse Interests in the European Union." *Suffolk Transnational Law Review* 22: 349.

Agence Europe. 1997a. "EU/Infringements." January 9.

———. 1997b. "EU/Environment." January 30.

———. 1997c. "Jacques Santer announces that Commission is to modify management of veterinary affairs." January 16.

———. 1997d. "EU:EU/EP/Health/Consumers—In Mrs. Bonino's presence, parliamentary committee strongly criticizes the forthcoming transfer of the FVO to Ireland." May 27.

———. 1997e. "EU/EP/'Mad Cow'—Interim Report." September 26.

———. 1998. "Food Control. Commission explains why it does not support creation of an independent agency for food control and inspections." January 6.

Allen, David. 1996. "Cohesion and Structural Adjustment." In Helen Wallace and William Wallace, eds., *Policy-Making in the European Union.* Oxford: Oxford University Press.

Alter, Karen. 1996. "The European Court's Political Power." *West European Politics* 19(3): 458–487.

———. 1998. "Who are the 'Masters of the Treaty'?: European Governments and the European Court of Justice." *International Organization* 52(1): 121–147.

———. 2001. *Establishing the Supremacy of European Law: The Making of an International Rule of Law in Europe.* Oxford: Oxford University Press.

Alter, Karen, and Sophie Meunier-Aitsahalia. 1994. "Judicial Politics in the European Community." *Comparative Political Studies* 26(4): 535–561.

Alter, Karen, and Jeannette Vargas. 2000. "Explaining Variation in the Use of European Litigation Strategies: European Community Law and British Gender Equality Policy." *Comparative Political Studies* 33(4): 452–482.

Araiza, William D. 2000. "Alden v. Main and the Web of Environmental Law." *Loyola of Los Angeles Law Review* 33: 1513.

Baar, Carl. 1991. "Judicial Activism in Canada." In Kenneth Holland, ed., *Judicial Activism in Comparative Perspective*. New York: St. Martins.

Bakvis, Herman, and William M. Chandler, eds. 1987. *Federalism and the Role of the State*. Toronto: University of Toronto Press.

Bardach, Eugene, and Robert Kagan. 1982. *Going by the Book: The Problem of Regulatory Unreasonableness*. Philadelphia: Temple University Press.

Bates, Gerry. 1992. *Environmental Law in Australia*, 3rd ed. Sydney: Butterworths.

———. 1995. *Environmental Law in Australia*, 4th ed. Sydney: Butterworths.

Bednar, Jenna, William Eskridge, and John Ferejohn. 2001. "A Political Theory of Federalism." In John Ferejohn, Jack N. Rakove, and Jonathan Riley, eds., *Constitutional Culture and Democratic Rule*. New York: Cambridge University Press.

Bednar, Jenna, John Ferejohn, and Geoffrey Garrett. 1996. "The Politics of European Federalism." *International Review of Law and Economics* 16: 279–294.

Begg, Ian. 1996. "Introduction: Regulation in the European Union." *Journal of European Public Policy* 3(4): 525–535.

Benz, Arthur. 1991. "Perspektiven des Föderalismus in Deutschland." *Die Öffentliche Verwaltung*, no. 14.

Betlem, Gerrit. 2001. "Strict Environmental Liability and NGO Damages and Enforcement Claims: A Dutch and International Law Perspective." MS, University of Exeter.

Bird, Ian B., and Miguel A. Veiga-Pestana. 1993. "European Community Environmental Policy and Law." In Ralph Folsom, Ralph Lake and Ved Nanda, eds., *European Community Law after 1992*. Deventer, Netherlands: Kluwer Law and Taxation Publishers.

Blair, Philip M. 1981. *Federalism and Judicial Review in West Germany*. Oxford: Clarendon Press.

Blankenburg, Erhard, and Rüdiger Voigt. 1987. "*Implementation von Gerichtsentscheidungen*." *Jahrbuch für Rechtssoziologie und Rechtstheorie*, vol. XI. Opladen: Westdeutscher Verlag.

Blühdorn, Ingolfur. 1995. "Campaigning for Nature: Environmental Pressure Groups in Germany and Generational Change in the Ecology Movement." In Ingolfur Blühdorn, Frank Drause, and Thomas Scharf, eds., *The Green Agenda: Environmental Politics and Policy in Germany*. Keele, UK: Keele University Press.

Boardman, Robert, ed. 1992. *Canadian Environmental Policy: Ecosystems, Politics, and Process.* Toronto: Oxford University Press.

Boehmer-Christiansen, Sonja, and Jim Skea. 1991. *Acid Politics: Environmental and Energy Policies in Britain and Germany.* New York: Belhaven Press.

Bonyhady, Tim, ed. 1992. *Environmental Protection and Legal Change.* Sydney: Federation Press.

Börzel, Tanja. 1998. "Shifting or Sharing the Burden? The Implementation of EU Environmental Policy in Spain and Germany." *European Planning Studies* 6(5): 537–553.

Brinkhorst, Laurens Jan. 1996. "The Future of European Agencies: A budgetary Perspective from the European Parliament." In Alexander Kreher, ed., *The New European Agencies.* EUI Working Paper, RSC no. 96149. Florence: European University Institute.

Brown, M. Paul. 1992. "Organizational Design as Policy Instrument: Environment Canada in the Canadian Bureaucracy." In Robert Boardman, ed., *Canadian Environmental Policy: Ecosystems, Politics, and Process.* Toronto: Oxford University Press.

Brown, Neville, and Tom Kennedy. 1994. *The Court of Justice of the European Communities.* London: Sweet and Maxwell.

Brown, R. Steven. 2001. "States Put Their Money Where Their Environment Is: State Environmental Spending." Report of the Environmental Council of the States (ECOS). Available at *www.sso.org/ecos/*.

Bryner, Gary C. 1987. *Bureaucratic Discretion.* New York: Pergamon.

Bulmer, Simon, ed. 1989. *The Changing Agenda of West German Public Policy.* Brookfield, Vt.: Dartmouth Publishing Co.

Bundesrat. 1995. *The German Federal Council (Bundesrat).* Bonn: Bundesrat, Public Relations Office.

Burgess, Michael. 1989. *Federalism and European Union: Political Ideas, Influences and Strategies in the European Community, 1972–1987.* New York: Routledge.

———. 2000. *Federalism and European Union: The Building of Europe, 1950–2000.* London: Routledge.

Burley, Anne-Marie, and Walter Mattli. 1993. "Europe before the Court: A Political Theory of Legal Integration." *International Organization* 47: 41–76.

Bzdera, Andre. 1993. "Comparative Analysis of Federal High Courts: A Political Theory of Judicial Review." *Canadian Journal of Political Science* 26(1): 3–29.

Calvert, Randall, Matthew McCubbins, and Barry Weingast. 1989. "A Theory of Political Control and Agency Discretion." *American Journal of Political Science* 33: 588–611.

Calvert, Randall, Mark Moran, and Barry Weingast. 1987. "Congressional Influence over Policy Making: The Case of the FTC." In Matthew McCubbins and Terry Sullivan, eds., *Congress: Structure and Policy,* Cambridge: Cambridge University Press.

Canberra Times. 1999. "Environment Is a Federal Issue." June 28, pt. TVG, p. 8.

Caporaso, James, and Joseph Jupille. 2001. "The Europeanization of Gender Equality Policy and Domestic Structural Change." In Maria Green Cowles, James Caporaso, and Thomas Risse, eds., *Transforming Europe.* Ithaca: Cornell University Press.

Cappelletti, Mauro, Monica Seccombe, and Joseph Weiler. 1986. *Integration through Law: Europe and the American Federal Experience.* New York: W. de Gruyter.

Caulfield, Henry. 1989. "The Conservation and Environmental Movements: An Historical Analysis." In James Lester ed., *Environmental Politics and Policy: Theories and Evidence.* Durham: Duke University Press.

Cecchini, Paolo. 1988. *The European Challenge: The Benefits of a Single Market.* Aldershot: Wildwood House.

CCME (Canadian Council of Ministers of the Environment). 2000. "Two-Year Review of Canada-Wide Accord on Environmental Harmonization." Available at *www.mbnet.mb.ca/ccme/2e_new/2e.html.*

Chambers, Graham. 1999. "The BSE Crisis and the European Parliament." In Christian Joerges and Ellen Vos, eds., *EU Committees: Social Regulation, Law and Politics.* Oxford: Hart Publishing.

Chappell, Duncan. 1988. *From Sawdust to Toxic Blobs: A Consideration of Sanctioning Strategies to Combat Pollution in Canada.* Ottawa: Ministry of Justice.

Cichowski, Rachel A. 1998. "Integrating the Environment: The European Court and the Construction of Supranational Policy." *Journal of European Public Policy* 5(3): 387–405.

———. 2001. Litigation, compliance and european integration: The preliminary ruling procedure and EU nature conservation policy. Paper presented at the 2001 annual meeting of the European Community Studies Association, Madison, Wisconsin, May 31–June 2.

Collins, Ken, and David Earnshaw. 1993. "The Implementation and Enforcement of European Community Environment Legislation." In David Judge, ed., *A Green Dimension for the European Community: Political Issues and Processes.* Portland, Ore.: Frank Cass.

Commission of the European Communities. 1982. *Manual of Procedure.* 5th updating. March.

———. 1985. *Completing the Internal Market.* COM(85) 310 final.

———. 1991. *Eighth Annual Report to the European Parliament on Commission Monitoring of the Application of Community Law.* OJ C338/1.

———. 1995a. *VAT Collection and Control Procedures Applied in Member States.* Second Article 12 Report, Regulation EEC/Euratom no. 1553/89.

———. 1995b. *Twelfth Annual Report on Monitoring the Application of Community Law.* COM(95) 500 final.

———. 1996a. *Communication from the Commission: Implementing Community Environmental Law.* COM(96) 500 final.

———. 1996b. *Thirteenth Annual Report on Monitoring the Application of Community Law.* COM(96) 600 final.

———. 1996c. *Communication on Environmental Agreements.* COM(96) 561 final.

———. 1996d. *The Agencies of the European Union.* Luxembourg: Office for Official Publications of the European Communities.

———. 1996e. *Proposal for a Council Regulation (EC) Establishing a European Agency for Veterinary and Phytosanitary Inspection.* COM(96) 223 final.

———. 1997a. *Communication from the Commission: Consumer Health and Food Safety.* COM(97) 183 final.

———. 1997b. "Bonino Speech on Food Law and Food Policy." European Commission Press Release: Speech/97/233. November 5.

———. 1997c. *Final Consolidated Report to the Temporary Committee of the European Parliament on the Follow-up of Recommendations on BSE.* COM(97) 509 final.

———. 1998a. *Communication from the Commission to the European Parliament, The Council and the Economic and Social Committee on Food, Veterinary and Plant Health Control and Inspection.* COM(1998) 32 final.

———. 1998b. *Report on the Initial Visits by the Commission's Services to the Member States Pursuant to Article 5 of the Council Directive 93/99 EEC with a View to Evaluating the National Systems for the Official Control of Foodstuffs.* COM(1998) 37 final.

———. 1998c. *Proposal for a Council Decision on the prohibition of the Use of Material Presenting Risks as Regards Transmissible Spongiform Encephalopathies and Repealing Decision 97/534/EC.* COM(1998) 160 final.

———. 1998d. *Proposal for a Council Decision Concerning Emergency Measures to Protect against Bovine Spongiform Encephalopathy, Amending Decision 94/474/EC and Repealing Decision 96/239/EC.* COM(1998) 161 final.

———. 1998e. *Communication on the State of the Environment in the 6 Länder of the Former East Germany.* COM(1998) 33 final.

———. 1998f. *Proposal for a Council Recommendation Providing for Minimum Criteria for Environmental Inspections in the Member States.* COM(1998) 772 final.

———. 1999a. *White Paper on Food Safety.* COM(99) 719 final. January 12.

———. 1999b. *Food and Veterinary Office (FVO) Annual Report 1999.* Available at *www.europa.eu.int/comm/food/fs/inspections/policy_papers/vi_pol07_en.pdf.*

———. 1999c. *Sixteenth Annual Report on Monitoring the Application of Community Law.* COM(1999) 301 final.

———. 2000a. *Proposal for a Regulation of the European Parliament and of the Council Laying Down the General Principles and Requirements of Food Law, Establishing the European Food Authority, and Laying Down Procedures in Matters of Food.* COM(2000) 716 final. November 8.

———. 2000b. *Seventeenth Annual Report on Monitoring the Application of Community Law.* COM(2000) 92 final.

————. 2000c. *Second Annual Survey On the Implementation and Enforcement of Community Environmental Law—January 1998–December 1999.* Working Document of the Commission Services, Directorate General XI.

————. 2000d. *Green Paper on Legal Aid in Civil Matters.* COM(2000) 51 final. Brussels, February 9.

————. 2000e. *White Paper on Environmental Liability.* COM(2000) 66 final.

————. 2000f. *Food and Veterinary Office (FVO) Annual Report 1999.* Available at *www.europa.eu.int/comm/food/fs/inspections/policy_papers/ann_rep_2000_en.pdf.*

————. 2000g. *Report from the Commission on the Application of Directive 85/374 on Liability for Defective Products.* COM(2000) 893 final.

————. 2000h. "Bathing Water: Commission Acts Against Several Member States." European Commission Press Release: IP/00/14. January 11.

————. 2002. "Community Legislation on BSE." Available at *http://europa.eu .int/comm/food/fs/bse/bse15_en.pdf.*

Conant, Lisa. 2001. "Europeanization and the Courts: Variable Patterns of Adaptation among National Judiciaries." In Maria Green Cowles, James Caporaso, and Thomas Risse, eds., *Transforming Europe: Europeanization and Domestic Change.* Ithaca: Cornell University Press.

Conlan, Timothy J., James D. Riggle, and Donna E. Schwartz. 1995. "Deregulating Federalism? The Politics of Mandate Reform in the 104th Congress." *Publius* 25: 3.

Cooter, Robert, and Josef Drexl. 1994. "The Logic of Power in the Emerging European Constitution: Game Theory and the Division of Powers." *International Review of Law and Economics* 14: 307–326.

Cooter, Robert, and Tom Ginsburg. 1996. "Comparative Judicial Discretion: An Empirical Test of Economic Models." *International Review of Law and Economics* 16: 295–313.

Cotler, Irwin. 1996. "Can the Center Hold? Federalism and Rights in Canada." In Ellis Katz and G. Alan Tarr, eds., *Federalism and Rights.* London: Rowman and Littlefield.

Council of State Governments. 1996. *Resource Guide to State Environmental Management,* 4th ed. Lexington, Ky.: Council of State Governments.

Council of the European Union. 1997. "200th Meeting of the Council on 21 and 22 April 1997 in Luxembourg." Press Release, 7361/97 (Presse 109). April 22.

Cowles, Maria Green, James Caporaso, and Thomas Risse, eds. 2001. *Transforming Europe: Europeanization and Domestic Change.* Ithaca: Cornell University Press.

Craig, Robin Kundis. 2001. "Will Separation of Powers Challenges 'Take Care' of Environmental Citizen Suits? Article II, Injury-in Fact, Private 'Enforcers' and Lessons from Qui Tam Litigation." *University of Colorado Law Review* 72:93.

Crawford, James. 1992. "The Constitution." In Tim Bonyhady, ed., *Environmental Protection and Legal Change.* Sydney: Federation Press.

Cripps, J. S. 1992. "Administrative Law." In Tim Bonyhady, ed., *Environmental Protection and Legal Change*. Sydney: Federation Press.

Crook, Stephen, and Jan Pakulski. 1995. "Shades of Green: Public Opinion on Environmental Issues in Australia." *Australian Journal of Political Science* 30: 39–55.

Crombez, Christophe. 1996. "Legislative Procedures in the European Community." *British Journal of Political Science* 26: 199–218.

Currie, David P. 1993. "Separation-of-Powers in the Federal Republic of Germany." *American Journal of Comparative Law* 41: 201.

———. 1994. *The Constitution of the Federal Republic of Germany*. Chicago: University of Chicago Press.

Davies, J. Clarence, and Barbara Davies. 1975. *The Politics of Pollution*. Indianapolis, Ind.: Pegasus.

Davis, Charles E., and James P. Lester. 1989. "Federalism and Environmental Policy." In James Lester, ed., *Environmental Politics and Policy: Theories and Evidence*. Durham: Duke University Press.

De Búrca, Gráinne. 1995. "The Language of Rights and European Integration." In Jo Shaw and Sarah Moore, eds., *New Legal Dynamics of European Union*. Oxford: Oxford University Press.

Dehousse, Renaud. 1992. "Integration v. Regulation? On the Dynamics of Regulation in the European Community." *Journal of Common Market Studies* 30(4): 383–402.

———. 1997. "Regulation by Networks in the European Community: The Role of European Agencies." *Journal of European Public Policy* 4(2): 240–261.

———. 1998. "European Institutional Architecture after Amsterdam: Parliamentary System or Regulatory Structure?" *Common Market Law Review* 35: 595–627.

Den Boer, Monica, and Neil Walker. 1993. "European Policing after 1992." *Journal of Common Market Studies* 31(1): 3–28.

Derthick, Martha. 1999. "How Many Communities? The Evolution of American Federalism." In Martha Derthick, ed., *Dilemmas of Scale in America's Federal Democracy*. Cambridge: Cambridge University Press.

Dillon, Sara. 1999. "The Mirage of EC Environmental Federalism in a Reluctant Member State Jurisdiction." *New York University Environmental Law Journal* 8: 1.

Doern, G. Bruce, and Thomas Conway. 1994. *The Greening of Canada: Federal Institutions and Decisions*. Toronto: University of Toronto Press.

Downes, David. 1996. "Neo-corporatism and Environmental Policy." *Australian Journal of Political Science* 31(2): 175–190.

Doyle, Timothy. 2000. *Green Power: The Environmental Movement in Australia*. Sydney: University of New South Wales Press.

Doyle, Timothy, and Aynsley Kellow. 1995. *Environmental Politics and Policy Making in Australia*. South Melbourne: MacMillan.

Duncan, Allan G. 2000. The History of IMPEL. Available on European Union website at *www.europa.eu.int/comm/environment/impel/*.

Dunlap, Riley. 1989. "Public Opinion and Environmental Policy." In James Lester, ed., *Environmental Politics and Policy: Theories and Evidence*. Durham: Duke University Press.

Dwyer, John P. 1995. "The Practice of Federalism under the Clean Air Act." *Maryland Law Review* 54: 1183.

Dyson, Kenneth, ed. 1992. *The Politics of German Regulation*. Brookfield, Vt.: Dartmouth Publishing Co.

Economist. 1991. "The Dirty Dozen." July 20.

———. 2000. "Our Constitution for Europe." October 28.

EEA (European Environment Agency). 1997. *EEA Annual Report 1996*. Luxembourg: Office for Official Publications of the European Communities.

———. 2000. *Annual Report 2000. Annex: Key figures for budgetary and staff resources*. Available at *www.org.eea.eu.int/documents/ar2000/Annex*.

Elazar, Daniel J. 1987. *Exploring Federalism*. Tuscaloosa, Ala.: University of Alabama Press.

ELDR (Group of the European Liberal, Democrat and Reform Party in the European Parliament). 1995. *Deregulation in the Single Market*. Brussels: European Parliament.

Elliott, Donald E., Bruce A. Ackerman, and John C. Millian. 1985. "Toward a Theory of Statutory Evolution: The Federalization of Environmental Law." *Journal of Law, Economics and Organization* 1(2): 313–340.

EMEA (European Agency for the Evaluation of Medicinal Products). 1996. *First General Report—1995*. London: EMEA.

———. 1997a. *First General Report—1997*. London: EMEA.

———. 1997b. *Statement of Principles Governing the Partnership between the National Competent Authorities and the EMEA*. EMEA/MB/013/97. London: EMEA.

———. 2000. *Sixth General Report—2000*. London: EMEA.

———. 2001a. *Seventh General Report—2001*. London: EMEA.

———. 2001b. "Update December 2001: Medicinal Products Granted a Community Marketing Authorisation under the Centralised Procedure." EMEA/34608/02. Available at *www.emea.eu.int/pdfs/general/direct/listprod/3460802.pdf.*

Emison, Gerald. 1996. "From Compelling to Catalyzing: The Federal Government's Changing Role in Environmental Protection." *William and Mary Environmental Law and Policy Review* 20.

Ends Environment Daily. 2001. "Legal Actions Announced over EU Waste Rules." No. 1038. July 30.

Engel, Kirsten. 1997. "State Environmental Standard-Setting: Is There a 'Race' and Is It 'to the Bottom'?" *Hastings Law Journal* 48: 271.

Engel, Kirsten, and Susan Rose-Ackerman. 2001. "Environmental Federalism in the United States: The Risks of Devolution." In Daniel C. Esty and Damien Geradin, eds., *Regulatory Competition and Economic Integration: Comparative Perspectives*. Oxford: Oxford University Press.

Environment Australia 1992. *Intergovernmental Agreement on the Environment (IGAE)*. Available at *www.environment.gov.au/psg/igu/igae.html*.

EPA (Environmental Protection Agency). 1997a. *Water Enforcement Bulletin* 13. February. EPA, Office of Regulatory Enforcement, Office of Enforcement and Compliance Assistance, Water Enforcement Division.

———. 1997b. "EPA Memo." August 20, 1997. Available at *www.epa.go/ regional/pps/memo.html*.

———. 2001. "EPA Releases FY 2000 Enforcement and Compliance Assurance Data," EPA Press Release. January 19. Available at www.*es.epa.gov/oeca/r-20 .pdf*.

Epp, Charles. 1998. *The Rights Revolution: Lawyers, Activists, and Supreme Court in Comparative Perspective*. Chicago: University of Chicago Press.

Epstein, David, and Sharyn O'Halloran. 1994. "Administrative Procedures, Information, and Agency Discretion." *American Journal of Political Science* 38(3): 697–722.

———. 1999. *Delegating Powers: A Transaction Cost Politics Approach to Policy Making under Separate Powers*. Cambridge: Cambridge University Press.

Eskridge Jr., William N., and John Ferejohn. 1994. "The Elastic Commerce Clause: A Political Theory of American Federalism." *Vanderbilt Law Review* 47(5): 1355.

Esty, Daniel C., and Damien Geradin, eds. 2001. *Regulatory Competition and Economic Integration: Comparative Perspectives*. Oxford: Oxford University Press.

European Ombudsman. 1999. *Annual Report for 1999*. Available at *www.euro-ombudsman.eu.int/report/en/dEFSAult.htm*.

European Parliament. 1984. *European Parliament Resolution*. OJ C127/67. April 11.

———. 1994. *Jurisprudence de la Cour de Justice des Communautés Européenes dans le Domaine de L'environement*. Direction Générale des Etudes, Document de Travail, W-8. Luxembourg: Parlement Européen.

———. 1996. *Committee on the Environment, Public Health and Consumer Protection, Working Document on Implementation of Community Environmental Law*. PE 219.420. October 9.

———. 1997a. *Committee on the Environment, Public Health and Consumer Protection, Report on a Communication from the Commission on Implementing Community Environmental Law*. PE 221.176 final. March 21.

———. 1997b. *Report on Alleged Contraventions or Maladministration in the Implementation of Community Law in Relation to BSE*. DOCS.PE220.544 A/FIN, *Annexes I–IX and B*. February 7.

———. 1997c. "EP Committee Hears Bonino on Vet Service Transfer to Ireland." European Parliament News Report Press Release. May 22.

———. 1998. "EP Committee Hears Rapporteur Reimer Boge." European Parliament News Report Press Release. February 4.

Everson, Michelle. 1995. "Independent Agencies: Hierarchy Beaters?" *European Law Journal* 1: 180.

Everson, Michelle, Giandomenico Majone, Les Metcalfe, and Adrian Schout. 1999. *The Role of Specialised Agencies in Decentralising EU Governance. Report Presented to the Commission.* Available at *www.europa.eu.int/comm/governance/areas/group6/contribution_en.pdf.*

Fafard, Patrick C., and Kathryn Harrison, eds. 2000. *Managing the Environmental Union: Intergovernmental Relations and Environmental Policy in Canada.* Montreal: McGill-Queen's University Press.

Farber, Daniel A. 1992. "Politics and Procedure in Environmental Law." *Journal of Law, Economics and Organization* 8(1): 59–81.

Farrier, David, and Linda Tucker. 1998. "Beyond a Walk in the Park: The Impact of International Nature Conservation Law on Private Land in Australia." *Melbourne University Law Review* 22: 564.

Faure, Michael. 2001. "Regulatory Competition vs. Harmonization in EU Environmental Law." In Daniel C. Esty and Damien Geradin, eds., *Regulatory Competition and Economic Integration: Comparative Perspectives.* Oxford: Oxford University Press.

Federal Ministry for the Environment, ed. 1992. *Environmental Protection in Germany: National Report of the Federal Republic of Germany for the United Nations Conference on Environment and Development in June 1992 in Brazil.* Bonn: Economica Verlag.

Ferejohn, John. 1995. "Law, Legislation and Positive Political Theory." In Jeffrey Banks and Eric Hanushek, eds., *Modern Political Economy: Old Topics, New Directions.* New York: Cambridge University Press.

Ferejohn, John, and Barry Weingast. 1992. "Limitations of Statutes: Strategic Statutory Interpretation." *Georgetown Law Journal* 80: 565.

Ferejohn, John and Barry Weingast, eds. 1997. *The New Federalism: Can the States Be Trusted?* Stanford, Calif.: Hoover Institution Press.

Financial Times. 1992. "The High Costs of a Cleaner Europe." November 3.

———. 1994. "Can Europe Compete?" March 3.

Flynn, Leo. 1999. "The Implications of Article 13 EC—After Amsterdam, Will Some Forms of Discrimination Be More Equal Than Others?" *Common Market Law Review* 36: 1127.

Forsyth, Murray. 1981. *Unions of States: The Theory and Practice of Confederation.* Leicester: Leicester University Press.

Franchino, Fabio. 2000. "Control of the Commission's Executive Functions: Uncertainty, Conflict and Decision Rules." *European Union Politics* 1(1): 63–92.

———. 2001. "Delegation and Constraints in the National Execution of EC Policies: A Longitudinal and Qualitative Analysis." *West European Politics* 24(4): 169–92.

Friedrich, Carl J. 1968a. *Constitutional Government and Democracy: Theory and Practice in Europe and America,* 4th ed. Waltham, Mass.: Blaisdell Publishing.

———. 1968b. *Trends of Federalism in Theory and Practice.* New York: Praeger.

Galligan, Brian. 1987. *Politics of the High Court: A Study of the Judicial Branch of Government in Australia.* New York: University of Queensland Press.

———. 1991. "Judicial Activism in Australia." In Kenneth Holland, ed., *Judicial Activism in Comparative Perspective*. New York: St. Martin's Press.

———. 1995. *A Federal Republic: Australia's Constitutional System of Government*. Cambridge: Cambridge University Press.

Garrett, Geoffrey. 1992. "International Cooperation and Institutional Choice: The European Community's Internal Market." *International Organization* 46(2): 533–560.

———. 1995. "From the Luxembourg Compromise to Co-decision: Decision Making in the European Union." *Electoral Studies* 14(3): 289–308.

Garrett, Geoffrey, R. Daniel Kelemen, and Heiner Schulz. 1998. "The European Court of Justice, National Governments and Legal Integration in the European Union." *International Organization* 52(1): 149–176.

Garrett, Geoffrey, and George Tsebelis. 1996. "An Institutional Critique of Intergovernmentalism." *International Organization* 50(2): 269–299.

Garrett, Geoffrey, and Barry Weingast. 1993. "Ideas, Interests and Institutions: Constructing the European Community's Internal Market." In Judith Goldstein and Robert O. Keohane, eds., *Ideas and Foreign Policy*. Ithaca: Cornell University Press.

Garrett, Theodore L. 1991. "Citizen Suits." In Janet S. Kole and Larry D. Espel, eds., *Environmental Litigation*. Chicago: American Bar Association.

Gaynor, Kevin A., et al. 1991. "Environmental Criminal Prosecution." In Janet Kole and Larry Espel, eds., *Environmental Litigation*. Chicago: American Bar Association.

Geddes, Andrew C. 1995. *Protection of Individual Rights under EC Law*. Boston: Butterworths.

Gely, Rafael, and Spiller, Pablo T. 1992. "The Political Economy of Supreme Court Constitutional Decisions: The Case of Roosevelt's Court-packing Plan." *International Review of Law and Economics* 12: 45–67.

George, Alexander. 1979. "Case Studies and Theory Development: The Method of Structured, Focused Comparison." In Paul Lauren, ed., *Diplomacy: New Approaches in History, Theory and Policy*. New York: Free Press.

Gilles, Myriam E. 2001. "Representational Standing: U.S. ex rel. Stevens and the Future of Public Law Litigation." *California Law Review* 89: 315.

Gilpin, Alan. 1980. *Environmental Policy in Australia*. New York: University of Queensland Press.

Goldstein, Leslie Friedman. 2001. *Constituting Federal Sovereignty: The European Union in Comparative Context*. Baltimore: Johns Hopkins University Press.

Golub, Jonathan. 1994. "The Pivotal Role of British Sovereignty in EC Environmental Policy." EUI Working Paper, RSC no. 94/17. Florence: European University Institute.

———. 1996. "Why Did They Sign? Explaining EC Environmental Policy Bargaining." EUI Working Paper, RSC no. 96/52. Florence: European University Institute.

———. 1998. *New Instruments for Environmental Policy in the EU*. London: Routledge.

———. 1999. "In the Shadow of the Vote? Decision Making in the European Community." *International Organization* 50: 269–299.

Grande, Edgar. 1996. "The State and Interest Groups in a Framework of Multilevel Decision-making: The Case of the European Union." *Journal of European Public Policy* 3(3): 318–338.

Green, Andrew J. 1999. "Public Participation, Federalism and Evironmental Law." *Buffalo Environmental Law Journal* 6: 169.

Gress, Franz. 1996. "Interstate Cooperation and Territorial Representation in Intermestic Politics." *Publius* 26(1): 53–71.

Greve, Michael S. 1989. "The Non-Reformation of Administrative Law: Standing to Sue and Public Interest Litigation in West German Environmental Law." *Cornell International Law Journal* 22: 197.

Haagsma, Auke. 1989. "The European Community's Environmental Policy: A Case-study in Federalism." *Fordham International Law Journal* 12: 311.

Haas, Ernst B. 1958. *The Uniting of Europe: Political, Social and Economic Forces, 1950–57.* Stanford, Calif.: Stanford University Press.

Halberstam, Daniel. 2001. "Comparative Federalism and the Issue of Commandeering." In Kalypso Nicolaidis and Robert Howse, eds., *The Federal Vision: Legitimacy and Levels of Governance in the U.S. and the EU.* Oxford: Oxford University Press.

Harris, Michael, and Vicki Waye, eds. 1991. *Administrative Law.* Sydney: Federation Press.

Harrison, Kathryn. 1996. *Passing the Buck: Federalism and Canadian Environmental Policy.* Vancouver: UBC Press.

———. 2000a. "Intergovernmental Relations and Environmental Policy: Concepts and Context." In Patrick Fafard and Kathryn Harrison, eds., *Managing the Environmental Union: Intergovernmental Relations and Environmental Policy in Canada.* Montreal: McGill-Queens University Press.

———. 2000b. "The Origins of National Standards: Comparing Federal Government Involvement in Environmental Policy in Canada and the United States." In Patrick Fafard and Kathryn Harrison, eds., *Managing the Environmental Union: Intergovernmental Relations and Environmental Policy in Canada.* Montreal: McGill-Queens University Press.

Hartley, Trevor C. 1994. *The Foundations of European Community Law,* 3rd ed. New York: Oxford University Press.

Harlow, Carol. 1998. "European Administrative Law and the Global Challenge." EUI Working Paper, RSC no. 98/23. Florence: European University Institute. Available at *www.iue.it/RSC/WP-Texts/98_23.html.*

———. 1999. "Citizen Access to Political Power in the European Union." EUI Working Paper, RSC no. 99/2. Florence: European University Institue. Available at *www.iue.it/RSC/WP-Texts/99_2t.html.*

Haward, Marcus, and Graham Smith. 1992. "What's New About the 'New Federalism.'" *Australian Journal of Political Science* 27.

Héritier, Adrienne, Susanne Mingers, Christoph Knill, and Martina Becka. 1994. *Die Veränderung von Staatlichkeit in Europa: Ein regulativer Wettbewerb:*

Deutschland, Grossbritannien und Frankreich in der Europäischen Union. Opladen: Leske and Budrich.

Hesse, Joachim Jens, and Vincent Wright. 1996. *Federalizing Europe? The Costs, Benefits, and Preconditions.* Oxford: Oxford University Press.

Hessel, Bart, and Kamiel Mortelmans. 1993. "Decentralized Government and Community Law: Conflicting Institutional Developments?" *Common Market Law Review* 30: 905–937.

Hildebrand, Philipp M. 1993. "The European Community's Environmental Policy, 1957 to '1992': From Incidental Measures to an International Regime?" In David Judge, ed., *A Green Dimension for the European Community: Political Issues and Processes.* Portland, Ore.: Frank Cass.

Hix, Simon. 1999. *The Political System of the European Union.* New York: St. Martin's Press.

Hodas, David R. 1995. "Enforcement of Environmental Law in a Triangular Federal System: Can Three Not Be a Crowd When Enforcement Authority Is Shared by the United States, the States, and Their Citizens?" *Maryland Law Review* 54: 1552.

Hoffman, Stanley. 1966. "Obstinate or Obsolete? The Fate of the Nation State and the Case of Western Europe." *Daedalus* 95(4): 862–915.

———. 1982. "Reflections on the Nation-State in Western Europe Today." *Journal of Common Market Studies* 21(1,2): 212–37.

Holland, Kenneth, ed. 1991. *Judicial Activism in Comparative Perspective.* New York: St. Martins.

———. 1996. "The Role of the Courts in the Making and Administration of Environmental Policy in the U.S." In Kenneth M. Holland, F. L. Morton, and Brian Galligan, eds., *Federalism and the Environment: Environmental Policymaking in Australia, Canada, and the United States.* Westport, Conn.: Greenwood Press.

Holland, Kenneth M., F. L. Morton, and Brian Galligan. 1996. *Federalism and the Environment: Environmental Policymaking in Australia, Canada, and the United States.* Westport, Conn.: Greenwood Press.

Horn, Murray. 1995. *The Political Economy of Public Administration: Institutional Choice in the Public Sector.* Cambridge: Cambridge University Press.

Howlett, Michael. 1994. "The Judicialization of Canadian Environmental Policy 1980–1990: A Test of the Canada–United States Convergence Thesis." *Canadian Journal of Political Science* 27(1).

Hrbek, Rudolf. 1999. "The Effects of EU Integration on German Federalism." In Charlie Jeffery, ed., *Recasting German Federalism: The Legacies of Unification.* London: Pinter.

Hucke, Jochen. 1985. "Environmental Policy: The Development of a New Policy Area." In Klaus von Beyme and Manfred Schmidt, eds., *Policy and Politics in the Federal Republic of Germany.* Aldershot, UK: Gower Publishing.

Hughes, Elaine L., Alastair R. Lucas, and William A. Tilleman II. 1993. *Environmental Law and Policy.* Toronto: Emond Montgomery Publications.

Humphrey, Hubert H., and LeRoy C. Paddock. 1990. "The Federal and State

Roles in Environmental Enforcement: A Proposal for a More Effective and More Efficient Relationship." *Harvard Environmental Law Review* 14(1).

Hutton, Drew, and Libby Connors. 1999. *A History of the Australian Environmental Movement.* Cambridge: Cambridge University Press.

IMPEL (European Union Network for the Implementation and Enforcement of Environmental Law). 2000. *Complaint Procedures and Access to Justice for Citizens and NGOs in the Field of Environment within the European Union.* Available at *www.europa.eu.int/comm/environment/impel/access_to_justice.htm.*

Ingram, Helen, and Dean Mann. 1978. "Environmental Policy: From Innovation to Implementation." In Theodore Lowi and Alan Stone, eds., *Nationalizing Government: Public Policies in America.* Beverly Hills: Sage Publications.

Jachtenfuchs, Markus, and Beate Kohler-Koch, eds. *Europäische Integration.* Opladen: Leske and Budrich.

Jackson, Vicki. 2000. "Seductions of Coherence, State Sovereign Immunity and Denationalization of Federal Law." *Rutgers Law Journal* 31: 691.

Jacobs, Francis, Richard Corbett, and Michael Shackleton. 1995. *The European Parliament,* 3rd ed. London: Catermill Publishing.

Jarass, Hans D., and Joseph Dimento. 1993. "Through Comparative Lawyers' Goggles: A Primer on German Environmental Law." *Georgetown International Environmental Law Review* 6(1): 47.

Jeffery, Charlie. 1999. *Recasting German Federalism: The Legacies of Unification.* London: Pinter.

Joerges, Christian, Yves Mény, and Joseph Weiler, eds. 2001. *What Kind of Constitution for What Kind of Polity? Responses to Joschka Fischer.* Florence: European University Institute. Available at *www.jeanmonnetprogram.org/papers/00/symp.html.*

Joerges, Christian, and Ellen Vos, eds. 1999. *EU Committees: Social Regulation, Law and Politics.* Oxford: Hart Publishing.

Johnson, Stanley, and Guy Corcelle. 1995. *The Environmental Policy of the European Communities.* The Hague: Kluwer Academic Press.

Johnstone, C. 1997. "Calls for EU telecoms agency," European Voice. April 17–23, p. 2.

Jones, Charles O. 1975. *Clean Air: The Policies and Politics of Pollution Control.* Pittsburgh: University of Pittsburgh Press.

Jordan, Andrew, Rüdiger Wurzel, and Anthony Zito. 2001. European Governance and the Transfer of "New" Environmental Policy Instruments in the European Union. Paper presented at the 2001 Biennial International Conference of the European Community Studies Association, Madison, Wisconsin, May 29–June 2.

Judge, David, ed. 1993. *A Green Dimension for the European Community: Political Issues and Processes.* Portland, Ore.: Frank Cass.

Jupille, Joseph. 1997. "Contracts, Contingencies and Coordination: The European Court of Justice and the EC's Green Market." MS, University of Washington, Department of Political Science.

Kagan, Robert. 1991. "Adversarial Legalism and American Government." *Journal of Policy Analysis and Management* 10: 369.

———. 1993. "Regulatory Enforcement." In David Rosenblum and Richard Schwartz, eds., *Handbook of Regulation and Administrative Law.* New York: Marcel Dekker.

———. 1996. "The Political Construction of American Adversarial Legalism." In Austin Ranney, ed. *Courts and the Political Process: Jack W. Peltason's Contributions to Political Science.* Berkeley: Institute for Governmental Studies Press.

———. 1997. "Should Europe Worry about Adversarial Legalism?" *Oxford Journal of Legal Studies* 17(2): 165.

———. 2001. Adversarial Legalism: The America Way of Law. Cambridge: Harvard University Press.

Kagan, Robert A., and Lee Axelrad. 1997. "Adversarial Legalism: An International Perspective." In Pietro S. Nivola, ed., *Comparative Disadvantages? Social Regulations and the Global Economy.* Washington, D.C.: Brookings.

———. 2000. *Regulatory Encounters: Multinational Corporations and American Adversarial Legalism.* Berkeley: University of California Press.

Kalb, Claudia. 1998. "When Drugs Do Harm." *Newsweek.* April 27.

Katz, Ellis, and G. Alan Tarr, eds. 1996. *Federalism and Rights.* London: Rowman and Littlefield.

Kelemen, R. Daniel. 1995. "Environmental Policy in the European Union: The struggle between Court, Commission and Council." In Brigitte Unger and Frans van Waarden, eds., *Convergence or Diversity? Internationalization and Economic Policy Response.* Aldershot, UK: Avebury.

———. 1997. "The European 'Independent' Agencies and Regulation in the EU." Working Document no. 112. Brussels: Centre for European Policy Studies.

———. 2000. "Regulatory Federalism: EU Environmental Policy in Comparative Perspective." *Journal of Public Policy* 20(2): 133–167.

———. 2001. "The Limits of Judicial Power: Trade–Environment Disputes in the GATT/WTO and the EU." *Comparative Political Studies* 34(6): 622–650.

———. 2002. "The Politics of 'Eurocratic' Structure and the New European Agencies." *West European Politics* 25(4): 93–118.

Kelemen, R. Daniel, and Eric C. Sibbitt. 2003. "The Globalization of American Law." *International Organization,* forthcoming.

Kellow, Aynsley. 1996. "Thinking Globally and Acting Federally: Intergovernmental Relations and the Politics of Environmental Protection in Canada." In Kenneth M. Holland, F. L. Morton, and Brian Galligan, eds., *Federalism and the Environment: Environmental Policymaking in Australia, Canada, and the United States.* Westport, Conn.: Greenwood Press.

Keohane, Robert. 1984. *After Hegemony: Cooperation and Discord in the World Political Economy.* Princeton: Princeton University Press.

Keohane, Robert, and Stanley Hoffman, eds. 1991. *The New European Community: Decisionmaking and Institutional Change.* San Francisco: Westview Press.

Kerr, Michael. 2000. "Briefing Note: Slipsliding Away—Weaker Environmental Laws as Senate Rejects ALP/Green EPBC Regulation Disallowance." Australian Conservation Foundation. November 28. Available at *www.acfonline.org /au/campaigns/epbc/discussion/briefingepbc.htm.*

Kibel, Paul Stanton, and Stefan Klinski. 1994. "Rapping at the Courthouse Door: Judicial Access for Environmental Advocates in the U.S. and Germany." *Journal of Environmental Law and Practice* 5(1): 59.

Kiewiet, D. Roderick, and Matthew McCubbins. 1991. *The Logic of Delegation: Congressional Parties and the Appropriations Process.* Chicago: University of Chicago Press.

Kimber, Cliona J. M. 1995. "A Comparison of Environmental Federalism in the United States and the European Union." *Maryland Law Review* 54: 1658.

———. 2000. "Implementing European Environmental Policy and the Directive on Access to Environmental Information." In Christoph Knill and Andrea Lenschow, eds., *Implementing EU Environmental Policy: New Directions and Old Problems.* Manchester, UK: Manchester University Press.

Kincaid, John. 1994a. "The New Coercive Federalism." In Franz Gress, Detlef Fetchner, and Matthias Hannes, eds., *The American Federal System: Federal Balance in Comparative Perspective.* Berlin: Peter Lang.

———. 1994b. "Economic Union and Federal Diversity." In Anne Mullins and Cheryl Saunders, eds., *Economic Union in Federal Systems.* Sydney: Federation Press.

———. 1996. "Intergovernmental Costs and Coordination in U.S. Environmental Protection." In Kenneth M. Holland, F. L. Morton, and Brian Galligan, eds., *Federalism and the Environment: Enviornmental Policymaking in Australia, Canada, and the United States.* Westport, Conn.: Greenwood Press.

Kingham, Richard F, Peter W. L. Bogaert, and Pamela S. Eddy. 1994. "The New European Medicines Agency." *Food and Drug Law Journal* 49(2): 301.

Kitschelt, Herbert. 1986. "Political Opportunity Structures and Political Protest: Anti-nuclear movements in four countries." *British Journal of Political Science* 16(1): 57–85.

Klatt, Hartmut. 1987. "Interföderale Beziehungen im kooperativen Bundesstaat: Kooperation und Koordination auf der politischen Leitungsebene." *Verwaltungsarchiv* 78: 186–206.

———. 1999. "Centralizing Trends in Western German Federalism 1949–1989." In Charlie Jeffery, ed. *Recasting German Federalism: The Legacies of Unification.* London: Pinter.

Klatte, Ernst R. 1997. "The Role of the European Environment Agency in Support of Enforcement of European Law." Paper presented at International Bar Association Seminar on Enforcement of Environmental Law in Europe, Copenhagen, March 20–22.

Kloepfer, Michael. 1994. *Zur Geschichte des deutschen Umweltrechts.* Berlin: Duncker and Humblot.

Kloepfer, Michael, and Wolfgang Durner. 1997. Der Umweltgesetzbuch-Entwurf der Sachverständigenkommission. *Deutsches Verwaltungsblatt* (DVBl), no. 18.

Knill, Cristoph, and Andrea Lenschow. 1998. "Coping with Europe: The Impact of British and German Administrations on the Implementation of EU Environmental Policy." *Journal of European Public Policy* 5(4): 595–614.

Knill, Christoph, and Andrea Lenshow, eds. 2000. *Implementing EU Environmental Policy: New Directions and Old Problems.* Manchester, UK: Manchester University Press.

Knopff, Rainer, and J. E. Glenn. 1996. "Courts, Tribunals, and the Environment in Canada." In Kenneth M. Holland, F. L. Morton, and Brian Galligan, eds., *Federalism and the Environment: Environmental Policymaking in Australia, Canada, and the United States,* Westport, Conn.: Greenwood Press.

Kohler-Koch, Beate. 1996. "Catching Up With Change: The Transformation of Governance in the European Union." *Journal of European Public Policy* 3(3): 359–380.

Kole, Janet S. and Larry D. Espel, eds. 1991. *Environmental Litigation.* Chicago: American Bar Association.

König, Klaus, Hans Joachim von Oertzen, and Frido Wagener. 1983. *Public Administration in the Federal Republic of Germany.* Deventer, The Netherlands: Kluwer.

Kraft, Michael E. 1994. "Environmental Gridlock: Searching for Consensus in Congress." In Norman J. Vig and Michael E. Kraft, eds., *Environmental Policy in the 1990s,* 2nd ed. Washington, D.C.: Congressional Quarterly Press.

Kraft, Michael E., and Norman J. Vig. 1994. "Environmental Policy from the Seventies to the Nineties: Continuity and Change." In Norman J. Vig and Michael E. Kraft, eds., *Environmental Policy in the 1990s,* 2nd ed. Washington, D.C.: Congressional Quarterly Press.

Krämer, Ludwig. 1990. *EEC Treaty and Environmental Protection.* London: Sweet and Maxwell.

———. 1992. *Focus on European Environmental Law.* London: Sweet and Maxwell.

———. 1993. "The Interdependency of Community and Member State Activity on Nature Protection within the European Community." *Ecology Law Quarterly* 20(1): 25.

———. 1995. *E.C. Treaty and Environmental Law,* 2nd ed. London: Sweet and Maxwell.

———. 1996. "Public Interest Litigation in Environmental Matters before European Courts." *Journal of Environmental Law* 8(1): 1.

Krasner, Stephen. 1983. *International Regimes.* Ithaca, N.Y.: Cornell University Press.

———. 1984. "Approaches to the State." *Comparative Politics* 16(2): 223–246.

Kreher, Alexander, ed. 1996. *The New European Agencies.* EUI Working Paper, RSC no. 96/49. Florence: European University Institute.

———. 1997. "Agencies in the European Community." *Journal of European Public Policy* 4(2): 225–245.

Ladeur, Karl-Heinz. 1996. *The EEA and Prospects for a European Network of Environmental Administrations*. EUI Working Paper, RSC no. 96/50. Florence: European University Institute.

Lazarus, Richard J. 1991. "The Tragedy of Distrust in the Implementation of Federal Environmental Law." *Law and Contemporary Problems* 54: 334.

Lefevere, Jürgen G. J. 1996. "State Liability for Breaches of Community Law. *European Environmental Law Review* August/September: 237.

Lehmbruch, Gerhard. 1989. "Institutional Linkages and Policy Networks in the Federal System of West Germany." *Publius* 19: 221–235.

———. 1992. "The Institutional Framework of German Regulation." In Kenneth Dyson, ed. *The Politics of German Regulation*. Brookfield, Vt.: Dartmouth Publishing.

Le Monde. 2000. "Le face-à-face Chevenement-Fischer." June 21.

Lenaerts, Koen. 1993. "Regulating the Regulatory Process: 'Delegation of Powers' in the European Community." *European Law Review* 18(1): 23.

Leonardy, Uwe. 1994. "The German Model of Federalism." Paper prepared for Conference on Australian Federalism: Future Directions, Centre for Comparative Constitutional Studies, University of Melbourne, July 14–15.

Leonhardt, Klaus. 1983. "The German Administration and the European Communities." In Klaus König, Hans Joachim von Oertzen, and Frido Wagener, *Public Administration in the Federal Republic of Germany*. Deventer, The Netherlands: Kluwer.

Lester, James P., ed. 1989. *Environmental Politics and Policy: Theories and Evidence*. Durham: Duke University Press.

Lester, James P. 1990. "A New Federalism? Environmental Policy in the States." In Norman Vig and Michael Kraft, eds., *Environmental Policy in the 1990s*, 2nd ed. Washington, D.C.: Congressional Quarterly Press.

———. 1994. "A New Federalism: Environmental Policy in the States." In Norman Vig and Michael Kraft, eds., Environmental Policy in the 1990s, 2nd ed. Washington, D.C.: Congressional Quarterly Press.

Lijphart, Arend. 1999. *Patterns of Democracy*. New Haven: Yale University Press.

———. 1984. *Democracies: Patterns of Majoritarian and Consensus Government in Twenty-One Countries*. New Haven: Yale University Press.

Lowi, Theodore J. 1969. *The End of Liberalism: Ideology, Politics and the Crisis of Public Authority*. New York: Norton.

Lowry, William R. 1992. *The Dimensions of Federalism: State Governments and Pollution Control Policies*. Durham: Duke University Press.

Lucas, A. R. and C. Sharvit. 2000. "Underlying Constraints on Intergovernmental Cooperation in Setting and Enforcing Environmental Standards." In Patrick Fafard and Katherine Harrison, eds., *Managing the Environmental Union: Intergovernmental Relations and Environmental Policy in Canada*. Montreal: McGill-Queen's University Press.

Ludlow, Peter. 1991. "The European Commission." In Robert O. Keohane and Stanley Hoffman, eds., *The New European Community: Decision-making and Institutional Change*. San Francisco: Westview Press.

Lynch, Georgina, and Brian Galligan. 1996. "Environmental Policymaking in Australia: The Role of the Courts." In Kenneth M. Holland, F. L. Morton, and Brian Galligan, eds., *Federalism and the Environment: Environmental Policy-making in Australia, Canada, and the United States*. Westport, Conn.: Greenwood Press.

Macpherson, Robert. 2001. "EU leaders move forward on reforms, stumble on agencies." *Agence France Press*, December 16.

Macrory, Richard. 1992. The Enforcement of Community Environmental Laws: Some Critical Issues. *Common Market Law Review* 29: 347.

———. 1994. "Community Supervision in the Field of the Environment." Paper presented at Enforcement of EC Environmental Law Conference, University of Warwick, July 7–8.

Madison, James. (1987 [1788]). "Federalist No. 51." In James Madison, Alexander Hamilton, and John Jay. *The Federalist Papers*. London: Penguin.

Majone, Giandomenico. 1993. The European Community between Social Policy and Social Regulation. *Journal of Common Market Studies* 31(2): 153–170.

———. 1994a. "The Rise of the Regulatory State in Europe." *West European Politics* 17(3): 78–102.

———. 1994b. "Understanding Regulatory Growth in the European Community." EUI Working Paper, SPS no. 94/17. Florence: European University Institute.

———. 1994c. "Independence vs. Accountability?" EUI Working Paper, SPS no. 94/3 Florence: European University Institute.

———. 1995. "Mutual Trust, Credible Commitments and the Evolution of Rules for a Single European Market." EUI Working Paper, RSC no. 95/1. Florence: European University Institute.

———. 1996. *Regulating Europe*. London: Routledge.

———. 1997. "The New European Agencies: Regulation by Information." *Journal of European Public Policy* 4(2): 262–275.

———. 2000. "The Credibility Crisis of Community Regulation." *Journal of Common Market Studies* (38)2: 273–302.

Marcus, Alfred A. 1980. *Promise and Performance: Choosing and Implementing an Environmental Policy*. Westport, Conn.: Greenwood Press.

Marks, Gary, Liesbet Hooghe, and Kermit Blank. 1996. "European Integration from the 1980s: State-Centric v. Multi-level Governance." *Journal of Common Market Studies* 34(3): 341–378.

Martin, Isabelle. 1994. "The Limitations to the Implementation of a Uniform Environmental Policy in the European Union." *Connecticut Journal of International Law* 9: 675.

Martin, Lisa. 1993. "Credibility, Costs and Institutions: Cooperation on Economic Sanctions." *World Politics* 45(3): 406–432.

Mashaw, Jerry. 1990. "Explaining Administrative Process: Normative, Positive and Critical Stories of Legal Development." *Journal of Law, Economics and Organization* 6: 267–298.

Mashaw, Jerry L., and Susan Rose-Ackerman. 1984. "Federalism and Regulation." In George C. Eads and Michael Fix, eds., *The Reagan Regulatory Strategy.* Washington, D.C.: Urban Institute Press.

Mayhew, David R. 1974. *Congress: The Electoral Connection.* New Haven: Yale University Press.

Mayntz, Renate, et al. 1978. *Vollzugsprobleme der Umweltpolitik.* Stuttgart: Kohlhammer.

Mayntz, Renate, and Fritz W. Scharpf. 1975. *Policy-making in the German Federal Bureaucracy.* New York: Elsevier.

Mazey, Sonja, and Jeremy Richardson. 1993. "Environmental Groups and the EC: Challenges and Opportunities." In David Judge, ed., *A Green Dimension for the European Community: Political Issues and Processes.* Portland, Ore.: Frank Cass.

McCloskey, Robert G. 1960. *The American Supreme Court.* Chicago: University of Chicago Press.

McCubbins, Matthew, Roger Noll, and Barry Weingast. 1987. "Administrative Procedures as Instruments of Political Control." *Journal of Law Economics and Organization* 3(2): 243–277.

———. 1989. "Structure and Process, Politics and Policy: Administrative Arrangements and the Political Control of Agencies." *Virginia Law Review* 75(2): 432–482.

———. 1999. "The Political Origins of the Adminstrative Procedures Act." *Journal of Law, Economics and Organization* 15(1): 180–217.

McCubbins, Matthew, and Thomas Schwartz. 1984. "Congressional Oversight Overlooked. Police Patrols versus Fire Alarms." *American Journal of Political Science* 28(1): 165–179.

McGowan, Francis, and Hellen Wallace. 1996. "Towards a European Regulatory State." *Journal of European Public Policy* 3(4): 560–576.

McKay, David. 1999. *Federalism and European Union: A Political Economy Perspective.* Oxford: Oxford University Press.

———. 2001. *Designing Europe: Comparative Lessons from the Federal Experience.* Oxford: Oxford University Press.

Melnick, R. Shep. 1983. *Regulation and the Courts: The Case of the Clean Air Act.* Washington, D.C.: Brookings Institution.

———. 1996. "Federalism and the New Rights." *Yale Journal on Regulation and Yale Law Journal,* Symposium Issue 23.

Mendrinou, Maria. 1996. "Non-compliance and the European Commission's role in integration." *Journal of European Public Policy* 3(1): 1–22.

Mény, Yves, Pierre Muller, and Jean-Louis Quermonne, eds. 1996. *Adjusting to Europe: The Impact of the European Union on National Institutions and Policies.* New York: Routledge.

Milgrom, Paul, Douglas North, and Barry Weingast. 1990. "The Role of Institutions in the Revival of Trade: The Law Merchant, Private Judges and the Champagne Fairs." *Economics and Politics* 2(1): 1–23.

Milgrom, Paul, and John Roberts. 1992. *Economics, Organization and Management*. Englewood Cliffs, N.J.: Prentice Hall.

Milward, A. S. 1992. *The European Rescue of the Nation-State*. Berkeley: University of California Press.

Moe, Terry. 1984. "The New Economics of Organization." *American Journal of Political Science* 28.

———. 1989. "The Politics of Bureaucratic Structure." In John E. Chubb and Paul E. Peterson, eds., *Can the Government Govern?* Washington, D.C.: Brookings.

———. 1990. "The Politics of Structural Choice: Towards a Theory of Public Bureaucracy." In Oliver E. Williamson, ed., *Organization Theory: From Chester Barnard to the Present and Beyond*. Oxford: Oxford University Press.

———. 1991. "Politics and the Theory of Organization." *Journal of Law, Economics and Organization* 7: 107–129.

Moe, Terry, and Michael Caldwell. 1994. "The Institutional Foundations of Democratic Government: A Comparison of Presidential and Parliamentary Systems." *Journal of Institutional and Theoretical Economics* 150(1): 171–195.

Moravcsik, Andrew. 1991. "Negotiating the Single European Act: National Interests and Conventional Statecraft in the European Community." *International Organization* 45(1): 19–56.

———. 1993. "Preferences and Power in the European Community: A Liberal Intergovernmentalist Approach." *Journal of Common Market Studies* 31(4): 473–524.

———. 1995. "Liberal Intergovernmentalism and Integration: A Rejoinder." *Journal of Common Market Studies* 33(4): 611–628.

———. 1998. *The Choice for Europe: Social Purpose and State Power from Messina to Maastricht*. Ithaca, N.Y.: Cornell University Press.

Morton, F. L. 1995. "The Effect of the Charter of Rights on Canadian Federalism." *Publius* 25(3).

———. 1996. "The Constitutional Division of Powers with Respect to the Environment in Canada." In Kenneth M. Holland, F. L. Morton, and Brian Galligan, eds., *Federalism and the Environment: Environmental Policymaking in Australia, Canada, and the United States*. Westport, Conn.: Greenwood Press.

Mulgan, Richard. 1996. "The Australian Senate as a 'House of Review.'" *Australian Journal of Political Science* 31(2): 191–204.

Mullan, David. 1983. "Alternatives to Judicial Review of Administrative Action: The Commonwealth of Australia's Administrative Appeals Tribunal." In Canadian Insititute for the Administration of Justice, *Judicial Review of Administrative Rulings*. Montreal: Les Éditions Yvon Blais.

Müller-Brandeck-Boquet, Gisela. 1993. "Von der Fähigkeit des deutxchen Föderalismus zur Umweltpolitik." In Volker von Prittwitz, ed. *Umweltpolitik als Modernisierungsprozess*. Opladen: Leske and Budrich.

Murchison, Kenneth M. 1995. "Environmental Law in Australia and the United

States: A Comparative Overview." *Boston College Environmental Affairs Law Review* 22:503.

Nelson, Robert. 1997. "Public Lands and Federalism." In Terry Anderson and Peter Hill, eds., *Environmental Federalism*. Lanham: Rowman and Littlefield.

NEPC (National Environmental Protection Council—Australia). 1998. *Revised Impact Statement for the Ambient Air Quality National Environment Policy Measure*. Available at *www.ephc.gov.au*.

Nicolaidis, Kalypso, and Robert Howse, eds. 2001. *The Federal Vision: Legitimacy and Levels of Governance in the U.S. and the EU*. Oxford: Oxford University Press.

Noam, Eli. 1982. "The Choice of Government Level in Regulation." *Kyklos* 35: 276–291.

Noll, Roger G., ed. 1971. *Reforming Regulation: An evaluation of the Ash Council Proposals*. Washington D.C.: Brookings.

———. 1991. "The Economics and Politics of Deregulation." Jean Monnet Chair Paper, European Policy Unit." San Domenico: European University Institute.

Nolte, Georg. 1994. "General Principles of German and European Administrative Law: A Comparison in Historical Perspective." *Modern Law Review* 57: 191.

Nugent, Neil. 1994. *The Government and Politics of the European Union*, 3rd ed. Durham: Duke University Press.

Oates, Wallace. 1997. "On Environmental Federalism." *Virginia Law Review* 83: 1321.

O'Brien, Denis. 1991. "The Impact of Administrative Review on Commonwealth Public Administration." In Michael Harris and Vicki Waye, eds., *Administrative Law*. Sydney: Federation Press.

Orzack, Louis, Kenneth I. Kaitin, and Louis Lasagna. 1992. "Pharmaceutical Regulation in the European Community: Barriers to Single market Integration." *Journal of Health Politics, Policy and Law* 17: 847–868.

Page, Thomas J. 1997. "The Limits of Devolution in Environmental Law: A Comparison of Regional and Statewide Ambient Air Quality Planning the United States and Germany." *University of Chicago Legal Forum* 1997: 527–550.

Papadakis, Elim. 1994. "Development and the Environment." *Australian Journal of Political Science* 29: 66–80.

Paterson, William. 1989. "Environmental Protection, the German Chemical Industry and Government: Self-Regulation under Pressure." In Simon Bulmer, ed., *The Changing Agenda of West German Public Policy*. Brookfield, Vt.: Dartmouth Publishing.

Peake, Ross. 1999. "Green Lobby Divided over Deal." *Canberra Times*, June 23.

Pelkmans, Jacques. 1995. "Does Regulatory Competition Yield a Better Internal Market?" Paper prepared for the conference "Competition or Harmonisation? Fiscal Policy, Regulation and Standards," Lake Starnberg, Munich, October 30–November 2.

Pelkmans, Jacques, and David Young. 1995. "European Telecommunications:

How to regulate a Liberalised Single Market?" CEPS Working Party Report no. 13. Brussels: Centre for European Policy Studies.

Percival, Robert V. 1995. "Environmental Federalism: Historical Roots and Contemporary Models." *Maryland Law Review* 54: 1141.

Peterson, Paul E. 1981. *City Limits*. Chicago: University of Chicago Press.

Pfander, James E. 1996. "Environmental Federalism in Europe and the United States: A Comparative Assessment of Regulation through the Agency of Member States." In John B. Braden, Henk Folmer, and Thomas S. Ulen, eds., *Environmental Policy with Political and Economic Integration: The European Union and the United States*. Cheltenham: Edward Elgar.

Phillips, Joseph T. 2000. "Comment: Friends of the Earth v. Laidlaw Environmental Services: Impact Outcomes, and the Future Viability of Environmental Citizen Suits." *University of Cincinnati Law Review* 68: 1281.

Pierson, Paul. 1996. "The Path to European Integration: A Historical Institutionalist Analysis." *Comparative Political Studies* 29(2).

Pinder, John. 1993. "The New European Federalism: The Idea and the Achievements." In Michael Burgess and Alain Gagnon, eds., *Comparative Federalism and Federation*. Toronto: University of Toronto Press.

Pollack, Mark. 1994. "Creeping Competences: The Expanding Agenda of the European Community." *Journal of Public Policy* 14(2): 95–145.

———. 1997. "Delegation, Agency and Agenda Setting in the European Community." *International Organization* 51(1): 99–134.

Prechal, Sacha. 1995. *Directives in European Community Law*. Oxford: Oxford University Press.

Quirk, Paul. 1980. "Food and Drug Administration." In James Q. Wilson, ed., *The Politics of Regulation*. New York: Basic Books.

Rasmussen, Hjalte. 1986. *On Law and Policy in the European Court of Justice*. Dordrecht, The Netherlands: Martinus Nijhoff Publishers.

Rehbinder, Eckard. 1976. "Controlling the Environmental Enforcement Deficit: West Germany." *American Journal of Comparative Law* 24: 373.

———. 1989. "The Federal Republic of Germany." In Turner T. Smith and Pascale Kromarek, eds., *Understanding U.S. and European Environmental Law: A Practitioner's Guide*. Norwell, Mass.: Kluwer Academic Publishers.

———. 1993. "Environmental Regulation through Fiscal and Economic Incentives in a Federalist System." *Ecology Law Quarterly* 20: 57.

———. 1996. "Locus Standi, Community Law and the Case for Harmonisation." In H. Somsen, ed., *Enforcement of EC Environmental Law*. Oxford: Oxford University Press.

Rehbinder, Eckhard, and Richard Stewart. 1985. *Environmental Protection Policy*. New York: W. de Gruyter.

Revesz, Richard. 1992. "Rehabilitating Interstate Competition: Rethinking the 'Race-to-the-Bottom' Rationale for Federal Environmental Regulation." *NYU Law Review* 67: 1210.

———. 1997a. "Federalism and Environmental Regulation: A Normative Critique." In Ferejohn and Weingast, eds., *The New Federalism: Can the States be Trusted?* Stanford, Calif.: Hoover Institution Press.

———. 1997b. "Federalism and Environmental Regulation: Lessons for the European Union and the International Community." *Virginia Law Review* 83: 1331–1346.

———. 2001. "Federalism and Regulation: Some General Considerations." In Daniel C. Esty and Damien Geradin, eds., *Regulatory Competition and Economic Integration: Comparative Perspectives.* Oxford: Oxford University Press.

Riechenberg, Kurt. 1999. "Local Administration and the Binding Nature of Community Directives: A Lesser Known Side of European Legal Integration." *Fordham International Law Journal* 22: 696.

Riker, William. 1964. *Federalism: Origin, Operation, Significance.* Boston: Little, Brown.

Ringquist, Evan J. 1993. *Environmental Protection at the State Level: Politics and Progress in Controlling Pollution.* Armonk, N.Y.: M. E. Sharpe.

Rittberger, Berthold, and Jeremy Richardson. 2001. "(Mis-)Matching Declarations and Actions? Commission Proposals in Light of the Fifth Environmental Action Programme." Paper presented at the Seventh Biennial International Conference of the European Community Studies Association (ECSA), Madison, Wisconsin, May 31–June 2.

Rose-Ackerman, Susan. 1981. "Does Federalism Matter? Political Choice in a Federal Republic." *Journal of Political Economy* 89: 1.

———. 1990. Deregulation and Reregulation: Rhetoric and Reality. *Journal of Law and Politics* 6: 287–309.

———. 1992. *Rethinking the Progressive Agenda: The Reform of the American Regulatory State.* New York: Free Press.

———. 1994. "Environmental Policy and Federal Structure: A comparison of the United States and Germany." *Vanderbilt Law Review* 47: 1587.

———. 1995. *Controlling Environmental Policy: The Limits of Public Law in Germany and the United States.* New Haven: Yale University Press.

Rosenbaum, Walter. 1994. "The Clenched Fist and the Open Hand: Into the 1990s at EPA." In Norman Vig and Michael Kraft, eds., Environmental Policy in the 1990s, 2nd ed. Washington D.C.: Congressional Quarterly Press.

Rosenberg, Gerald. 1992. "Judicial Independence and the Reality of Political Power." *Review of Politics* 54(3): 369–398.

Sandholtz, Wayne, and Alec Stone Sweet. 1998. *European Integration and Supranational Governance.* New York: Oxford University Press.

Sands, Philippe. 1990. "European Community Environmental Law: Legislation, the European Court of Justice and Common Interest Groups." *Modern Law Review* 53: 685.

Saunders, Cheryl. 1996. "The Constitutional Division of Powers with Respect to the Environment in Australia." In Kenneth M. Holland, F. L. Morton, and Brian Galligan, eds., *Federalism and the Environment: Environmental Policymaking in Australia, Canada, and the United States.* Westport, Conn.: Greenwood Press.

Sbragia, Alberta, ed. 1992a. *Euro-politics: Institutions and Policymaking in the "New" European Community*. Washington, D.C.: Brookings.

———. 1992b. "Environmental Policy in the European Community: The Problem of Implementation in Comparative Perspective." In *Towards a Transatlantic Environmental Policy: Conclusions from an International Roundtable Seminar*. Washington D.C.: European Institute.

———. 1993a. "EC Environment Policy: Atypical Ambitions and Typical Problems?" In Alan W. Cafruny and Glenda Rosenthal, eds., *The State of the European Community*, vol. 2. Boulder: Lynne Riener.

———. 1993b. "The European Community: A Balancing Act." *Publius* 23(3): 23–28.

———. 1996. "The Push-Pull of Environmental Policy Making." In Helen Wallace and William Wallace, eds., *Policy Making in the European Union*. Oxford: Oxford University Press.

Scharpf, Fritz W. 1970. *Die Politischen Kosten des Rechtstaats*. Tübingen: J. C. B. Mohr.

———. 1988. "The Joint Decision Trap: Lessons from German Federalism and European Integration." *Public Administration* 66(3): 239–278.

———. 1994. *Optionen des Föderalismus in Deutschland und Europa*. Frankfurt: Campus Verlag.

———. 1995. "Federal Arrangements and Multi-Party Systems." *Australian Journal of Political Science* 30: 27–39.

———. 1996a. "Politische Optionen im vollendeten Binnenmarkt." In Markus Jachtenfuchs and Beate Kohler-Koch, eds., *Europäische Integration*. Opladen: Leske and Budrich.

———. 1996b. "Negative and Positive Integration in the Political Economy of European Welfare States." In Gary Marks, Fritz Scharpf, Philippe Schmitter, and Wolfgang Streeck, eds., *Governance in the European Union*. London: Sage Publications.

———. 1996c. "Can There Be a Stable Federal Balance in Europe?" In Joachim Jens Hesse and Vincent Wright, eds., *Federalizing Europe? The Costs, Benefits, and Preconditions*. Oxford: Oxford Publishing Press.

———. 1999. *Governing in Europe: Effective and Democratic?* Oxford: Oxford University Press.

Schink, Alexander. 1993. "Vollzugsdefizite im Umweltschutz." *Zeitschrift für angewandte Umweltforschung* 1: 16–21.

Schlemminger, Horst, and Holger Wissel, eds. 1996. *German Environmental Law for Practitioners*. The Hague, the Netherlands: Kluwer Law International.

Schmitter, Philippe. 1996a. "Some Alternative Futures for the European Polity and Their Implications for European Public Policy." In Yves Mény, Pierre Muller and Jean-Louis Quermonne, eds., *Adjusting to Europe: The Impact of the European Union on National Institutions and Policies*. New York: Routledge.

———. 1996b. "Examining the Present Euro-Polity with the Help of Past Theories." In Gary Marks, Fritz Scharpf, Philippe Schmitter, and Wolfgang Streeck, eds., *Governance in the European Union*. London: Sage Publications.

————. 1996c. "Imagining the Future of the Euro-Polity with the Help of New Concepts." In Gary Marks, Fritz Scharpf, Philippe Schmitter, and Wolfgang Streeck, eds., *Governance in the European Union*. London: Sage Publishers.

Schneider, Hans-Peter. 1999. "German Unification and the Federal System: the Challenge of Reform." In Charlie Jeffery, ed., *Recasting German Federalism: The Legacies of Unification*. London: Pinter.

Schreckenberger, Waldemar. 1983. "Intergovernmental Relations." In Klaus König, Hans Joachim von Oertzen, and Frido Wagener, eds., *Public Administration in the Federal Republic of Germany*. Deventer, the Netherlands: Kluwer.

Schrecker, Ted. 1992. "Of Invisible Beasts and the Public Interest: Environmental Cases and the Judicial System." In Robert Boardman, ed., *Canadian Environmental Policy: Ecosystems, Politics, and Process*. Toronto: Oxford University Press.

Schuck, Peter H., and E. Donald Elliott. 1990. "To the Chevron Station: An Empirical Study of Federal Administrative Law." *Duke Law Journal* 1990: 984.

Schulz, Heiner, and Thomas König. 1999. "Institutional Reform and Decision Making Efficiency in the European Union." *American Journal of Political Science* 44(4): 653–666.

Schwarze, Jürgen, ed. 1996. *Administrative Law under European Influence: On the Convergence of the Administrative Laws of the EU Member States*. Baden-Baden: Nomos Verlagsgesellschaft.

Schwarze, Jürgen, Eberhard Schmidt-Assmann, eds. 1992. *Das Ausmass der gerichtlichen Kontrolle im Wirtschafts-, verwaltungs- und Umweltrecht*. Baden-Baden: Nomos Verlagsgesellschaft.

Shackleton, Michael. 2000. "The Politics of Codecision." *Journal of Common Market Studies* 38(2): 325–42.

Shapiro, Martin. 1981. *Courts: A Comparative and Political Analysis*. Chicago: University of Chicago Press.

————. 1988. *Who Guards the Guardians?* Athens: University of Georgia Press.

————. 1992. "The European Court of Justice." In Alberta Sbragia, ed., *Europolitics: Institutions and Policymaking in the "New" European Community*. Washington, D.C.: Brookings.

————. 1996a. "The Frontiers of Science Doctrine: American Experiences with the Judicial Control of Science-Based Decision-Making." EUI Working Paper, RSC no.96/11. Florence: European University Institute.

————. 1996b. "Independent Agencies: U.S. and EU." Jean Monnet Chair Paper no. 34. Florence: European University Institute.

————. 1997. "The Problems of Independent Agencies in the United States and the European Union." *Journal of European Public Policy* 4(2): 276–291.

————. 2001. "The Institutionalization of the European Adminstrative Space." In Alec Stone Sweet, Wayne Sandholtz, and Neil Fligstein, eds., *The Institutionalization of Europe*. Oxford: Oxford University Press.

Sharpe, Jennifer M. 1986. *The Administrative Appeals Tribunal and Policy Review*. Sydney: Law Book Company.

Shaw, Jo. 1997. "European Citizenship: The IGC and Beyond." European Integration online Papers (EIoP), vol. 1, no. 3. Available at *www.eiop.or.at/eiop/texte/1997–003.htm.*

Shepsle, Kenneth. 1992. "Bureaucratic Drift, Coalitional Drift, and Time Consistency: A Comment on Macey." *Journal of Law, Economics and Organization* 8: 111–18.

Shipan, Charles. 2000. "The Legislative Design of Judicial Review: A Formal Analysis." *Journal of Theoretical Politics* 12(3): 269–304.

Siedentop, Larry. 2001. *Democracy in Europe.* New York: Columbia University Press.

Siedentopf, Heinrich, and Jacques Ziller. 1988. *Making European Policies Work: The Implementation of Community Legislation in the Member States.* London: Sage Publications.

Skogstad, Grace. 1996. "Intergovernmental Relations and the Politics of Environmental Protection in Canada." In Kenneth M. Holland, F. L. Morton, and Brian Galligan, eds., *Federalism and the Environment: Environmental Policymaking in Australia, Canada, and the United States.* Westport, Conn.: Greenwood Press.

Skogstad, Grace, and Paul Kopas. 1992. "Environmental Policy in a Federal System: Ottawa and the Provinces." In Robert Boardman, ed. *Canadian Environmental Policy: Ecosystems, Politics, and Process.* Toronto: Oxford University Press.

Skowronek, Stephen. 1982. *Building a New American State: The Expansion of National Capacities, 1877–1920.* Cambridge: Cambridge University Press.

Smith, Mitchell P., and R. Daniel Kelemen. 1997. "The Institutional Balance: Formal and Informal Change." Centre for European Policy Studies, Working Document no. 111, July.

Smith Jr., Turner T., and Pascale Kromarek, eds. 1989. *Understanding U.S. and European Environmental Law: A Practitioner's Guide.* Norwell, Mass.: Kluwer Academic Publishers.

Somsen, Han. 1994. "Francovich and Its application to EC Environmental Law." Paper presented at the Conference on the Enforcement of EC Environmental Law, University of Warwick. July 7–8.

Soper, Philip. 1974. "The Constitutional Framework of Environmental Law." In E. Dolgin and T. Guilbert, eds., *Federal Environmental Law,* vol. 20. Washington, D.C.: Environmental Law Institute and West Publishing.

Southey, Caroline. 1996. "Fischler proposes European-type FDA." *Financial Times,* December 4.

Stein, Eric. 1981. "Lawyers, Judges and the Making of a Transnational Constitution." *American Journal of International Law* 75f: 1–27.

Stewart, Richard B. 1975. "The Reformation of American Administrative Law." *Harvard Law Review* 88: 1667.

———. 1977. "Pyramids of Sacrifice? Problems of Federalism in Mandating State Implementation of National Environmental Policy." *Yale Law Journal* 86: 1196.

———. 1993a. "Antidotes for the 'American Disease.'" *Ecology Law Quarterly* 20.

———. 1993b. "Environmental Regulation and International Competitiveness." *Yale Law Journal* 102: 2039.

Stewart, Richard, and Cass R. Sunstein. 1982. Public Programs and Private Rights. *Harvard Law Review* 95: 1193.

Stone Sweet, Alec. 1999. "Judicialization and the Construction of Governance." *Comparative Political Studies* 32: 147–184.

———. 2000. *Governing with Judges: Constitutional Politics in Europe*. Oxford: Oxford University Press.

Stone Sweet, Alec, and James Caporaso. 1998. "From Free Trade to Supranational Polity: The European Court and Integration." In Sandholtz and Stone Sweet, eds., *European Integration and Supranational Governance*. New York: Oxford University Press.

Strauss, Peter L. 1984. "The Place of Agencies in Government: Separation-of-Powers and the Fourth Branch." *Columbia Law Review* 84(3): 573.

Streeck, Wolfgang, and Philippe Schmitter. 1991. "From National Corporatism to Transnational Pluralism: Organized Interests in the Single European Market." *Politics and Society* 19(2): 133–164.

Sun, Jeanne-Mey, and Jacques Pelkmans. 1995. "Regulatory Competition in the Single Market." *Journal of Common Market Studies* 33(1): 67–89.

Sunstein, Cass. 1990. *After the Rights Revolution: Reconceiving the Regulatory State*. Cambridge: Harvard University Press.

Swanson, Elizabeth, and Elaine Hughes. 1990. *The Price of Pollution: Environmental Litigation in Canada*. Edmonton: Environmental Law Center.

Swire, Peter P. 1996. "The Race to Laxity and the Race to Undesirability: Explaining Failures in Competition among Jurisdictions in Environmental Law." *Yale Journal on Regulation* 14: 67–138.

Taggart, Michael, ed. 1986. *Judicial Review of Administrative Action in the 1980s: Problems and Prospects*. Oxford: Oxford University Press.

Tallberg, Jonas. 2000a. "Supranational Influence in EU Enforcement: the ECJ and the Principle of State Liability." *Journal of European Public Policy* 7(1): 104–21.

———. 2000b. The Anatomy of Autonomy: An Institutional Account of Variation in Supranational Influence. *Journal of Common Market Studies* 38(5): 843–864.

Thatcher, Mark. 2001. "The Commission and National Governments as Partners: EC Regulatory Expansion in Telecommunications 1979–2000." *Journal of European Public Policy* 8(4): 558–584.

———. 2002. "Delegation to Independent Regulatory Agencies: Pressures, Functions and Contextual Mediation." *West European Politics* 25(1): 125–147.

Thatcher, Mark, and Alec Stone Sweet. 2002. "Theory and Practice of Delegation to Non-Majoritarian Institutions." *West European Politics* 25(1): 1–22.

Thelen, Kathleen, and Sven Steinmo. 1992. "Historical Institutionalism in Comparative politics." In Sven Steinmo, Kathleen Thelen, and Frank Longstreth, eds., *Structuring Politics*. New York: Cambridge University Press.

Thomas, Ian. 1996. *Environmental Impact Assessment in Australia: Theory and Practice*. Annandale, New South Wales: Federation Press.

Tolley, Michael C., and Bruce A. Wallin. 1995. "Coercive Federalism and the Search for Constitutional Limits." *Publius* 25(4): 73–90.

Toyne, Phillip. 1994. *The Reluctant Nation: Environment, Law and Politics in Australia*. Sydney: Australian Broadcasting Corporation.

Tsebelis, George. 1994. "The Power of the European Parliament as a Conditional Agenda Setter." *American Political Science Review* 88(1): 128–142.

———. 1995. "Decision Making in Political Systems: Veto Players in Presidentialism, Parliamentarism, Multicameralism and Multipartyism." *British Journal of Political Science* 25: 289–325.

———. 1999. "Veto Players and Law Production in Parliamentary Democracies: An Empirical Assessment." *American Political Science Review* 93(3): 591–608.

———. 2002. *Veto Players: How Political Institutions Work*. Princeton: Princeton University Press.

Tsebelis, George, and Geoffrey Garrett. 2000. "Legislative Politics in the European Union." *European Union Politics* 1(1): 9–36.

———. 2001. "The Institutional Foundations of Intergovernmentalism and Supranationalism in the European Union." *International Organization* 55(2): 357–390.

Union des Confédérations de l'Industrie et des Employeurs d'Europe. 1996. UNICE Statement on EU Environmental Liability. Brussels: UNICE.

Vandermeersch, Dick. 1987. "The Single European Act and the Environmental Policy of the EEC." *European Law Review* December: 407.

Van Miert, Karel. 1996. "The Proposal for a European Competition Agency." *Competition Policy Newsletter*, vol.2, no. 2. Brussels: European Commission.

VanNijnatten, Debora. "Intergovernmental Institutions and Environmental Policy-Making: A Cross-National Perspective." In Patrick Fafard and Katherine Harrison, eds., *Managing the Environmental Union: Intergovernmental Relations and Environmental Policy in Canada*. Montreal: McGill-Queen's University Press.

Varis, Tuula. 1996. "Towards Credibility? Proposals for Improving the Implementation and Enforcement of EU Environmental Law." Paper presented at European Environment Bureau Public Hearing on Challenges to Environmental Protection—Making Legislation Work, Brussels, May 30.

Verhoeve, B., Bennett, G., and Wilkinson, D. 1992. *Maastricht and the Environment*. London: Institute for European Environmental Policy.

Vig, Norman J. 1994. "Presidential Leadership and the Environment: From Reagan to Bush to Clinton." In Norman J. Vig and Michael E. Kraft, eds., *Environmental Policy in the 1990s*, 2nd ed. Washington, D.C.: Congressional Quarterly Press.

Vig, Norman J., and Michael E. Kraft, eds. 1994. *Environmental Policy in the 1990s*, 2nd ed. Washington, D.C.: Congressional Quarterly Press.

Vogel, David. 1981. "The 'New' Social Regulation in Historical and Comparative

Perspective." In Thomas K. McGraw, ed., *Regulation in Perspective: Historical Essays.* Cambridge, Mass.: Harvard University Press.

———. 1986. *National Styles of Regulation: Environmental Policy in Great Britain and the United States.* Ithaca, N.Y.: Cornell University Press.

———. 1993a. "The Making of EC Environmental Policy." In Svein Andersen and Kjell Eliassen, eds., *Making Policy in Europe: The Europeification of National Policy-Making.* London: Sage Publications.

———. 1993b. "Representing Diffuse Interests in Environmental Policy Making." In R. Kent Weaver and Bert Rockman, eds., *Do Institutions Matter? Government Capabilities in the United States and Abroad.* Washington D.C.: Brookings.

———. 1995. *Trading Up: Consumer and Environmental Regulation in a Global Economy.* Cambridge, Mass.: Harvard University Press.

———. 1998. "The Globalization of Pharmaceutical Regulation." *Governance* 11(1): 1–22.

Von Annegret, Lorenz. 1991. "Vollzugsdefizite im Umweltrecht." *Umwelt- und Planungsrecht (UPR), Zeitschrift für Wissenschaft und Praxis* 7: 253–257.

Von Oertzen, Hans Joachim. 1983. "The Control of Public Administration by the Courts." In Klaus König, Hans Joachim von Oertzen, and Frido Wagener, eds., *Public Administration in the Federal Republic of Germany.* Deventer, the Netherlands: Kluwer.

Vos, Ellen. 1997. "The Rise of Committees." *European Law Journal* 3(3): 210–229.

Wallace, Helen, and William Wallace, eds. 1996. *Policy-Making in the European Union.* Oxford: Oxford University Press.

Watts, Ronald. 1970. *Administration in Federal Systems.* London: Hutchison Educational.

———. 1996. *Comparing Federal Systems in the 1990s.* Kingston: Institute of Intergovernmental Relations, Queen's University.

Weale, Albert. 1992. "*Vorsprung durch Technik?* The Politics of German Environmental Regulation." In Kenneth Dyson, ed., *The Politics of German Regulation.* Aldershot, UK: Dartmouth.

Weale, Albert, Geoffrey Pridham, Michelle Cini, Dimitrios Konstadakopulous, Martin Porter, and Brendan Flynn. 2000. *Environmental Governance in Europe: An Ever Closer Ecological Union?* Oxford: Oxford University Press.

Weaver, R. Kent. 1986. "The Politics of Blame Avoidance." *Journal of Public Policy* 6(4): 371–98.

Weaver, R. Kent, and Bert Rockman, eds. 1993. *Do Institutions Matter? Government Capabilities in the United States and Abroad.* Washington D.C.: Brookings.

Weiler, Joseph H. H. 1991. "The Transformation of Europe." *Yale Law Journal* 100: 2403.

Weiland, Paul S. "Federal and State Preemption of Environmental Law: A Critical Analysis." *Harvard Environmental Law Review* 24: 237.

Wenner, Lettie M. 1994. "Environmental Policy in the Courts." In Norman J. Vig and Michael E. Kraft, eds., *Environmental Policy in the 1990s*. Washington, D.C.: Congressional Quarterly Press.

Wessels, Wolfgang. 1991. "The EC Council: The Community's Decisionmaking Center." In Robert Keohane and Stanley Hoffman, eds., *The New European Community: Decisionmaking and Institutional Change*. San Francisco: Westview Press.

Wessels, Wolfgang, and Dietrich Rometsch. 1996. "German Administrative Interaction and the European Union: The Fusion of Public Policies." In Yves Mény, Pierre Muller, and Jean-Louis Quermonne, eds., *Adjusting to Europe: The Impact of the European Union on National Institutions and Policies*. New York: Routledge.

Westlake, Martin. 1995. *The Council of the European Union*. London: Catermill Publishing.

———. 1997. "Keynote Article: 'Mad Cows and Englishment': The Institutional Consequences of the BSE Crisis." *Journal of Common Market Studies* 35(Annual Review): 11–36.

Wey, K. G. 1982. *Umweltpolitik in Deutschland*. Opladen: Westdeutscher Verlag.

Wilcox, Murray. 1992. "Retrospect and Prospect." In Tim Bonyhady, ed., *Environmental Protection and Legal Change*. Sydney: Federation Press.

Wilhelm, Sighard. 1992. *20 Jahre Umweltpolitik in der Bundesrepublik*. Berlin: Publikationen der Fachhochschule für Verwaltung und Rechtspflege.

Wilson, James Q. 1989. *Bureaucracy: What Government Agencies Do and Why They Do It?* New York: Basic Books.

Winter, Gerd, ed. 1994. *German Environmental Law: Basic Texts and Introduction*. Boston: Martinus Nijhoff/Graham and Trotman.

Wurzel, Rudiger. 1993. "Environmental Policy." In Juliet Lodge, ed., *The European Community and the Challenge of the Future*. New York: St. Martin's Press.

Yataganas, Xénophon. 2001. "Delegation of Regulatory Authority in the European Union: The Relevance of the American Model of Independent Agencies." Harvard Jean Monnet Working Paper no. 03/01, Harvard Law School. Available at *www.jeanmonnetprogram.org/papers/01/010301.html*.

Cases Cited

European Union Cases

C-9/56, *Meroni v. High Authority*, [1957–1958] ECR 133.

C-10/56, *Meroni v. High Authority*, [1957–1958] ECR 157.

C-26/62, *van Gend en Loos v. Nederlandse Administratie der Belastingen*, [1963] ECR 1.

C-6/64, *Costa v. Ente Nazionale per L'Energia Elettrica (ENEL)*, [1964] ECR 585.

C-41/74, *Van Duyn v. Home Office*, [1974] ECR 1337.

C-33/76, *Rewe v. Landwirtschaftskammer*, [1976] ECR 1989.

C-120/78, *Rewe-Zentral A.G. v. Bundesmonopolverwaltung (Cassis de Dijon)*, [1979] ECR 649.

C-148/78, *Pubblico Ministero v. Tullio Ratti*, [1979] ECR 1629.

C-91/79, *Commission v. Italian Republic*, [1980] ECR 1099.

C-92/79, *Commission v. Italian Republic*, [1980] ECR 1115.

C-240/83, *Procureur du Roi v. Association de défense des bruleurs d'huiles usagées*, [1985] ECR 531.

C-322/86, *Commission v. Italy*, [1988] ECR 3955.

C-131/88, *Commission v. Germany*, [1991] ECR I-825.

C-361/88, *Commission v. Germany*, [1991] ECR I-2567.

C-58/89, *Commission v. Germany*, [1991] ECR I-4893.

C-59/89, *Commission v. Germany*, [1991] ECR I-2607.

C-300/89, *Commission v. Council*, [1991] ECR I-2867.

C-56/90, *Commission v. United Kingdom*, [1993] ECR I-4109.

C-6/90 and C-9/90, *Francovich and Others v. Italy*, [1991] ECR I-5357.

C-237/90, *Commission v. Germany*, [1992] ECR I-5973.

C-355/90, *Commission v. Spain*, [1993] ECR I-4221.

C-45/91, Commission v. Greece, [1992] ECR I-2509.

C-155/91, *Commission v. Council*, [1993] ECR I-939.

C-396/92, *Bund Naturschutz in Bayern e.V. and Richard Stahnsdorf and Others v. Freistaat Bayern, Stadt Vilsbiburg and Landkreis Landshut*, [1994] ECR I-3717.

C-422/92, *Commission v. Germany,* [1995] ECR I-1097.

C-431/92, *Commission v. Germany,* [1995] ECR I-2189.

C-46/93 and C-48/93, *Brasserie du Pêcheur SA v. Germany and R. v. Transport Secretary ex parte Factortame III,* [1996] ECR I-1029.

C-392/93, *R. v. HM Treasury ex parte British Telecommunications,* [1996] ECR I-1631.

C-5/94, *Hedley Lomas v. Agriculture and Fisheries (MAFF),* [1996] ECR I-2553.

C-178, 179, and 188–190/94, *Dillenkofer and Others,* [1996] ECR I-4845.

C-325/94, *An Taisce—The National Trust for Ireland and World Wide Fund for Nature (WWF) v. Commission,* [1996] ECR I-3727.

C-105/95, *WWF UK (World Wide Fund for Nature) v. Commission,* [1997] ECR II-0313.

C-72/95, *Kraaijeveld BV v. Gedepudteerde Staten van Zuid-Holland,* [1996] ECR I-5403.

C-262/95, *Commission v. Germany,* [1996] ECR I-5729.

C-297/95, *Commission v. Germany,* [1996] ECR I-6739.

C-301/95, *Commission v. Germany,* [1998] ECR I-6135.

C-321/95, *Stichting Greenpeace Council (Greenpeace International) v. Commission,* [1998] ECR I-1651.

C-3/96, *Commission v. Netherlands,* [1998] ECR I-3031.

C-387/97, *Commission v. Greece,* [2000] ECR I-5047.

C-435/97, *World Wildlife Fund (WWF) and Others v. Autonome Provinz Bozen and Others,* [1999] ECR I-5613.

C-427/00, *Commission v. United Kingdom,* [2001] ECR I-8535.

United States Cases

Alden v. Maine, 119 S. Ct. 2240 (1999).

Chevron, U.S.A., Inc., v. NRDC, Inc., 467 U.S. 837 (1984).

College Sav. Bank v. Florida Prepaid Postsecondary Educ. Expense Bd., 119 S. Ct. 2219 (1999).

Duke Power Co. v. Carolina Environmental Study Group Inc., 438 U.S. 59 (1978).

Environmental Defense Fund v. Ruckelshaus, 3 Envt'l L. Rep. 20173 (1973).

Federal Energy Regulatory Comm'n v. Mississippi, 456 U.S. 742 (1982).

Florida Prepaid Postsecondary Educ. Expense Bd. v. College Sav. Bank, 119 S. Ct. 2199 (1999).

Friends of the Earth, Inc. v. Crown Cent. Petroleum Corp., 95 F.3d 358 (5th Cir. 1996).

Friends of the Earth, Inc. v. Laidlaw Envtl. Serv., Inc., 120 S. Ct. 693 (2000).

Heckler v. Chaney, 470 U.S. 821 (1985).

Hodel v. Surface Mining & Reclamation Ass'n, Inc., 452 U.S. 264 (1981).

Kennecott Copper Corp v. EPA, 462 F.2d 846 (D.C. Cir. 1972).

Kentucky v. Dennison, 65 U.S. 66 (1861).
Long Island Soundkeeper Fund v. New York Athletic Club, U.S. Dist. LEXIS 3383 (S.D.N.Y. Mar. 20, 1996).
Lujan v. National Wildlife Fed'n, 110 S. Ct. 3177 (1990) *(Lujan I).*
Lujan v. Defenders of Wildlife, 112 S. Ct. 2130 (1992) *(Lujan II).*
Missouri v. Illinois, 180 U.S. 208 (1901).
Monroe v. Pape, 365 U.S. 167 (1991).
Natural Resources Defense Council v. EPA, 475 F.2d 968 (D.C. Cir. 1973).
Natural Resources Defense Council v. Train, 545 F.2d 320 (2d Cir. 1976).
New York v. New Jersey, 256 U.S. 296 (1921).
New York v. United States, 505 U.S. 144 (1992).
Printz v. United States, 521 U.S. 898 (1997).
Seminole Tribe v. Florida, 517 U.S. 44 (1996).
Sierra Club v. Morton, 405 U.S. 727 (1971).
Sierra Club v. Ruckelshaus, 344 F. Supp. 253 (D.D.C. 1972).
The Steel Co., aka Chicago Steel and Pickling Co. v. Citizens for a Better Environment, 523 S. Ct. 83 (1998).
United States v. Students Challenging Regulatory Agency Procedure ("SCRAP"), 412 U.S. 669 (1973).
Vermont Agency of Natural Resources v. United States ex rel. Stevens, 120 S. Ct. 1858 (2000).
Vermont Yankee Nuclear Power Corp. v. Natural Resources Defense Council Inc., 435 U.S. 519 (1978).
Wickard v. Filburn, 317 U.S. 111 (1942).

Australian Cases

Commonwealth v. Tasmania, 46 A.L.R. 625 (1983).
Murphyores Inc. Pty. Ltd. v. Commonwealth, 136 C.L.R. 1 (1976).
Queensland v. Commonwealth, 62 ALJR 143 (1988).
Victoria v. Commonwealth, 99 C.L.R. 575 (1957).

Canadian Cases

Canadian Wildlife Fed'n Inc. v. Canada (Minister of the Environment), [1989] 3 F.C. 309 (T.D.)
Finlay v. Canada, [1986] 2 S.C.R. 607.
Friends of the Oldman River Soc'y v. Canada (Minister of Transport), [1992] 1 S.C.R. 3.
R. v. Crown Zellerbach Ltd. et al., [1988] 1 S.C.R. 401.

Index